SECURITY IN NEW RUSSIA

SECURITY IN NEW RUSSIA

DR. AMARENDRA MISHRA

KALPAZ PUBLICATIONS
DELHI-110052

Security in New Russia

Rs. 690

ISBN: 81-7835-581-1

Published in 2007 in India by
Kalpaz Publications
C-30, Satyawati Nagar,
Delhi-110052
E-mail: kalpaz@hotmail.com

Lassertype Setting by: Rudra Computer Graphics, Delhi
Printed at: Salasar Imaging System, Delhi

Dedicated

to

My

Parents

Contents

Preface and Acknowledgements

As the humanity ushers in a different phase of history, it is as unsure about its progress as it is about existence. An advancing civilization and its wheels i.e. modern technology leaves humanity in a precarious state. The question arises: Will humanity prevail or perish? The question is not imposed, it is self-imposed. Infact, this question is the driving force for me to explore the contradictions and complexities involved in the concept of security. That too, in Soviet Union and Russian context, exploring its concept of security is both a fascinating and a difficult task. Former Soviet Union has not only witnessed ups and downs and quick changes during Gorbachev era, which led to the demise of the Soviet empire, but also defied a fixed pattern for the study of its development and decay and made it difficult for a researcher to predict the future of Russia (the true inheritor of Soviet union). Further, the situation was worse after the disintegration of Soviet Union when there was a state of uncertainty in Russia for a long period for which the formulation of the national security concept was delayed. The National Security Concept of 1997 and 2000 are two milestones in the history of new Russia. The National Security Concept of 2000 formulated by Putin reflected his pragmatism and vision and concern for the people of Russia and the entire mankind. In fact, Putin is the only leader who has learnt lessons from history and tried to take right course of actions at the right time.

This book addresses the security questions that are mind bugling and also analyses security doctrines propounded and practised by the leaders of Soviet Union and Russia. The views and comments of strategic experts of Russia and other countries have been incorporated in it. But here, my primary concern is to study the entire history of Soviet Union and present Russia with special focus on Soviet concept of security during *Perestroika* and to explore the reasons for the demise of the great empire, and at the same time to critically observe and assess the security of Russia in the post cold war era, which went through a painful process of redefining its national interests and tailoring its security strategy to cope up with realities and to regain its super power status.

In this book, I have made an attempt to study the security concept of Russia within a theoretical framework applying historic-analytical method, of course, putting importance on the security of Russia, which is at present moving in a positive direction from the state of uncertainty to certainty.

Again, I write this book from my own standpoint as an individual and researcher. In applying a theoretical framework for the study of the subject matter, I have tried to pick up the most suitable and relevant paradigm for enquiry without diluting its historical context.

The major part of the book was written in Jawaharlal Nehru University when I was a Doctoral Research Scholar. The last but the most important chapter was written in my working place in a secluded room staying away from my family for months together. I was bit *roomy* those days, which was painful but much interesting. It was only possible due to cheerful tolerance of my parents, in- laws, family members, and my wife **Jeeta** and my little baby **Anwesha**. I would like to dedicate this book to them.

Many of the ides in the book were formulated and developed when I was doing research seriously in the Center for Russian, Central Asian and East European Studies, School of International Studies, JNU. I am very grateful to **Prof. Ajay Pattnaik** and **Dr. Talir Asghar** for their comments, suggestions and guidance.

I owe my gratitude to **Prof. R.R.Sharma, Prof. Devendra Kaushik, Prof. Zafar Imam, Prof. Shams-ud-din, Prof. Anuradha Chenoy, Dr. Tulsi Ram, Dr. Sanjoy Pandey** of Russian and Central Asian Studies; **Prof. S.K.Jha, Dr. Gulshan Sachdeva** of European Studies; **Prof. Zuberi, Prof. Kanti Bajpei, Prof. B.D.Ghoshal, Dr. Aswini Mohapatra** and other faculty members of SIS; **C.Uday**

Bhaskar, Satbir Singh, **Santosh Meherotra**, (formerly) of IDSA; and **Prof. Anand Mohan** of City University, New York, (USA) for sharing their intellectual views with me which helped me in sharpening my ideas and developing a broader frame work on my topic.

I am equally grateful to **Prof. Amareswar Mishra**, **Prof. Brahmananda Satpathy**, **Prof. Sudhanshu Pattinaik**, and **Prof.Surya Narayan Mishra** of Utkal University for their advice and encouragement.

I am really indebted to **Dr. Narottam Gaan**, a renowned expert in International Studies, **Dr.Ashok Ku. Behuria**, Senior Research Fellow in IDSA, and **Neil**, formerly Research Fellow at Keele University, (U.K.) in providing immense intellectual inputs and going through draft papers and raising questions that have helped me clarify my thought.

I would particularly like to thank **Behuria** and **Gaan** family, and my friends **Phoobadan, Usha K.B., Archana, Jajati, Ganesh, Sailendra, Prakash** and **Santosh** for their help at the time of need.

Needless to say that, I am thank full to my colleagues and staff in my working place, and **Sunil ch. Prusty** of Hingula Area, MCL, for encouraging me to publish this book.

Last but not least, I extend my heart-felt thanks to my relatives for providing emotional support and eagerly waiting for the successful completion of this work.

Amarendra Mishra
South Balanda
Angul,Orissa
May 2006

Introduction

Since the dawn of human civilization, man's concern for a safe and secure life has led to a constant search for security. In order to thrive amidst prosperity, man has devised an ingenious approach towards his surroundings by which he can secure his interests. Safeguarding the interest of one group of individuals from the onslaught of another group was the cardinal principle of security right since the inception of human civilization. With the passage of time and progress of civilization, the notion of security has undergone several changes from this pristine approach. With the emergence of the nation-state in Europe in the early nineteenth century, security occupied a prominent position in the policy matters of the state. The upsurge of nationalism in the recent times around the world has given rise to multi-dimensional security perspectives. The military, political, economic, environmental and humanitarian aspects of security have come to shape the policy of one state towards the other nations. Security matters have always been framed in a manner so as to accommodate the interest of the concerned state, whereas the interests of other states get marginalised and relegated to the background. In the traditional security perspective, a nation hardly takes the security interest of other nations into account while pursuing its own security. Nations, very often, seek to attain highest strategic parity while espousing the policy of military security. This tendency to pursue one's own security by attaining highest strategic parity has always made room for arms race, thus jeopardizing the security of everybody and promoting acrimony and mutual distrust. A state of uncertainty is forced to prevail thereby. Pursuit of traditional security was marked by the espousal of a policy of mutually exclusive security. Balance of forces as the highest possible level of strategic parity and that was the general feature of traditional security characterized by conflict, competition and block antagonism. With the advancement of military technology and invention of sophisticated weaponry system, security priorities of nations have taken a different orientation characterized by arms race and arms build-up. Piling up of deadly weapons and formation of block alliances with friendly countries became synonymous with security of a nation. Striving for security at the cost of others' interests was the main consideration of the security policy of a nation.

The upsurge of nationalism and nation's concern for exclusive security lays emphasis on the security of one nation-state, without caring for its implication of the security of others neighbouring nations in the international community. Common security or universal security was just inconceivable in the security system where national security did not encompass mutual security and this had become the norm of the national security system around the world. Soon after the end of Second World War, the rise of super powers marked the accentuation of power politics leading to emergence of a bi-polar, competitive and conflicting security system. The formation of North Atlantic Treaty Organisation (NATO) and Warsaw Pact (dismantled now) was the culmination of the bipolar model characterized by alliance and counter alliance. Both the power blocks believed in a model where security could be attained by means of highest possible level of strategic parity.

The concept of security thrived on principle of balance of power. With the nuclearisation of international politics, security of nations, especially of power blocks revolved around the principle of balance of terror. Each other's destructive capability having been enhanced to several times with the invention of sophisticated nuclear weapons and with the modernization of military set up, security of nations in general and of the power blocks specifically got jeopardized. Balance of power and balance of terror were the decisive factors that maintain a stable and secure international system. But at the same time, it led to a situation where zero-sum game became the sub-structure on which the entire international politics was built up.

In the initial years of Soviet regime and during Second World War, Soviet leaders tried to strengthen their nation's security in the face of internal discontentment and external threat. Security was conceived within the framework of widespread militarisation and military alliance. Soviet pursuit of security was characterized by variable policy approaches starting from forward strategy of war communism to trade-cum-arms control orientation of the 1970s. In the late 1970s and early 1980s an aggressive approach that swerved from the line of rapprochement with the West. A steady effort to modernize the military and prop up anti-American left wing Governments in the Third World became the characteristic of forward strategy. Soviet security policy especially détente and cooperation proved to be a mere eyewash whereas hardline militancy dominated the Soviet policy. During the phase preceding to Perestroika, Soviet leaders rarely pursued any policy in its purest form from across the border; rather they picked and choose calibrating strategy and tactics to time and place. Thus, Soviet sought détente with the West and at the same time went on supporting anti-imperialist activities in the Third World. Soviet leaders, during this period, wanted to have the best of both worlds: economic relationship with the First World combined with enhanced Soviet influence in the Third World. This sort of pragmatism, although, had advantages yet often produced contradictory policies that garnered few gains in either spheres.

Soviet Union during Perestroika proposed an accord on a strategy of "military sufficiency" restructuring armed forces so that they could resist aggression but would be unable to become offensive. A first step in this direction could be a controlled withdrawal of nuclear and other offensive weapons and zones of reduced and or no armaments between adversaries. The new Soviet leadership called for accords to prevent the outbreak of nuclear war and stop nuclear piracy. If imbalance disproportion existed in the marks of NATO and Warsaw Pact that was to be removed.

The Soviet Union declared that "peace is indivisible". The new Soviet leadership put forth a number of proposals for incorporation into an all-embracing system of peace and security. Gorbachev pledged that Soviet Union would shift from confidence building measures in individual spheres to a large-scale policy of trust that would gradually shape a comprehensive security. In line with Western theories of conflict reduction, Gorbachev laid out his broad strategy in advance affirming his priority for rejection of nuclear deterrence as a basis for security. He emphasized on compromise as the way to resolve disputes and issued a declaration outlining a plan to eliminate all nuclear arms by the year 2000 and sharply limit other weapons as well. In stead of upgrading nuclear and conventional arms, Soviet Union proposed shifting Warsaw Pact and NATO forces towards a posture of "reasonable sufficiency" adequate for defense but insufficient to threaten attack. Soviet leadership declared its willingness to make conventional as well as nuclear reductions. If there were asymmetries in the assets of both sides Soviet Union was ready to remove them even if this meant reducing more Eastern than Western forces. Gorbachev proposed steps to maintain a balance at even low levels.

In January 1989 Gorbachev went to the extent of reducing of half a million troops from Soviet military. The Soviet spending on military hardware and armaments was reduced and Soviet troops from Mongolia and Eastern Europe were pulled out. In 1989-90, Soviet Union unilaterally reduced its armed forces by 500,000 with reduction in arms and ammunitions. In the late 1980s the Soviet Union cut back its involvement in costly Third World ventures. Soviet forces initiated withdrawal from Afghanistan in early 1988 and completed it on February 15, 1989 under a deadline set by Gorbachev. Soviet Union acknowledged realities and did its best to retreat with dignity. Soviet forces were reduced on the Chinese border and SS-20s were removed that were at one time targeted on China, Japan and Korea.

Soviet Union sought a constructive role in solutions for conflicts in Angola, Cambodia, and Middle East and created external conditions for people to settle the issues themselves to remove foreign interference. In December 1988, Soviet Union endorsed a US brokered accord to end Angolan-South African fighting accompanied by withdrawal of Cuban forces from Angola. In early 1989 Soviet Union expressed willingness before Norway to alter moderately proposals for a boundary in a strategically vital zone of Barents Sea. This novel step deviated from earlier Soviet refusal to negotiate any of its borders. These initiatives taken by the Soviet Union reflected its willingness to resolve the international conflicts through mutual goodwill and by reducing its military influence abroad.

Economic concerns that featured more perceptibly in Soviet Union during Perestroika was perceived as another vital aspect of security. In the years preceding Perestroika, Soviet economic growth rate had crawled for decades with wide-scale stagnation. Gorbachev believed that the ills of the Soviet economy and society demanded total and revolutionary restructuring. The main thrust and agenda of the new economic policy during Perestroika was to make life better for the people and to put an end to excessive arms production which the new leadership considered to be wasteful as well as immoral. The economic policy during Perestroika revolved around mutual advantages provided by reciprocal scientific and technological cooperation. Soviet Union, in the days of Perestroika, had grandiose plans in the domestic sphere, mainly economic. And it needed congenial and peaceful external conditions in order to translate the economic plans to reality. Among the measures Soviet Union wanted to take inorder to streamline and strengthen the economic security were its desire to join G-7 and international financial and trade organizations such as International Monetary Fund (IMF), the World Bank and General Agreement on Trade and Tariff (GATT, presently known as WTO-World Trade Organisation). During this phase, Soviet declared that they would welcome joint ventures in business and commerce with West and the world community.

On the international front, all forms of discrimination and economic blockades and sanctions recommended by the world community were condemned and adequate steps were taken to remove all those practices. Serious efforts were made for the settlement of the problems of debts as most of the Third World countries were under the debt trap. Soviet Union also supported the establishment of New International Economic Order (NIEO), which was taken up by the Third World countries, for strengthening the economic security of all countries. During this phase the Soviet leaders tried to divert the resources from defence expenditure to developmental projects, particularly to the Third World countries, by cutting down the defence budget and supplying arms. The humanitarian aspects of security had not been underscored on Soviet security plans. Thus, they swerved from the line of command economy of Stalin's Russia and Brezhnev's stagnation to Grobachev's notion of restructuring and integrating Soviet economy with global economy.

After the demise of the Soviet empire, the new Russia, a true successor of Soviet Union struggled hard to cope with realities and to formulate, security concept to meet the emerging challenges on account of the shifting sands of Russian politics. At the early stage, Yeltsin and his government lacked a clear vision of the security policy and could not prepare themselves to chalk out a right strategy at the right time. Perhaps, Yeltsin's best performance was the fight for the cause of democracy during the August coup-de-etat in 1991. After that, his performance deteriorated, and the script rain dry. He was more serious to wear a democratic garb rather than to solve the genuine problems, be it political, social, economic and environmental and hence things started deteriorating before his eye. His rule 'resulted in economic stagnation, massive corruption, military disintegration and court politics of a kind that resembled those of Boris Godunov'.

The only achievement of Yeltsin in the field of Russian security was the National Security Concept of 1997, which was even not well formulated and balanced one. What ever it may be, it opened up the way for Putin to formulate the National Security Concept of 2000, which put much importance on expediency and reflected his pragmatism and vision. In fact, he rightly learnt lessons from history and also had a clear idea of the direction in which he would have to move. His concept of security not only stresses on military aspects but also political, economic and human aspects too. Indeed, his holistic approach to security reflects his concern for the all round development of the people of Russia and at the same time the problems of the world, which have serious implications for ensuring global peace and security.

In the military security, he brought changes by introducing military reforms to develop the military capabilities of Russia to ward off any sort of eventualities against Russia and to strengthen its foot hold for regaining its lost super power status. In the political security, he tries to democratize the Russian Federation through redrawing the federal map by introducing reformative measures and abolishing the inequitable tax disadvantages, curtailing the powers of governors and thus tightening his grip over administration. In the external dimension, his approach to security is well thought up and his decision for shifting the policy according to the call of the time, be it the case of Kosovo or the event of 9/11 is a real testimony of his political insight and wider vision. In the economic security, Russia under the leadership of Putin tries seriously to overcome the negative impacts of the Russian economy by neutralizing it through various ways and gaining economic stability by revamping Russian economy and integrating it to global economy through the process of liberalization, privatization and globalization (LPG). In order to strengthen Russian economy and foster economic growth economic reforms were introduced and structural and functional changes were made in the Russian economy. In the security framework of Russia, Human Security was not even undermined. Putin not only concerned for the well being of the people of Russia but also the people of the entire world and for ensuring it he took various measures which are since sine-qua-non for a healthy society.

But his Security Concept is not free from flaws. His biggest weakness is his ex--colleagues, *silovakis* and *chekisties* which often create troubles for him. Hence, the need of the time is to maintain neutrality and honesty in dealing with the complex security problems of New Russia.

The book is an attempt to analyse and assess the concept of security, propounded and practised by the leaders of Soviet Union during Perestroika and Present Russia. The broader notion of security, in its military, political, economic and human aspects, has been explored within a specific context. The book has been organised into seven chapters. In chapter one "Concept of Security: A Framework for Analysis", the theoretical and conceptual aspects of security have been analysed. Further, the role of international institutions like the United Nations, Non-Aligned Movement (NAM), in the field of international security, has been studied too. Besides military and political security, special focus has been put on economic, environmental, societal, and humanitarian security issues that have much more relevance in the present context.

In chapter two "Soviet Concept of Security: Historical Perspective", the historical background of Soviet security from the era of Lenin to Gorbachev has been elaborated. The views of strategic experts of the Soviet Union have been incorporated in it. This chapter has emphasized Gorbachev's concept of comprehensive universal security and the way it is different from his predecessors. It is argued that Gorvachev's concept of security is a complex combination of realism and idealism by combining socio-economic matrix both at domestic and international level.

In the chapter three "Military Aspects of Security during Perestroika", different proposals and measures taken by Soviet leaders for making a secured and peaceful world have been analysed. The doctrine of reasonable sufficiency and its relevance for maintaining security of the world in general and Soviet Union in particular has been dealt with. The American reaction to Soviet's military security has been critically reviewed. Hence the linkage has been established between internal and external dimension of security and the way this military security was responsible for the disintegration of the Soviet Union.

In the chapter four "Political Aspects of Security during Perestroika", various proposals and measures taken by "New Thinkers", for ensuring security of the Soviet Union and the world have been discussed. The concept of "Common European Home", the solution of the regional conflicts with special focus on Asia-Pacific regions has been elaborated. It has also stressed on the confidence building measures; prevention of international terrorism for strengthening the security of the world. The changes in Eastern

Europe, which were no doubt products of internal changes in Soviet Union, have been stressed upon and answers to questions like how far the changes shattered the fabric of Soviet security and encouraged secessionist movements in various parts of the Soviet Union which ultimately led to collapse of communism have been sought in the present study.

In chapter five, "Economic Security during Perestroika", both internal and external reforms with its structural and functional changes in Soviet security have been elaborated. It has explored the processes that hastened the integration of the Soviet economy to the world economy and enough light has been thrown on import and export relations of Soviet Union with the West, joint ventures, and relation with the European Community. The Asian dimension has not been underscored in it. This chapter has also dealt with various proposals and measures taken by Soviet Union for ensuring economic security of the world.

The sixth chapter "Humanitarian Aspects of Security" deals with the issues of human rights of the Soviet Union and the world. It has mainly concentrated on the main proposals of the humanitarian security during Perestroika phase and its impact on global peace and security and the Western reactions to the changes of the Soviet Union. This chapter further explores the humanitarian aspects of security and its implications in strengthening the security of the world and particularly the security of erstwhile Soviet Union.

The seventh chapter 'The Security in New Russia' deals with the security concept of New Russia. Here the focus has been given to various aspects of the security of New Russia. Hence, it has been divided into four sections, military, political, economic and human security. In each section, various issues and problems have been elaborated. In this chapter, the steps taken by Yeltsin and particularly Putin to sort out the problem in Russian security have been highlighted. An attempt has also been made to evaluate their efforts in this direction and the remedial measures need to be taken to strengthen the security structure of New Russia.

The conclusion chapter has provided the summary of this research. Though this research largely concludes that there had been serious flaws in the Soviet concept of security during Perestroika, it had enormous impact on ensuring peace and security in the world. Nevertheless, this research claims that introduction of a new theoretical paradigm, i.e., "Rational Contextual Analysis", could have solved the Soviet security complexity during Perestroika phase and the problems of the world.

Further, it also explores the reasons for the disintegration of the Soviet Union and also analyses its impact on the security of New Russia. Various problems and issues have been analysed, and the steps taken by Yeltsin and particularly Putin to solve the problems in Russia security have been discussed.

1

Concept of Security: A Framework for Analysis

1.1. The Concept of Security

The concept of security plays a vital role in formulating the domestic and foreign policy of a nation. It has broader connotation than the terms, self-preservation, survival, defence-preparedness, guarding one's frontiers etc., though they are often interchangeably used. It relates not only to the ultimate desire of the survival of State but also to live without serious external threat to its interests or values that are regarded as important or vital.[1]

The policies that the States follow to promote their security rest on a series of judgements and choices. In the first place, the State should find out the vital interests and prepare to preserve it.[2] In the second place security-judgements should be taken with proper consideration of the changing conditions of the State, its relationship with other States and their intentions and capabilities. In the third place, the degree of threats for a State should be properly studied while making policies relating to security. Even while facing similar threats, States differ in their security-arrangements; some tend to spend relatively high while others relatively low proportion of their resources on security.[3] In the fourth place, methods for ensuring security differ from State to State. Dangers may be warded off or countered through conflicts or peaceful means. When some States prefer peaceful negotiations and co-operation, others resort to war, conflict alliance, and counter-alliance for preserving their security.[4]

In a conflict situation, an actor with enough power attains a dominating position in the power politics and feels secure thereby.[5] In some other situations, co-operation replaces confrontation in resolving conflicts of interest.[6] Such cooperative endeavors minimize the probability of use of power and helps in sorting out the differences among the countries through peaceful negotiations, positive policies, and programmes, which lead to a state of peace and ultimately make everybody feel immensely secure.

In common parlance, concept of security is identified with military preponderance. However, this is a narrow concept. Recently, it has undergone a qualitative change. Besides military security, now it includes political, economic, environmental and socio-psychological security. In the present context, it is not possible to maintain security solely through military preponderance. Robert McNamara highlights this aspect of security when he says: "It is not a military force though it may involve it. Security is not traditional military activity though it may encompass it".[7] Thus the objective of security now has been "all round development focussing national attention on political and economic power". The latter, in particular, in the context of the developing countries, is an essential ingredient of security".[8] Today security concerns encompass not only the defence of the territory but also the problem of access to raw materials at reasonable prices and how to alter and satisfy the expectations of social and economic stability.[9] In the post Second World War, particularly in 1980s unstable economic conditions of a state posed a threat to the concept of domestic security. Higher the expectations of the people, more the threats to the domestic concept of security in the industrial world. Developments during the post war period have enlarged the problem of security within industrial societies to include not only the question of physical but also questions of individual well-being such as job security, maintenance of standard of living, health care and retirement pensions. Though these problems are not new to the government but they are now perceived as security problems by the large segments of Western population.[10]

Besides military and economic aspects of security, political dimensions also play a vital role in the policy of national security. Domestic and foreign policies of a nation are largely influenced by it.[11] Political instability, class and community conflicts, secessionist tendencies of states shatter the internal fabric of security. Thus security involves not only freedom from physical danger but also from psychological danger and is therefore a subjective concept.[12] In the concept of security, national and international security is intertwined in such a manner that it is too difficult to differentiate one from the other. In the present context, international security is getting prominence as bi-polar conflictual world is heading towards a multi-polar consensus world. Instead of warfare, peace is the prime mover of nations. In a broader canvass, international security encompasses regional security, international strategic doctrines, and political, economic and socio-psychological security of nations.[13] Its objective is global peace and all round development of the world. These views on security are expressed by the writings of the idealist thinkers.

Nevertheless, political realists think that international security is to be understood on the basis of actions and interest of nations. They put least emphasis on international problems, humanitarian issues, and global security problems. They clearly discount the questions of inter-group relations at levels other than the state, issues relating to the economic, political and socio-psychological problems of the world.[14]

In the present world particularly after 1985 when Gorbachev assumed power, the concept of international security was given a new twist. It sought to blend political realism with idealism and de-ideologize the socio-political matrix in which concept of security is embedded'. Attempts were made to solve individual and national security problems through international security measures.[15]

For a better understanding of this novel concept of security, one should analyse the various approaches to the security. In the analysis of security, the realist model of international politics, conceived broadly as a struggle for power, had its relevance in the polarized environment of the Second World War. During the subsequent Cold War days such realism determined the course of super power politics. Such was the sway of realist paradigm that states in the international arena were perceived to be locked in perennial power struggles, and the concern for security was conceived of as a derivative of power.[16]

Idealists rejected this realist model, but emphasized more on arms control, disarmament, and international cooperation. Thus their approach to security indirectly attested the realist contention that security was a mere derivative of the power-struggles perennially going on at the international level.[17]

With such tentative appreciation of the concept of security, now attempts has been made to discuss various approaches to security in details. The approaches to "security" can be broadly classified under two headings: classical approaches to security and rational scientific approaches to security.

1. 2. Classical Approach to Security

Classical approach is otherwise known as traditional approach. This approach analyses security from normative, qualitative and value-judgement point of view. This approach was adopted by most of the scholars until scientific approach made its appearance. It nourished two important streams of thought: realism and idealism, which contributed greatly to the understanding of the nature, determinants and dynamics of the concept of security.

1.2.i. Realism

Realism, which is the prime mover of the security paradigm, emerges out of the individual's fear psychosis that others are trying to destroy him for which he must take protective measures.[18] This approach is developed under the basic assumption that rivalry and strife among nations continue in some form or the other. As it emphasizes on the struggle for power or the contest for powers, most of the nations revolve around this power paradigm for protecting their security. They adopt various means like balance of power, deterrence for effective check of the contest for power. Hans J. Morgenthau; George F. Kennan; Reinhold Niebuhr; Stanley

Hoffman; Arnold Wolfers; E. H. Carr; Hedley Bull and Raymond Aron are the leading advocates of the realist school of thought.

The best exposition of realistic theory of international politics has been given by Hans J. Morgenthau. Security is the prime concern in his theory. He says, "international politics like all politics is a struggle for power. Whatever be the ultimate aim of international politics, power is always supreme".[19] It is obvious that a nation can be secured if it enjoys power. Power occupies a cardinal position in the realist security-paradigm as it helps in preserving security, which is a part of national interest. The struggle for power leads to the balance which nations try for their protection against others' attack.[20] Kenneth Thompson and Hans J. Morgenthau laid stress on balance of power. They tend to view balance of power as an effort by the nations to increase their strength at least to equal level with other nations if not superior to other nations' strength to counteract the power of other nations.[21] Balance of power also helps to protect the vital interest of nations by adopting various methods like war and aggression.[22] It is obvious that security is the prime concern as it is the vital interest of nations.[23] A country ignoring the balance of power is poorly armed; thus its security is at stake, as it cannot check the attack of belligerent nations.

The idea of equilibrium is the basis of balance of power. But in reality nations prefer preponderance, not equilibrium of power. They prefer disequilibrium as it works out in their favour. Realists hold that it is in the interest of every nation to prevent other nations to be more powerful than itself as it may bring threats for its security and survival.[24] Morgenthau argues in favour of national interest at the cost of morality as it helps in ensuring security. On the other hand, George Kennan tries to make a striking balance between national interest and morality ingrained in our civilization for conducting foreign policy of a nation.[25] From the above analysis, it is reflected that Kennan supported the idea of moral relativism and Morgenthau the idea of transcendental relativism.[26]

Raymond Aron emphasizes on maximum security of a nation as it helps in protecting a nation and simultaneously increases its prestige by helping less powerful nations as the leaders of the coalition. In other words "to want the maximum of security means to want the maximum of power which in turn means the greatest number of allies the fewest possible enemies".[27] A great power also does not ignore the significance of ideology. They help their allies on ideological grounds and pave the way for opposite ideological nations to make counter allies in the struggle for power. Aron maintains that most of the conflicts and rivalry continues, as most of the nations do not agree either to a common law or compromises.[28] However, Aron differs with Morgenthau and others in his analysis and distinguishes between power as a means and power as an end.

Prominent realist Quinçy Wright examines that since World War II, states had relied more on military force for preserving their security than international law and organization.[29] Studies of the course of public opinion also supported this conclusion. Since World War II, nationalism and state sovereignty and security overshadowed internationalism and world community. International problems were solved militarily than peaceful means. According to Wright, realism, which defined national interest in terms of power, represented short-term national policies, which would be helpful for the fulfillment of immediate requirements of nations.[30] Balance of power as a method for ensuring security cannot prevent nuclear war prematurely as balance of military power always required occasional wars to make their operation effective. As Wright put in this way: *"in actual aggression impossible, the development of military geniuses, military interventions, military alliances or effective military preparation has always in time stimulated some states to attempt to break the balance of power, especially if a long peace has induced some states to relax military preparation, to ally themselves with the potential aggressor, or to pursue policies of permanent neutrality, thus reducing the potential exposition to the aggressor".*[31]

Hedley Bull critically reviewed one of the strategic experts, Noel-Baker, for his theory of collective security. He, in fact, rejected it and gave his own theory in stead. Unlike other realists, he argued against excessive self-interest in approaches to security. He tried to introduce a link between common interest and national security.[32] He pointed out *"the military balance is itself most important source of security, and it is not necessarily made more important by being reduced to a lower level in terms of strategic or limited war forces".*[33] *He argued that "there is no necessary presumption in favour of disarmament rather than rearmament in the design of a system of arms control".*[34] His writing on arms control suggest that he considered military balance very important for the preservation of security, especially when the world is under the shadow of a nuclear holocaust. In the 1980s, he became concerned about the defence policies of super powers and stressed more on armaments than arms control to enhance their security. Hedley Bull analysis on arms control outlined five ideas, which would be helpful for preserving security. These are:

- Arms control is not an end in itself but a means to an end: security against nuclear war;
- Arms control rests on the assumption that there is some perceived area of common interest between the antagonistic powers;
- Arms control and defence strategy are not mutually contradictory by nature and must be developed in harmony with an overall security policy;
- Arms control embraces a wider area of military policy than simply that which is covered by formal agreements. The most important immediate goal of arms control is to stabilise the relationship of mutual deterrence between the super powers.[35]

Nevertheless, he was very much sceptical about the response of the super powers to arms-control as they wanted to spread their ideological and military hegemony over the rest of the world.

Arnold Wolfers believes that life of the individuals and national community can be saved by sacrificing moral values. But the advent of nuclear has made the situation worse and it is doubtful whether the security of nations can be protected through war which is detrimental for human existence ultimately throw human race to catastrophe.[36] Wolfers emphasized on the concept of national security and critically analysed the many dimensional complexities of this concept. He characterized security as an ambiguous symbol – at one point he argues that it does not have any precise meaning.[37]

Stanley Hoffman compared the present power struggle in politics for ensuring security with a game of 'roulette in a cellar', and noted that "as long as the competition goes on, the player cannot be asked to behave as if it were over". He argued that it was absurd to want states to give up their separate interests merely because they had a common interest— divergently perceived— in survival or in a modicum of order. But it is not absurd for states to refrain from pursuing separate interest with means that are capable of throwing not only their immediate rivals but all by-standers and themselves to abyss".[38]

1. 2.ii. Neo-Realism

Neo-realism is a synthesis between classical realism and elements of various critiques of realism. Modern neo-realists emphasize on international system and the structure than the nation states in their analysis of power paradigm. The leading advocates of Neo-realism are Kenneth Waltz, Robert Gilpin, Barry Buzan and Bjørn Møller.

Kenneth Waltz's structural realism reflected that in the structure of international system, states, though important, are not the only actors. It is obvious that national interest is the prime concern of the states in taking important decisions including decisions on national security. But this self-help attitude of the states shatters the fabric of the system.[39] Waltz argued that this anarchy was a lesser evil than the hierarchical structure, such as collective security, world government, which regulated balance of power but often favoured the powerful nations. He argued in favour of nuclear revolution and even he rejoiced at the prospects of nuclear proliferation as he felt "it restrains and imparts a sense of caution among those states that are in possession" and such kind of a nuclear deterrence, in the ultimate analysis helped in preserving security rather than endangering it. In his opinion there is an important correlation between degree of freedom and security. Higher the freedom, more the social threats to the individuals and thus individual security was threatened. In the same way, freedom of the states leads to insecurity, as that will lead to a state of chaos where states will be groping for direction.

Neo-realists like Robert Gilpin would seek a terrain away from the realists' obsession with power. Even he substantially modifies the realists' overall conceptual position of the state. He would call a state a 'coalition of coalitions' rather than a unitary actor as was emphasized in earlier times and even go to the extent of banishing the concept of state from the realm of conceptual possibility.[40] He ridicules the realists' weakness for *status quo* and situates the problematic of security against such a backdrop where *status quoist* states bent on preserving the *status quo* would seek power for the sake of it in overtly military terms. Gilpin rather emphasizes on economic factors. He argues that calculation of cost and benefits very often determines the locus of decision-making of nations in preparation for war and peace.[41] The recognition of economy as the most important ingredient of power makes Gilpin's neo-realist study sounds very logical in the context of happenings all round the globe right now. His concern for security, therefore, has more to do with strengthening of economic factors and considerations of them than the preparedness of war strictly in military-power terms.

Barry Buzan analyses the concept of security holistically. According to Buzan, security is a complex combination of individual, national and international security, which he considers as three levels in his analysis of security paradigm. He discusses security in relation to specific threats. He emphasizes on social threats that are intertwined in human environment with unavoidable social, political and economic consequences. Freedom is the most important factor that regulates the social security of a man. To overcome the threats that spring up from freedom and to maintain adequate level of security against social threats, people seek the mechanism of the state. The paradox is that, the state, instead of ensuring individual security, becomes a source of social threat against the individual because of its so called 'defence dilemma'. The objective of the state is to guarantee security to its citizens for which it seeks to go nuclear in the modern age, which ultimately leads to their extinction. Thus states in stead of acting as a vehicle of individual security acts as a source of insecurity. In his opinion, national security depends upon the relationship between the nation and the state. The vulnerability of national security depends upon the components of the state, i.e. the institution of state and physical base of it. The different character of the components, which constitute the state, suggests that threats to the state can come in variety of ways. They can be military, political and ecological. In the same way they can be averted by a variety of means among which military power may not be considered as the most important one.[42] Thus he tries to modify the conceptual position of realists and their over-emphasis on power paradigm.

According to Buzan, the two major systems, which constitute the security environment of the state, are: international political system and international economic system, which he characterizes as 'anarchical'. He distinguishes between immature and mature anarchies. The former variety resembles the popular image of anarchy; the latter seems to be an utopian concept of anarchy where "the benefits of fragmentation can be enjoyed without the costs of continuous struggle and instability". Hence such mature anarchy will lead to a better existence of the state system by mutual respect and understanding.[43] This condition of anarchy suggests that the security concerns of the subsystems do not spread uniformly throughout the system and complex patterns of alignments seek to promise security at different levels. He calls these arrangements as 'security complexes'. He defines a "security complex" as a group of states whose primary security concern link together with their national securities so closely that their individual security cannot be considered in isolation of the overall security arrangements.[44]

Bjørn Møller emphasizes a new type of defence structure 'Non Offensive Defence' (NOD) for ensuring security of nations, which is at stake. He argues in favour of it as it leads to arms control and disarmament, increased crisis stability and the elimination of incentives for preventive war and pre-emptive attack. He compared Non-Offensive Defence (NOD) with military strategy and elaborates its feature in the context of military, maritime forces and nuclear strategy. He analysed its implication in making alliances in general and NATO in particular and considered NOD as a corollary of 'common security'.[45]

1.3. Collective Security: Prospects and Peril

Collective security plays a significant role in preserving global peace and security. It promises peace by preventing wars, settling international disputes and discouraging warmongers. In the present world the United Nations –the regulator of 'collective security measures'— is stressing more on disarmament programmes as it feels collective security and disarmament programmes are inter-related and should go together. Benjamin Cohen states in U.N. General Assembly:

"I should like to stress the fact that there is an intimate relationship between a programme of collective security and a programme of disarmament. The two by their nature go hand in hand. In the disarmament field, we look to the day when no nation will have armed forces or armaments, which could pose a threat to a neighbor. In the collective security field, we look to the day when nations will not rely so much on their own forces as on the United Nations for their security. If states are assured that in case of attack they will not stand alone, they will need fewer arms for their defence As progress is made in disarmament, the task of building collective security becomes simpler. The two march together.... disarmament and collective security are the two great enterprises for peace that this General Assembly has before it".[46]

In the recent times, the UN took collective measures when Iraq illegally occupied Kuwait and succeeded in resolving this crisis. Before the existence of the UN, the League of Nations also tried its best for the settlement of problems collectively. In some of the disputes before it, especially in the early years, it rendered useful service. But in every major case involving open defiance of the covenant by great powers its security structure did not match to the test. It did not play that much effective role in Manchurian crisis, Poland crisis at the beginning of the Second World War and in Ethiopian crisis. However, the fact that collective security measures contribute to the maintaining of peace can never be denied.

The analysis of the theory and practice of collective security reveals that it wants to preserve *status quo.* Walter Lippmann rightly considers it as the 'custodian of *status quo'*. Collective security measure aims at observing peace by preventing wars, suppressing aggression by collective efforts but ignores the fact that *status quo,* which it wants to preserve, is unjust and must be replaced by peaceful means. The dark side of the collective security measure is that instead of preventing war, it universalizes war by converting local and regional wars to world war. It does so not by welcoming small and medium size nations to power struggle but also by preparing the people of a powerful nation with scientific technology to eliminate another nation.[47] Thus, the basic purpose of collective security— to maintain peace and security—gets defeated. In the nuclear world, collective security measure gets a new turn and twist. It is too difficult to control a powerful nation which may cause nuclear war leading to the extinction of the world.

Secondly, the victim of an aggression may be completely destroyed before this collective measure is taken. Collective security cannot be effective unless it takes a bold and impartial step in preventing wars by not dancing to the tune of powerful nations. Its objective should be 'security through disarmament' and not by war to counter another war, which may breed violence, thus jeopardize security.

1.4. Security and the Paradigm of Idealism

The concept of security gets a new dimension by the exponents of idealism who regard realists view of 'power politics' as a 'passing phase of history'.

The idealists outrightly rejected their ideas and came forward with a new idea that visualized a new order free from 'power politics, immorality and violence'. The basic objective of this theory is to look after the interests of various groups, nations and ensure the welfare of the entire humankind. In the year 1795, Condorcet wrote a treatise which elaborated the main ideas of idealism in international politics. He visualized a New World order free from war, violence, inequality, and tyranny and based on peace, amity and mutual cooperation.

In the modern age Kant, Tolstoy, Gandhi, Woodrow Wilson are considered as the chief exponents of idealism. Kant insisted on peace which he considered as pre-requisite for human kind's ultimate societal and moral progress. He condemned war, tried to eliminate it as it breeds violence. In his opinion, individuals should work for peace so should states. Kant regarded an end to war as something, which was not only desirable but whose historical progress was making peace increasingly realizable. He thought that the major force in history was the tension between humankind's desire to satisfy its own wants, without regard to the well being of others, and the realization that it is only through cooperation with others that it can have any real chance for happiness. As civilization develops, said Kant, people see increasingly clearly the truth that they must cooperate with one another, even if this means denial of their own passion and desires."[48]

Kant argued in favour of peaceful relationship between states and despised war, as it runs counter to the most desirable goal of survival of the mankind. In case of war, state would spend a lot of money for that, but if it were defeated, it would have to face the horrors of conquest and humiliation of defeat. Kant's ideas of *perpetual peace* had a tremendous impact all over the world. It gave a powerful stimulus to much of the nineteenth century thinking on how to limit and ultimately eliminate war on both sides of the Atlantic.[49] Thus Kant was a true champion of peace and tried to ensure security of the world through peaceful means.

Tolstoy was the champion of 'pacifism' and a great preacher of morality. His study of peace lies chiefly in his commitment to pacifism. He supported the idea of total non-resistance than passive resistance to violence. Tolstoy who was regarded as a 'Christian Anarchist' criticized state vehemently for producing war, legitimizing violence and endangering the existence of mankind. State propagates false values like inequality, cruelty, and brutality, and suppresses noble virtues by its coercive structure. "If state compelled the individual to do violence, then the individual should peaceably but decisively go on strike against it until the state ceased to exist".[50] Tolstoy was criticized by realists as he denied State its power and by Christians who admitted moral validity of much that he had to say but saw the impracticability of its realization. For without State it is impossible to think of social existence. Because of the State, there could be order based on law, morality and education. Tolstoy, who was a believer of transcendental and supernatural power, hoped for the change of the world through changes in the human heart. Though his ideas seemed to be utopian, he was an ardent advocate of peace who strived his best to guarantee the security of the entire world through peace.[51]

Mahatma Gandhi was a true champion of non-violence and peace. Though he did not evolve a complete theory of security, the twin principle of truth and non-violence (*satya* and *ahimsa*) formed the core of Gandhi's philosophy. Gandhi said that truth and non-violence could bring about a total transformation in the world. Like other idealists, he supported the eternal idea of peace and denounced violence and immorality, as they corrupt human relationship and souls of the people of the world. He wanted to preserve peace through mutual respect and mutual promotion of each other's interest.[52] He wanted to fight against the force of an invading army with the force of love but he wished for a moral victory not by reconciling with aggressor but by forcing him to surrender to his eternal principle of non-violence and peace. In this context Gandhi said: "Peace, I want, among all mankind, but I don't want peace at any cost and certainly not by placating aggression".[53] The idea of *Shanti Sena* (Peace Army) which was his brain-child was effective in containing the Chinese incursion into Tibet as well as in other conflicts. He also proposed the concept of 'civilian based defence' which has more relevance in the present world. This is considered by many including strategic thinkers as the panacea to save the world from nuclear catastrophe, for it is the only form of defence which neither threatens the attacking party by provoking them to attack, nor calls for militarization of society.[54] Gandhi extended his idea of non-violence and peace to national and international defence and strived for preserving security through these weapons.

Woodrow Wilson brought a renaissance in the world with his ideas of federalism, which laid the foundation stone of 'League of Nations'. He is the founding father of 'modern idealism', which he thought could be reflected in the world order and federalist traditions and advocated the abolition of states in favour of 'world government', peace societies, peace movements and other such organizations those are influenced by his ideas. He stressed on 'world government' and strived for replacing occidental with oriental cosmology.[55] Thus Wilsonian ideas of peace have much more relevance in the present world for creating a New World Order and preserving global security. In the words of Ruth C. Reynolds:

"He bequeathed his generation, and following generations, with a faith that such an order might be possible, and in the United Nations, much of Wilson's work and idealism came to fruition".[56]

1.5. Institutional Approach to Security

In the present time, various institutions, peace movements and organizations are devoted to the achievement of peace and security. They facilitate in disseminating these ideas all over the world, promoting cooperation and multilateral relations among various nations. This is an important approach to the concept of security. Various institutional frameworks which aimed at universal peace are discussed below.

1.5.i. Non-Alignment Movement and Security

The Non-Alignment Movement (NAM) is an anti-imperialist and anti-colonial movement, which strives towards peaceful co-existence and international security. When the entire world is under the spell of nuclear war, NAM is playing a decisive role in sorting out regional and super power conflicts and thereby has had a dampening influence on the East-West crisis.[57] It has also challenged the regressive forces, those that are trying to destabilize the world and disturbing the oneness of humanity. Its effective role and sincere efforts in solving Afghanistan, Nicaragua, Angola, Kampuchea and other West Asian problems is really worth praising. The political declaration adopted by the Delhi Conference stressed on this aspect: *"It is a struggle against imperialism, apartheid, racism including Zionism and against all forms of foreign aggression, occupation, domination, interference or hegemony as well as against great power and bloc policies".*[58] Apart from maintaining peace "it is also striving for the establishment of a New World Order based on respect for independence, equality and cooperation".[59]

NAM has really restructured the social, political and economic set up of the world. In the economic sphere it has tried for the establishment of a New International Economic Order (NIEO) which has saved the Third World, particularly Afro-Asian countries from colonialism and neo-colonialism. In 1961, Non-Aligned Summit at Belgrade tried to remove the economic disparities, which they inherited from colonialism and imperialism. It also tried to bridge the gap between developed and developing nations by accelerating the growth of economic, industrial and agricultural sectors of the Third World.

NAM has also stressed on the political dimension of security. It has encouraged super-powers and other important powers for the solution of the military, economic and other issues through summit diplomacy. It has also accelerated the pace for concluding various treaties, particularly during Cold War and new Cold War period, which ushered in a new phase of *détente*. From the above analysis, it is clear that this movement gave a new direction to the concept of security as it emphasizes military, political, economic and social security of the world. Now scholars like Galtung, Robert Gilpin and Paul Kennedy are successful in conceptualizing this dimension of security.[60]

1.5.ii. The United Nations and Security

The United Nations was formed after the Second World War to avert future wars and to maintain global peace and security. This world organization has been working successfully for last fifty years in promoting peace, security and human welfare.

The purpose of the United Nations is:

1. "To maintain international peace and security, and to that end, to take effective collective measures for the prevention and removal of threats to the peace, and for the suppression of acts or other breaches of the peace, and to bring about by peaceful means, and in conformity with the principles of

justice and international law, adjustment or settlement of international disputes or situations which might lead to a breach of the peace;

2. To develop friendly relations among nations based on respect for the principle of equal rights and self-determination of peoples, and to take other appropriate measures to strengthen universal peace;
3. To achieve international cooperation in solving international problems of an economic, social, cultural or humanitarian character and in promoting and encouraging respect for human rights and for fundamental freedoms for all without distinction as to race, sex, language, or religion; and
4. To be a centre for harmonizing the actions of nations in the attainment of these common ends".[61]

An Agenda for Peace was prepared at the level of Heads of State and Government at the level of U.N. Security Council meeting in January 1992. The report summarized the United Nations' approach to peace, security and the implications of its involvement in regional and intra-state conflicts. The then Secretary-General Boutros-Boutros Ghali defined three important functions that the Security Council asked him to address.

1. *Preventive Diplomacy* – It is action to prevent disputes from arising between parties, to prevent existing disputes from escalating into conflicts and to limit the spread of the latter.

2. *Peace Making* – It is a technique that expands the possibilities for both the prevention of conflict and the making of peace.

3. *Peace Enforcement* - which enforces peace in case of needs.[62]

Preventive diplomacy seeks to resolve disputes before violence breaks out. Peace making, peace keeping and peace enforcement are essential to halt conflict and to preserve peace, once it is attained. If it is successful it leads to 'post conflict peace building', which helps in preventing the recurrence of conflicts between states. It encompasses more than the reconstruction of peace after the cessation of hostilities. It is related to the developmental efforts – political, economic, socio-cultural of the U.N. Its prime-motive is to settle down conflicts of various magnitudes amicably and to open up the path for socio-economic development of nations by reinforcing ever-lasting peace. It strives for restoring civil society through its efforts in revamping its polity, economy and settling the migration problem.[63]

Preventive Diplomacy is playing a vital role in the present world for the solution of international conflicts. Mutual confidence and good faith are essential to reducing the likelihood of conflicts between states.[64] United Nations use good offices, good missions, despatching special envoys to tense areas and bringing parties to a conflict to the negotiating table for this purpose. It is the most effective technique of United Nations for tackling variety of challenges, which it faces in its day to day activities. More than one hundred missions of representation, fact finding and good will offices were undertaken by U.N. The U.N. Secretary General and other diplomats have travelled extensively to extend good offices and represent the organization throughout the world.[65] It played a positive role for the solution of South African problem and ensuring peace in that country. In the first time in the U.N. history military units have been deployed as a measure of preventive diplomacy in the former Yugoslav Republic of Macedonia. *"Under United Nations auspices, Greece and former Yugoslav Republic of Macedonia are engaged in talks intended to reduce tensions brought about by the recognition of the independence of the latter".*[66]

Various Humanitarian assistance programmes of the UN help in maintaining an atmosphere of peace world-wide by catering to the basic needs of the people in moments of crisis. The "Joint U.N.-South Africa Development Community Drought Emergency in South Africa Programme" played a significant role in mitigating the effects of drought, famine and migration problem. Its effective role in solving natural calamities and other natural disasters are really worth praising.

In many respects *An Agenda for Peace* was an effort to identify the new requirements of peace keeping and new role of

United Nations in the quest of international peace and security. The functions of the peace-keepers have already undergone a change. Nowadays, they have been working as a police force rather than an army for helping people and keeping order, so that government mechanisms will function smoothly. Founding fathers of the United Nations Charter rightly made the UN system flexible enough to accommodate the wider role of peace-keeping upon which the 'New Collective Security' system now operates.[67]

The United Nations has taken collective action against aggression only on two occasions – Korea in 1950 and Kuwait in 1991. Except for Kuwaiti case, the United Nations has faced problems with different variations since the end of the cold war for which there is no provision in the U.N. Charter. In the recent time, it is very difficult to distinguish between the functions of peace making and peace keeping. U.N. operation in the Congo in 1960 was the example of peace making in the traditional sense. With the end of the Cold War, the peace-making model has been stretched as U.N. has involved itself in various operations in Somalia, Cambodia, the former Yugoslav, Mozambique, Angola and Afghanistan with variety of missions to project humanitarian and programmes and to preserve peace and security.[68]

1.6. New Collective Security

The 'New Collective Security' stresses on both conceptual and practical levels for its operation. In the practical level, it emphasizes on three important aspects: United Nations operational capacity; stable source of funding; and well trained troops for peace keeping operation.

In the conceptual level, it tries to solve the security problems particularly transnational issues that are economic, social and ethical in nature. Nowadays, economic, political and social security has more relevance than military security in the traditional sense of the term. Paul Kennedy has rightly elaborated these aspects of security in *Rise and Fall of Great Powers*.[69] The United Nations security approach should be broad based for ensuring ever-lasting peace and security.

1.7. The Rationalist Perspective

Concept of security could be analyzed through 'system' and 'rational' approaches, as they would provide scientific insight into the complex and wider issues involved in it.

1.7. (i). The Systems Approach

The systems approach holds that international politics was full of anarchy. There was chaos, confusions, no fixed patterns to govern it. In this environment states used to fend for themselves as they pursued their contradictory interests.[70] The need for a system was the need of the time to systematize the activities of the states and to study intricate issues in a scientific manner. Thus the idea of system emerged from out of the chaos, which sought to bring about order and harmony.

Thus "a system is considered to exist in an environment and to be composed of parts which, through interaction, are in relation to each other".[71] In this sense, there are discernable regular patterns of action. As conflicts are inevitable in international politics and the 'games nation play' with certain fixed patterns and principles, international system helps in conducting this game. But the management of conflicts is more important than the conflict itself as it ensures peace and security.

1.7. (ii). The Rational Approach

The rational approach to security includes various models. Models could be mutually contradictory, while some of the models advocate building up of arms to secure peace, some others emphasize on complete disarmament. Some may argue in favour of perpetuating conflict at a low scale, others may stand for attempting decisions at a domestic level to pre-empt conflict. Attempts have been made to assess some of the significant models of security below.

Deterrence is one of the most important theoretical concept of security, in which one party tries to influence the behaviour of another in a desired direction. It rests directly upon threats, sanctions or deprivation.[72] Thus it deters the opposition from initiating armed actions and restraining escalation in case of war. The far-reaching consequences of deterrence are as follows:

- It views the world order in terms of allies and opponents. It emphasizes military build up and war for preserving security.
- Its prime motive is to prevent opponents from attack. For this, it keeps a vigilant eye on the opponents' moves, political behaviours and above all military strategies.
- Deterrence emphasizes on the capability of the attacker. It should be convinced about the potentiality of the other side and his motive to use force in case of war.
- In this game of deterrence, each side tries to win against the other; convincing other that it has potentiality to win.[73]

According to Phil Williams, the basic requirements for the functioning of the concept of deterrence are communication, capability and credibility.[74] In case of absence of any one of those requirements, deterrence would not be effective and it would lead to a war. Ultimately the security would be at stake. With the advent of nuclear age, traditional deterrence was replaced by 'nuclear deterrence'. The conflicts were not confined to states or between two powerful states, but extended to blocs. In 1960's bloc antagonism was intensified by both the super powers. Both the North Atlantic Treaty Organization (NATO) and the Warsaw Pact (dismantled now) amassed sophisticated nuclear arms and weapons like Intercontinental Ballistic Missile (ICBM) and Sea Launched Ballistic Missiles (SLBM) to deter each other. Thus Mutual Assured Destruction (MAD) restrained both the power hungers from nuclear war and played a positive role in ensuring security. Robert McNamara, the then U.S. Secretary of Defence stressed on MAD and analysed its effective role in deterrence. As the basic premise of nuclear deterrence is that its opponent cannot win a nuclear war, so to materialize this assurance power hungry nation tries for continuous development and military technology, improved methods of conducting war and increased killing capabilities.[75]

During the 1970s and early 1980s both the power blocs had sophisticated missiles, hydrogen bombs, long-range strategic bombers and other nuclear means for maintaining strategic purity. Higher the options of nuclear deterrence; more acute the arms race. In 1980's arms race between two super powers reached at its height, U.S.A. started its Strategic Defence Initiative (SDI) programme. During this time it increased its nuclear capabilities, MX missile programmes, the Trident, SLBM programmes. Similarly, Soviet Union started its missile programmes i.e., (ICBM) to counter the nuclear capability of U.S.A. and to deter U.S.A. from its imperialistic design.

The most important premises of deterrence, which restrained rational actors like super powers from nuclear attack was the cost-benefit considerations, horrors and irreparable damage which it would cause to civilian population, the possibility of escalating nuclear war beyond bounds which was a irrational and unethical.[76]

Soviet perception of nuclear deterrence was different from the American one. In the opinion of Soviet strategic thinkers, even though U.S.A. stressed more on the concept of nuclear sufficiency, but in real sense, its capabilities were developed beyond this which could be identified with 'deterrence through punishment'. Even U.S.A. was not ready to compromise with its S.D.I. programmes at the time of negotiation with USSR. The most dangerous part of nuclear arms race was that the surplus nuclear weapons were used for political bargaining which impeded the peaceful negotiations between the super powers. Soviet strategists thought that real operation of deterrence could be possible only through close inspection, fair evaluation and due application to mutuality.[77]

In late 1980s this nuclear deterrence was given a new twist. Gorbachev, the then leader of USSR came forward with his new concept of security, i.e. comprehensive universal security including delegitimization of the use of nuclear weapons as a viable alternative to the theory of nuclear deterrence.

Disarmament and Arms Control are the two important theories of the concept of security. At the outset, both seem to be straight forward approaches to the problems of peace and security, but in reality they are too complex with far reaching consequences.[78] The most accepted definition of both the theories are given by Hedley Bull: *"disarmament is the reduction or abolition of armaments; it may be unilateral or multilateral; general or local;*

comprehensive or partial, controlled or uncontrolled. Arms control on the other hand is restraint internationally exercised upon armaments policy, whether in respect of the level of armaments, their character deployment or use".[79]

Though the term 'disarmament' and 'arms control' are used interchangeably but both are not synonymous. Disarmament is related to reduction in armaments whereas arms control refers to restraint. One thing common about both is that there can be disarmament and arms control without formal agreement, arms control encompasses wider range of issues than the reduction of armament. Another important difference is that disarmament is the older but arms control is newer approach.[80]

Elimination of war and maintenance of peace and security are the catchwords of the disarmament programmes. The nation of disarmament springs up from the threat perception, which arises out of a situation of armed hostility. Each nation perceives the other as a threat to the national security and such perception is akin to the estimated capability and estimated intent of the opposition. Higher the capability and higher the intent of the opposition, the more the threat perception to a nation, but with the absence of anyone, threat perception diminishes drastically. The problem is that to come out of this 'arms tension circle' threat perception should be reduced. It could only possible through the reduction of both military capability and estimated military intent.[81]

Taking this threat perception into consideration, David Singer mentions three approaches to the theory of disarmament.[82]

1. Tension – First approach, otherwise known as UNESCO approach attempts to reduce tension through education, understanding and by changing the attitudes of the people. It believes that changing attitudes would be helpful in decreasing inter-governmental tension. It rejects the need for armaments. David Singer does not accept this approach as it has little merit.

2. Political Settlement Approach – This approach believes that arms tension circle which causes threat perception can be

eliminated through the proper settlement of underlying political problems. In this connection, Walter Lippmann says, "The power will not and cannot disarm while they are in conflict on vital issues". Similar views are also expressed by the writings of Morgenthau, Kennan, and de Madriaga. Singer sees little merit in this approach as it undermines the role of weapons in threat perception.[83]

3. Armament First Approach – This approach favours disarmament. It believes that tension can be reduced and political conflicts can be resolved when the process of disarmament begins.

Scholars of the *Gradualist School* argue that elimination of weapons should be done in a careful and controlled manner, which would generate an atmosphere of trust between the countries involved. They stressed on the Graduated Reciprocation in Tension Reduction (GRIT) scheme. David Singer, E. Osgood and L. B. Sohn are the exponents of this school of thought. But the scholars of 'armament-first school' believe that "the way to disarm is to disarm". When the States are serious and the environment for multilateral treaty is ready, the process of disarmament should begin.[84]

The popularity of this disarmament theory is clearly revealed from its history. The first disarmament agreement took place in 1817 between UK and USA which resulted in US-Canadian border becoming the largest demilitarized border in the world and thereafter large number of agreements have been taking place every year. This theory is acceptable internationally as it is supported by social, ethical and economic arguments. Socially, it argues that military power if not restrained and controlled properly is a threat to the society thus disarmament is the best way for preserving security. Ethically it supports the view of pacifists that preparation for war is not justifiable. Economically it is not advisable to go for armaments, as it would incur heavy cost.[85] However, the critics of disarmaments do not agree with the above arguments and support the arguments for armaments for preserving security. But the real problem of this disarmament is the problems of inspection, verification, and enforcement. American and the

Russian scholars have their own opinions on it and they do not agree with each other. But this problem could be solved only through unanimous decision and common approach to it.

The theory of arms control plays an important role in the concept of security. At the end of 1950s this theory assumed prominence as it provided the stimulus for the development of 'arms control'. Hedley Bull has described the central idea of this theory as follows:

"Arms control is a concern about the dangers of nuclear war, and a dissatisfaction with existing policies; a suspicion of the goal of negotiated general and comprehensive disarmament agreement; an insistence upon the unity of strategy and arms control; a broadening of the scope of the subject and a perception of the links between varieties of military activity hitherto thought separate, a criticism of the assumption that disarmament (arms reduction) should be the objective of arms control policy; and a determination to destroy the illusion of disarmament discussion while remaining optimistic about the contribution of the social sciences to improving the prospects of peace and security".[86]

The strategic experts Schelling and Halperin also emphasized on this theory. According to them, it reduces the scope of war and violence and recognizes the common interest and helps in developing a friendly and healthy relationship between potential enemies.[87] It is clear from the above discussion that national interest is the prime mover of this theory and the participants of the arms race believe that it is economically wasteful or strategically self defeating to develop a particular weapon system. It is wise to go for arms control, as it does not require the same degree of mutual trust line disarmament because it affects small sector of nation's armory. Secondly, it does not involve the complication of inspection, verification and other problems.

But there are two divergent views about the international conditions for this arms control measures. Some scholars believe that without political settlement there will be no arms control as it involves greater risk if war breaks out and the national distrust of uncertainty makes the international actors more skeptic. Others believe that arms control must precede political settlement as it ensures a right type of environment for mutual agreements for the solution of the political problems.[88] It is obvious that national interest is the most important factor for arms control proposals, but military security is the most important consideration for Soviets particularly during Khrushchev era. Lincoln P. Bloomfield emphasized on strategic, economic, external political and internal leadership as four important areas, which had an impact on the erstwhile Soviet disarmament policies. They conclude that:

"the military strategic factor best accounts for both the stability and fluctuations in Soviet policy towards arms control. Moscow's deep concern to avoid general war and its acquisition of a credible minimum deterrent account in large part for the fixed elements among Soviet interests and policies on arms control, while the changing balance between Soviet and US strategic forces appear to have been the key factor in inducing the shifts in Soviet arms control policies throughout the decade".[89]

Another important theory which has been developed during the past few decades is the decision-making theory which is associated in the names of Richard C. Snyder, H. W. Bruck and Burton Sapin. These writers tried to provide a theoretical framework to the complex question of international politics. This theory has utmost relevance for the analysis of the concept of security. This theory provides deep insights into the complex problems of security and helps the decision-makers in taking right decision, which is essential for international actor. In the words of Robinson, "It is a social process that selects a problem for decision (i.e. choice) and produces a limited number of alternatives, from amongst which a particular alternative is selected for implementation and execution".[90] This theory insists that the behaviour of the decision-makers should be treated as "actors in a situation". It also emphasizes on the perception of the situation by the actors as the most important basis of the decision. The situation, which includes both internal, and external factors motivate the decision-makers to take various steps for security reasons. Sprout and Sprout emphasize on the post-decisional results and compare the judgement of the decision-makers with those of outsiders.[91] They justify the action of the decision-makers not by the decision-makers perception of the situation but by the effective action taken by the actors to safeguard the national security. Another important factor is the personality of the decision-makers, which can never be undermined. It involves courage, conviction, intelligence and the studies of security policies before taking an important decision on security. It is obvious that the security policies of Henry Truman and John Kennedy were different than that of Joseph Stalin or Nikita Khrushchev.

The recent contribution to an understanding of this theory has been made by John Burton. In his opinion, the attitude of decision-makers is determined by the ideology of a country, the manner in which change is received, the knowledge of the leaders about international situation, past memory of the community as well as experience and the study of foreign policies of a nation. Some writers like Niou, Ordeshook and Rose emphasize on the people's preference than leaders decisions in this theory. According to them, stable or unstable international system emerges not by the decision of leaders but by the preference of the people. If it is assumed that nations seek peace or conflict, then that goals are the logical result of the operation of international political system. Because nations do not want to assume that a particular system leads to peace and others lead to conflict. Thus their motives begin with more fundamental objectives and derive the circumstances under which peace or conflict will prevail as the logical consequence of the relationship among States.[92] Most of the decision-makers of the security are guided by this idea while formulating security policies for a nation. Rosenau stresses on the reasoning and motivation as important factors in the analysis of decision-making. In his opinion, some analysts stress on the rationality which provides the requisite stimuli for decision-making. According to some others, personality traits, private prejudices of the officials play a decisive role in the process of decision-making.[93]

Game Theory and Bargaining Theory are two important theories in international policies that play a decisive role for the analysis of the concept of security. Game theory assumes that international politics is a game of power politics among international actors. As the game in international politics is inevitable, so the States try to advance their interests offensively or defensively but in either case, the players must weigh carefully the alternative means of achieving their objectives and then choose the option that will maximize their gains and minimize their losses, as well as their risks and costs.[94] In international politics, there are lots of games going on, such as adversary games in which two or more States engaged in conflict, alignment game in which States seek helps from other States and attract allies away from their opponents through de-alignment or realignment. Arms competition or preparedness game continues as each nation tries to safeguard its security by resisting the attack of the opponents or by gaining superiority over other nations.[95] This theory has five important concepts – the first is the concept of strategy. This emphasizes on the skillful plan of an international actor to maximize his chance of victory over the opponents. This strategy takes into account the potential behaviour of the opponents and helps the State in applying rationality before taking an important decision. It is clear that the strategy is chalked out taking the potentiality of the opponents. Thus, this theory assumes an 'opponent' which is the second important concept of this theory. Third concept is 'pay off' which evaluates the worth of this game. The fourth concept is a rule that regulates the game. In social and international situations, rules are the laws governed by geographical, social, economic, biological and psychological considerations. The fifth concept of this game is information, which is essential for making a sound strategy.[96] Game theory be it two persons game or n-person game is guided by the above concepts and the crux of this theory is nothing but to safeguard its security. It is simply an innovative way for the survival of the State.

Bargaining theory is the extension of the orthodox game theory. But it is usually applied in the field of international negotiations. As international negotiations play a decisive role for the solution of international conflicts, so the bargaining theory has much relevance. There have been three approaches adopted for the development of the theories of negotiations. First approach is known as the orthodox approach, which requires that preferences of the negotiating party must remain constant and no way it should be compromised. But some writers argue that there must be some sort of change in the process of negotiation.[97] On the basis of this possibility, second kind of approach has been developed. The third approach to negotiations expounded by Joseph Nogee. The basic premise of this approach is that negotiation is the last thing that a party wants to reach. No party ever wants to break off the negotiations either by withdrawing from it or by compelling the other party to go out of it. So, the only way is to find out a strategy, which would be acceptable by both the parties. Thus, this theory helps the international actor in this critical situation and compels the nation to go for a right type of negotiation. This theory can hardly be applied in a situation characterized by pure conflict or/ and pure co-operation. In a pure conflict situation, the participants do not have common interest, they go for straight forward contest of physical strength. So, this theory is meaning less. It has relevance when the conflict is not pure, though they have conflicts on certain specific issues, but they have one common interest i.e. the avoidance of the use of force, which is the driving force behind this theory. In the situation of pure co-operation, they go for joint planning for common benefit. Thus it does not have any relevance. The relevance of this bargaining theory is only in mixed situation i.e. situation in between pure conflict and pure cooperation.[98] But the most important aspect of this theory is the protection of national interest. As security interests dominate over other interests, so the need for this theory is a must in international politics.

Security is always the prime concern of a nation for which each nation tries to manage the crisis effectively, which arises out of its interactions with other nations. In the nuclear age crisis management is indispensable; otherwise national security will be at stake. Conflict is inevitable in international politics and this ultimately leads to settlement,[99] but in this game of conflict winner is always in a better position to bargain and usually the loser compromises with the winner. So, nations in general and super powers in particular took deliberate moves to counter or control the risks of war for security reasons. Decisions are made in rational and calculating manner as possible to overcome this crisis.[100] In the post Cold War period, both the sides recognize the significance of national security for which each rational takes ration steps of not entering into conflict where the security of both the nations will be at danger. The best example of crisis management are Cuban missile crisis and Berlin crisis where situational factors influenced the outcome of super power confrontations probably to a greater extent that it was acknowledged.[101]

In the crisis management theory there are three major tenets. First tenet is limiting one's objective. There must be rational bargaining otherwise the crisis cannot be overcome. Second tenet is that two powers should try to solve the crisis on terms that are satisfactory without considering gains and loss. The third tenet is that two powers should try to keep the situation under the control, which would provide them freedom of choice for the solution of the crisis.[102]

From the above analysis, it is clear that crisis management is a strange mixture of ruthless and moderation, determination and prudence, intransigence and accommodation.[103] International actors particularly USA and erstwhile USSR applied these qualities in a judicious way for preserving their national security.

As discussed, besides military security, there are other areas— economic, environmental, societal— in which security threats are perceived. In the present world, particularly after the end of the Cold War, these relatively newer sectors have much significance.[104] Post-structuralists have also stressed on the expansion of this concept of security. It is argued by Ole Wæver that the security is a discursive practice, so the concept of security cannot be confined to military domain. The most important point is not to establish an objective relationship between the concept and possible domains of security, but "to study whether and how this issue can be securitized". He argues in favour of problematizing the possible and relationship between the state and the other, asking whether security politics has to be built on a conquest of the other.[105]

1.8. Economic Security

Economic security concerns "access to the resources, finance and market necessary to sustain acceptable levels of welfare and state power".[106] The Third World countries are more economically insecure than the developed nations. These countries are unable to meet the needs of the people as they have been exploited by the centre (centre-periphery model). Nations like Sudan, Bangladesh, Ethiopia, Liberia are still struggling to better up their economy. Nations like Brazil, Argentina, Tanzania are unable to resist the pressure of outside institutions in return for needed supplies of capital. The centre-periphery relation is still imbalance where periphery occupies a weak position in global market whose prices, trade, finance and technical evolution are controlled by the centre. There is hardly any hope for periphery to overcome this problem because of declining commodity prices, divergence of interests among the developing nations, strategy by the centre to divide and rule, debt crisis of developing nations, lack of facilities to utilize cheap labour in a productive way.[107]

Some scholars argue that the plight of the Third World countries arose from their dependent economic position which they had inherited from their colonial past. Others view that these countries are politically independent but penetrated by outside market and political interests and problems in leadership and society whose traditions, skills, resources and internal divisions often impeded the development of a modern political economy.[108]

Besides the economic insecurity of the third world, economic crisis have been faced by developing nations. Of course with the introduction of liberalization in world economy and followed by disintegration of Soviet Union, rise of Japan, Germany as economic powers for global leadership and burden sharing have tremendous impact on economic security.

The contemporary economic security is dominated by the strong globalizing tendencies. Now nations are trying their best to integrate with new Liberal International Economic Order (LIEO). The costs of world wide shipping and communication are very low. Now many firms and markets operate globally. It is the global economic system which marginalizes the powers of the states. Now the financial institutions like G7, the World Bank, World Trade Organisation (WTO), the International Monetary Fund (IMF), are playing significant role. Particularly these developments change the discourse in economic security by putting importance on liberal agenda in the area of trade, production and finance. Liberal ascendance means the contemporary discourse on economic security concerns about instability and inequality. Instability is due to relative economic decline of US and about the domestic and international management problems arising from the integration and liberalization of world economy. Concerns about inequality questions the role of the State in the domestic level and takes into consideration the problems of Third World States.[109] The decline of USA is due to its unfamiliarity with the pains of economic interdependence. By the 1970s US economy faced crisis and began to feel threatened by dependence on imported oil, trade deficits and pressure on the dollar.[110] In the 1970s, another important problem relating to economic security was the problem of integration and liberalization of global economy in trade and particularly in finance sector. Due to excessive competition in global market and presence of Transnational Corporations (TNC), in financial markets in this liberalization phase, unemployment and de-industrialization became a threat to both welfare and sovereignty of nation, those were unable to do well within it.

Secondly, the problem of systemic crisis arose in States due to adaptability of nations to the emerging global and trading financial system for maintaining stability and smooth functioning.[111] Thirdly, the need for aid to poor States and economically crippled socialist States has not been taken seriously by the economic powerful nations on liberal economic agenda was overshadowed socialist thinking in economy during this phase.[112]

The above mentioned problems, if not tackled properly, may create serious crisis. In the worlds of Buzan et.al.,

"the crisis may not come to pass, but the prospect of it and awareness of its possibility provide the basis for securitization of system-level regimes, consultative mechanisms, and organizations that sustain the LIEO. A major economic breakdown would have repercussions not only on the economic sector but also in terms of political and military security. Attempting to prevent such a breakdown and to retain the known productive efficiencies of the LIEO is the main globalizing dynamic for economic security".[113]

There is a strong connection between global concerns about security of the LIEO and security set up at the regional level.

Economic regionalism has gained its popularity as a result of integration in the European Union since 1980s and the formation of North American Free Trade Association (NAFTA). Other regional set ups like Association of South East Asian- Nations (ASEAN), Asian Pacific Economic Cooperation (APEC), linking Australia and North America, the Southern core common market (MERCOSUR) covering the southern core of South America, Asian Free Trade Area in South East Asia, ECOWAS in West Africa, SAARC in South Asia, the South African Development Community (SADC) in South Africa, the Commonwealth of Independent States (CIS) covering the former Soviet Union are trying to play a significant role in the process of regional integration.

Now the most pertinent question comes to the mind of a researcher – why do economic regionalism is strong when there is a globalizing tendencies. The answer is that the economic regionalism is a response to globalization. It helps the nation in their day to day operation. The logic of economic regionalism can be considered as a response to manage the threats emanating from globalization. In the words of Buzan et.al.,

"Unlike the situation in 1930s, most contemporary regional blocs have fairly liberal internal trading structures and in many ways are open to world markets. Their purpose is to reduce the pressures of an open global economy without sacrificing all economics of scale and to try to reduce the over-stretched management demands of an open global economy by moving many of those demands to a more intimate regional scale".[114]

Another important part of economic regionalism is the desire to preserve societal security. In this line one can see the Islamic economics as a separate type which has regionalizing tendencies. Some realists have also viewed regionalization as an effort to be in the super powers race, but it has lost its relevance after the disintegration of USSR which led to the demise of second Cold War.

As discussed, the concept of economic security is related to military, political, environmental and societal security and it is too difficult to separate it. This over spill quality means that has been talked about economic security is also related to the survival in other sectors, not the economic one.[115]

But liberals have attempted to separate the economic sector from politics and other sectors which is helpful to understand the concept of security from the perspective of wider security agenda. But still there are problems as we mentioned in this economic security. It can only be solved through concerted efforts of countries on the basis of multilateral constructive and mutual co-operation.

1.9. Environmental Security

Environmental security which is called the 'ultimate security issue' has broadened the security agenda further. Though security experts like Walt rejects the expansion of this concept to include *inter alia* AIDS, the drug problem and ecological hazards, because they think that this could destroy the coherence of the security paradigm.[116] But the demands of the people of the developed and developing nations to save the world from environmental degradation, resource depletion and environmental change which causes social turmoil either within a country or with neighbouring countries draw the attention of security experts to give importance to 'environmental security' in the new framework for security analysis.[117]

A wide range of problems and issues are included within the environmental security agenda: disruption of eco-systems which include climate change, bio diversity, deforestation, desertification and other forms of erosion, depletion of the ozone layer and various kinds of pollution. Energy problems include depletion of natural resources such as fossils, fuels and forests. To this can be added various forms of pollution including management disasters (related in particular to nuclear energy, oil transportation and chemical industries); and scarcities and uneven distribution.

Population Problems: It is the most important problem, which threatens to overload the earth's carrying capacity. This population growth produces epidemics of dangerous diseases and creates enormous problems like poor health conditions; declining literacy rates; politically and socially uncontrolled migration including the problem of urbanization.

Food problems include poverty, famine, over consumption, loss of fertile soil and water resources; epidemic and poor health conditions and scarcities and uneven distribution. *Economic problems* include the protection of unsustainable production modes, societal instability and structural asymmetries and inequality.

Civil strife includes war related environmental damage and violence related to environmental degradation.[118] In the view of Homer Dixon – "environmental securities are already leading to violent confrontations and there are early signs of increasing conflict in the coming decade, either induced or aggravated by ecological scarcities.[119]

In theory, environmental security threats can be either natural or man- made. A volcanic explosion which devastated the island of Mont Serrat in 1997, earthquakes in various parts of the world and other natural calamities are the examples of natural threats to mankind whereas Exxon Valdez accident, Chernobyl or French nuclear testing on Muroroa are manmade.

National governments and international communities are taking up several measures to reduce the death and destruction caused by such events; for example, through Satellite monitoring weather patterns and data relating to earthquake activity and tidal waves on the pacific region.

The focus on environmental security is on the environmental changes, which question the survival of the planet as a sustainable home. There are certain environmental problems like the earth's forests are shrinking; its deserts are expanding; soil eroding at record rates; thousands of plants and animal species disappear; the ozone layer in the upper atmosphere that protects us from ultraviolet radiation is thinning; the earth's temperature is increasing, posing a threat to all like support systems.[120]

There are many issues where the attitudes of States vary widely and in many instances ecological decay is due to politics of

States. Powerful national and international commercial interests have to be accommodated.[121]

Some States are more sensitive to these environmental issues than others and therefore, take lead role in this environmental diplomacy. Australia took the lead role in creating an international environment regime for Antarctica, as did Sweden to create an international legal regime to prevent trans-boundary pollution through 'acid rain'. Besides States, Non-Governmental Organizations (NGO) are playing significant role for environmental security. The shining example was green peace, which played a decisive role in the efforts to preserve the declining number of whale in the oceans of the world.

Environmental security is the most sensitive part of the whole security system, which cannot be preserved by the efforts of some States only. International community including NGOs must come forward to take serious international actions either at global or at regional level to deal with the problem effectively or soon it will lead to environmental conflict.

1.10. Societal Security

Societal security is the most prominent issue in the present world. It is "about the threats and vulnerabilities that affect patterns of communal identity and culture"[122]. A wide range of problems and issues are included within it. But the most common issues that have been considered as threats to societal security are outlined here.

The first problem is the issue of migration, which dilutes and changes the identity of one community with the influx of other people (e.g. Chinese migration into Tibet, Russian migration into Estonia). The second problem is the issue of horizontal competition, which changes the ways of a community because of cultural and linguistic influence from neighbouring culture. The third issue, which is a threat to societal security, is the issue of vertical competition where people lose their identity and identify with wider or narrower identities because there is either an integrating project (e.g. Yugoslavia, the EU) or a secessionist "regionalist" project g., Quebec, Catalonia). The fourth issue relating to societal security could be de population, whether by plague, war, famine, natural catastrophe or policies of extermination.[123]

The focus of societal security is on the 'sustainability within acceptable conditions for evolution, of traditional patterns of language, culture and religions and national identity and custom. But there is a class called elite those are the product of the globalizing economy of the information age, do not identify with rest of the people and values of the nation state. The emotional attachment to the nation state is weakened for this group. In some cases, these elite with cosmopolitan attitude owe their loyalty to MNCs, where they are working as its substitute. In most cases, pure individualism prevails. In numerous instances the conflict goes between cosmopolitan, liberal, internalized part of society and more locally tied communitarian resistance. In this context, Buzan et. al., said

"Much of societal security in the richest part of the world is related to this possibly over-arching conflict, that is, the opposition is more between universalizing and particularizing cultures than between different particularizing cultures (Hassner 1996). In less privileged parts of the world, the patterns are different, either because wider segments expect to gain from internalization (e.g. EU support in southern Europe) or because much of the elite takes part in nationalist operations (the former Yugoslav area)."[124]

Besides the above mentioned conflict, "the clash of civilizational identities is as strong on the other side of Islam, where it about Hindu civilization, as between Islam and the West."[125] As already discussed, various sectors of security, but in the present world security experts also have not undermined 'Humanitarian Security' and 'Security Communities'. Humanitarian Security concerns 'inter-state relations, contacts among the people of various states for good relations, mutual trust and understanding and rational solution to the problems of the world.

Security community concerns 'one in which there is real re-assurance that the members of the community will not fight each other physically, but will settle their disputes in some other way.'

According to Karl Deutsch, the factors for successful security community are, first a high co-relation of certain shared values such as democracy, social market economies and respect for the rule of the law and second, a degree of mutual understanding, solidarity and responsiveness among the states that made up the political community.[126]

From the above analysis, one can conclude that the concept of security has broadened its purview and it is not confined to military security issues which would definitely create misunderstanding to those who are associated with this wider agenda. True security requires government, NGOs and international organizations to address such objectives as social economic justice, political freedom and the protection of the planetary eco-system.

References

1. Vernon Van Dyke, *International Politics*, (Bombay: Vakils, Feffer and Simons, 1969), p. 35.
2. Arnold Wolfers, *Discord and Collaboration*, (Baltimore: John Hopkins Press, 1962), pp.147-66.
3. *Ibid.*
4. Ibid. This line of arguments are also expressed by Barry Buzan's, *People, States and Fear*, (Great Britain: Wheatsheaf Books, 1989), and Gregory Flynn, *The Internal Fabric of Western Security*, (Allanheld: Osmun & Co, 1981).
5. See Buzan, *People, States and Fear*, op. cit,.
6. Olof Palme, *Common Security: A Programme for Disarmament, Report of the Independent Commission on Disarmament and Security*, (London: Pan Books, 1982), p. 56.
7. Robert S. McNamara,"The Limitations of Military Power", *Survival*, Vol. VIII. No. 7, (July 1966), pp. 212 –213.
8. *Ibid.*
9. Gregory Flynn, *The Internal Fabric of Western Security America*, (Allanheld: Osmun and Co. 1981), p. 2.
10. *Ibid.*, p. 5.
11. George E. Hudson, (ed.), *Soviet National Security Policy under Perestroika*, (Boston: Unwin Hyman, 1990) p. 11.

12. Donald M. Snow, *National Security: Emerging Problems of U.S. Defence Policy*, (New York: St. Martins, 1987), pp. 5-6.
13. K. Subrahmanyam, *Security in Changing World*, (Delhi: B. R. Publishing Corporations, 1990), p. X.
14. Robert A. Rubinstein and Mary Le Cron Foster (eds.), *The Soviet Dynamics of Peace and Conflict*, (Boulder, Colo.: Westview Press, 1988), pp. 19-20.
15. M. S. Gorbachev, "Political Report of the CPSU Central Committee to the 27th Congress of the CPSU", *Soviet Review*, Vol. XXIII, No. 10, (1986), p. 23. See also *Speeches of Gorbachev, Documents and Materials*, (Moscow: Novosti Press, 1986).
16. Buzan, *op. cit.*, p. 7.
17. *Ibid.*, p. 7.
18. John H. Herz, *Political Realism and Political Idealism*, (Chicago: Chicago University Press, 1951), p. 18.
19. Hans J. Morgenthau, *Scientific Vs. Power Politics*, (Chicago: University of Chicago Press, 1946) p. 101.
20. John Spanier, *Games Nations Play*, (New Delhi: Macmillan, 1990), p. 11.
21. K. W. Thompson and Hans J. Morgenthau (eds.), *Principles and Problems of International Politics*, (New York: Praegar, 1968), p. 103.
22. Martin Wight, *Power Politics*, (London: Penguin, 1978), pp. 35-39. see also Quincy Wright, *A Study of War, Vol. II*, (Chicago: University of Chicago Press, 1972), pp. 743-59.
23. Dyke, *International Politics, op. cit.*, p. 221.
24. Nicholas J. Spykman, *America's Strategy in World Politics*, (New York: Macmillan, 1942), pp. 21-22. Similar views are also expressed by Arthur Hassal, *The Balance of Power, 1751-89*, (New York: Macmillan, 1914) p. 361; Alfred Vogts, "The United States and the Balance of Power", *Journal of Politics*, Vol. 3. No. 4, (November 1941) p. 405. and Dyke, *International Politics, op.cit.*, pp. 220-224.
25. George F. Kennan, *The Realist of American Foreign Policy*, (Princeton, N.J.: Princeton University Press, 1954), pp. 212-214.
26. See for example, Robert Good, "National Interest and Moral Theory: The Debate Among Contemporary Political Realists", in Roger Hilsman and Robert C. Good (eds.), *Foreign Policy in the Sixties: The Issues and the Instruments*, (Baltimore: John Hopkins Press, 1965), p. 204.

27. Raymond Aron, "The Quest for a Philosophy of Foreign Affairs", in Stanley Hoffman (ed.), *Contemporary Theory in International Relations*, (New Delhi, Prentice Hall, 1964), p. 80.
28. Raymond Aron, *The Philosopher in History, Vol. 1*, (London: Sage Publication, 1986), p. 402.
29. Quincy Wright, *On Predicting International Relation, The Year 2000*, Morgenthau Series in World Affairs, Monograph No. 1, (Colorado: University of Denver, 1969-70), p. 9.
30. Quincy Wright, "Realism and Idealism in International Politics", *World Politics*, (October 1954), pp. 126-127.
31. Quincy Wright, *op.cit.,* p. 22.
32. Hedley Bull, *The Control of the Arms Race*, (London: Weidenfeld and Nicholson, 1961). pp. 25-29.
33. *Ibid.,* pp. 37-62.
34. *Ibid.,* p. 55.
35. Hedley Bull, "The Classical Approach to Arms Control: Twenty Three Years After", in Clive Nerlich (ed.), *Soviet Power and Western Negotiating Policies*, Vol. 2, (Ballinger, 1983.), pp. 119-125.
36. Arnold Wolfers, "Statesmanship and Moral Choice", *World Politics*, (January 1949), pp. 1763-94.
37. Arnold Wolfers, *Discord and Collaboration*, (Baltimore, John Hopkins University Press, 1962), ch 10. see also Buzan, *People, States and Fear, op.cit.* p. 4.
38. Stanley Hoffman, *The State of War: Essay on the Theory and Practice of International Politics*, (London: Pall Mall, 1965), p. 154.
39. Kenneth Waltz, *Theory of International Politics*, (Reading, MA: Addison- Wesley, 1979), pp. 93-97, 105.
40. Robert Gilpin, *War and Change in World Politics*, (Cambridge: Cambridge University Press, 1981), pp. 18-19, 35, 177.
41. Gilpin, op.cit., pp. 39-55, and 105-155. For comparable European views see e.g. Mary Kaldor, *The Disintegrating West*, (New York: Hill and Wang, 1978), pp. 14-28 and 173-208. See also Paul Kennedy, *The Rise and Fall of Great Powers: Economic Change and Military Conflict from 1500 to 2000*, (London: Unwin Hyman, 1988), pp. 514-535.
42. Buzan, *People, States and Fear*, op. cit., p. 20, pp. 24-92.
43. *Ibid.,* p. 96.
44. *Ibid.,* p. 106, 126.

45. Bjørn Møller, *Common Security and Non-Offensive Defence*, (Boulder: Lynn Rienner Publishers, 1992), pp. 1-9, 285.
46. *Department of State Bulletin*, XXVI, (January 21, 1982), pp. 101-102.
47. *International Sanctions*, (London: Royal Institute of International Affairs, 1930), pp. 208-210.
48. Garrett L. McAinsh (ed.), *World Encyclopadia of Peace Vol.I*, (Oxford: Pergamon Press, 1986), p. 517.
49. *Ibid.*, p. 518.
50. Brian E. Porter, *World Encyclopedia of Peace*, Vol. II, (Oxford: Pergamon Press, 1986), p. 465.
51. *Ibid.*, p. 466.
52. Eddy Asirvatham, *Political Theory*, (New Delhi: S. Chand and Co., 1988), p. 764.
53. *Bombay Chronicle*, August 9, 1942.
54. Eknath Easwaran, (ed.), *World Encyclopedia of Peace*, Vol. I, (Oxford: Pergamon Press, 1986), p. 355.
55. Møller, *Common Security and Non-Offensive Defence*, *op.cit.*, pp. 11.
56. Ruth C. Reynolds, (ed.), *World Encyclopedia of Peace*, Vol. 1-3, (Oxford: Pergamon Press, 1985), p. 229.
57. Linus Pauling (ed.), *World Encyclopedia of Peace*, Vol. II, (Oxford: Pergamon Press, 1986, p. 64.
58. *Seventh Conference of Heads of State or Govemment of Non-Aligned Countries*, Final Documents, (New Delhi: March 1983), p. 4. NAC/ Conf.7/ Doc.1/Rev. 2, March 10, 1983, p. 4.
59. *Ibid.*
60. See Gilpin, *War and Change in World Politics*, op.cit., pp. 186-210; and Kennedy, *Rise and Fall of Great Powers*, *op.cit.*, pp. 514-535.
61. *The Charter of the United Nations*, (New York: United Nations, 1996), pp. 3-4.
62. U.N. Report, New York, 1993, p. 96.
63. U.N. Report, on *An Agenda for Peace*, (New York: United Nations, 1993), p. 157.
64. Boutros Boutros Ghali, *An Agenda for Peace*: Report of the Secretary-General Pursuant to the statement adopted by the Summit meeting of the Security Council on 31 January 1992, (New York: United Nations, 1992), p. 24.

65. U.N. Report, on *An Agenda for Peace*, *op.cit.*, p. 97.
66. *Ibid.*, p. 99.
67. Gene M. Lyons, "A New Collective Security", *The Washington Quarterly*, (Spring 1994), p. 177.
68. *Ibid.*, p. 178.
69. *Ibid.*, p. 197.
70. Duncan Snidal, "The Game Theory of International Politics" in Kenneth A. Oye, (ed.), *Cooperation under Anarchy*, (Princeton: Princeton University Press, 1986), p. 39.
71. James N. Rosenau, *International Politics and Foreign Policy*, (New York: Free Press, 1961), p. 77.
72. Phil Williams, "Deterrence", in John Baylis, et.al., *Contemporary Strategy*, (London: Croom Helm, 1975), p. 69.
73. Barry Buzan (ed.), *The International Politics of Deterrence*, (London: Frances Pinter, 1987), pp. 17-19.
74. Phil Williams, *op. cit..*, p. 70.
75. Buzan (ed.), *op. cit.*, p. 25.
76. Møller, *Common Security of Non-Offensive Defence*, *op.cit.*, pp. 111-113.
77. John Erickson, "The Soviet View of Deterrence: A General Survey", in Jonathan Alford (ed.), *The Soviet Union Security Policies and Constraints*, (New York: St. Martin's Press, 1985), p. 143.
78. Ken Booth, "Disarmament and Arms Control", in John Baylis, et.al. *op.cit.* p. 89.
79. See, Hedley Bull, *The Control of the Arms Race, Disarmament and Arms Control in the Missile Age*, (London: Weidenfeld and Nicholson, 1961).
80. *Ibid.*, p. 89.
81. J. David Singer, *Deterrence, Arms Control and Disarmament*, (Ohio: Ohio State University Press, 1962), p. 172.
82. *Ibid.*, p. 174.
83. Ken Booth, "Disarmament and Arms Control", in John Baylis, et.al., *op. cit.*, p. 98.
84. *Ibid,* p. 98.
85. *Ibid,* p. 98.
86. *Ibid,* p.100.
87. T. C. Shelling and M. H. Halperin, *Strategy and Arms Control*, (New York: Twentieth Century Fund, 1961), p. 2.
88. David E. Edwards, *Arms Control in International Politics*, (New York: Holt, Rinhart and Winston Inc., 1969).

89. Summarized by Paul R. Benett, *The Soviet Union and Arms Control*, (New York: Praeger, 1989).
90. James A. Robinson, "Decision-Making: Political Aspects" in David L. Sills (ed.), *International Encyclopaedia of the Social Sciences*, (New York: Free Press, 1968), p. 55.
91. See Harold Sprout and Margaret Sprout, *Foundations of International Politics*, (Princeton: D. Van Nostrand, Inc, 1962).
92. Emersion M. S. Niou; Peter C. Ordeshook and Gregory F. Rose, *The Balance of Power*, (Cambridge: Cambridge University Press, 1989), p. 9.
93. James N. Rosenau, *The Scientific Study of Foreign Policy*, (London: Frances Pinter, 1979), pp. 304-305.
94. John Spanier, *Games Nations Play*, (New Delhi: Macmillan, 1990), p. 7.
95. Ibid, p. 7. This idea is also explained by Thomas W. Wolfe, *Soviet Power and Europe – 1945-1970,* (Baltimore: John Hopkins University Press, 1970), p.10.
96. For a comprehensive discussion of the game theory in respect of the five rules of strategy, see Richard C. Snyder, "Game Theory and the Analysis of Political Behaviour", in James N. Rosenau, (ed.), *International Politics and Foreign Policy,* (New York: Free Press, 1961), pp. 981-90.
97. Arthur Lee Burns, "Prospects of a General Theory of International Relations", in Klaus Knorr and Sidney Verba, (eds.), *The International System*, (Princeton: Princeton University Press, 1961), p. 41.
98. This idea is also expressed by Mahendra Kumar, *Theoretical Aspects of International Politics,* (Delhi: Shiva Lal Agarwala and Company, 1985), pp. 187-88.
99. For a comprehensive discussion of conflict theory, see Richard E. Barringer, *War Patterns of Conflict,* (Cambridge: The MIT Press, 1972), pp. 17-21. see also Stephen J. Cimbala and Keith A. Dunn, *Conflict Termination and Military Strategy*, (Boulder: Westview Press, 1987).
100. Phil Williams, "Crisis Management", in John Baylis, et.al., *op. cit.*, p.164.
101. R. F. Kennedy, *Thirteen Days*, (London: Pan Books 1969), p.124. see also J. L. Richardson, *Germany Atlantic Alliance*, (Cambridge, Mass.: Harvard University Press, 1966, p.286.
102. Phil Williams, *op. cit.,* p. 166.

103. *Ibid.*, p. 169.
104. Barry Buzan, "Rethinking Security After the Cold War", *Nordic Journal of International Studies*, Vol. 32. No. 1, (1997), pp. 5-28.
105. Lene Hansen, "A Case for Seduction? Evaluating the post-structuralist conceptualization of security", *Nordic Journal of International Studies*, Vol. 32. No. 4, (1997), pp. 369-397.
106. Barry Buzan, "New Patterns of Global Security in the Twenty-First Century", *International Affairs*, (July 1991), p. 445.
107. John Ravenhill, "The North-South Balance of Power", *International Affairs*, Vol. 66. No.4, (1996), pp. 731-748.
108. Galtung, John, "A Structural Theory of Imperialism", *Journal of Peace Research*, Vol. No. 2, (1971), pp. 81-118.
109. Barry Buzan, Ole Wæver, Jaap de Wilde, *Security: A New Framework for Analysis*, (Boulder: Lynne Reinner, 1998), p. 97.
110. *Ibid*, p. 97. See also Donald C. Hellman, "Economics and Security", in Richard Shultz, Roy Godson, Ted Greenwood (eds.), *Security Studies for the 1990s*, (Washington DC: Brassey's, 1993), p. 304.
111. *Ibid*, p.97.
112. Donal Hellman, op. cit., pp. 303-304. For liberal economic agenda, see Barry Buzan, Ole Wæver, Jaap de Wilde, *op.cit.*, p. 98.
113. Barry Buzan, Old Wæver, Jaap de Wilde, *op.cit.*, p.112.
114. *Ibid.*, pp.113-114.
115. *Ibid.*, p.116.
116. S. M. Walt, "The Renaissance of Security Studies", *International Studies Quarterly*, Vol. 35. No. 2, (1991), p. 213.
117. W. Harriet Critchley and Terry Terrif, "Environment and Security", in Richard Shultz, et.al., *Security Studies for the 1990s*, *op.cit.*, pp. 327-352.
118. Barry Buzan, et.al., have elaborated the above mentioned problems in the environmental security agenda, *op. cit.*, pp. 74-75.
119. Thomas F. Homer-Dixon, "Environmental Scarcities and Violent Conflict", *International Security*; Vol.19. No.1, (Summer 1994), p. 6.
120. Matthais Finger, "New Horizon for Peace Research: The Global Environment", in J. Kakonen, (ed.), *Perspectives on Environmental Conflict and International Politics*, (London: Frances Pinter, 1991), p. 9. See also M. Jane Davis (ed.), *Security Issues in the Post Cold War World*, (Cheltanham, U.K.: Edward Elgar, 1996), p.163.

121. J. Goldenberg, and E. Durham, "Amazonia and National Sovereignty", *International Environmental Affairs*, Vol. 4. No. 4, (Winter 1992), p.29.
122 Barry Buzan, "New Patterns of Global Security in the Twenty First Century", *International Affairs*, (July 1991), p . 447.
123 Barry Buzan, et.al., *op.cit.,* p.121.
124. *Ibid.,* p. 138.
125. Barry Buzan, "New Patterns of Global Security in Twenty-First Century", *op.cit.,* p. 450.
126. See K. Deutsch et. al., *Political Community and the North Atlantic Area*, (Princeton, N.J.: Princeton University Press, 1957).

2

Soviet Concept of Security : Historical Perspective

2.1. Historical Background of Soviet Security

Soviet concept of security had undergone a tremendous change from the days of Lenin to Gorbachev. One can surmise the Soviet perspectives on security; if one studies closely the approaches of the leaders, the security requirements of the erstwhile Soviet Union, the steps taken by the leaders for satisfying the requirements and the extent to which they succeeded in that mission. Really, it is a tough job to study a concept as dynamic as the concept of security, for there is no fixed criteria to determine the way the decision-makers approach issues relating to security from time to time. Another problem related to Soviet security system was the 'closed' nature of its operation for security was considered the most delicate and secret affair by the people at the helm.

However, Gorbachev was the first person to open the 'Pandora Box'. Before him Soviet leaders handled security questions in a very diplomatic manner as security was regarded as a very sensitive issue, especially in the wake of the cold war competition going on between the two super powers. The world outside was so convinced about the opacity of the security system operating within Soviet

Union that Churchill's famous pet-phrase that Soviet Union was "a riddle wrapped in an enigma" was passed off as the most acceptable elucidation of Soviet functioning in matters of security. Such obvious opacity led to lot of complexities and confusions.[1]

Before Gorbachev, security as a concept was analyzed within the framework of power paradigm; thus strategic dimension of security dominated over other dimensions of security. As perceptions vary so also the notion of security. Some nations feel secure with less power; others feel insecure with relatively more power. In the same way when some tried to overcome it by military strength, others sought to do it by relying on alliance and diplomacy.[2] From Stalin onwards, military was the prime consideration of Soviet policy makers. Soviet leaders laid more emphasis on military strength than on concepts like mutual friendship, interdependence and institution building. They tried their best to defend the State borders and protect the interests beyond the State borders. Thus, they intelligently combined both 'maximalist' and 'minimalist' approaches to security. The need of the time and national interest were the guiding factor for formulating security policies. From the above analysis it is reflected that it was a 'realist' approach to security rather than the combination of 'realism' and 'idealism' which they claimed.

2. 2. Lenin's Views on Security

Like Marx, Lenin did not write any book or article on security. But from his writings and speeches, it is possible to deduce his views on security. Lenin in his work *Imperialism: The Highest Stage of Capitalism*, analyzed the social contradictions of capitalism, which culminated in the imperialist stage and ultimately led to war. Lenin rightly mentioned that the motives of the great powers were to enslave other nations, seize colonies as source of raw materials and places for the export of the capital. The whole world is merging into a single economic organism and divided up among a handful of great powers. The objective conditions for society have fully matured and the present imperialist war is a war of the capitalists for privileges and monopolies to postpone the collapse of capitalism.[3] He argued that imperialist war made the time ripe for socialist revolution and transition to socialism. It could be possible only through transformation of imperialist war into civil war followed by seizure of power by workers. Thus, he advocated capture of power by the Bolsheviks in Tsarist Russia.[4] Lenin was convinced of the Marxist view that socialism could bring about peace and security.

The workers' movement will triumph and pave the way for socialism. After the socialist revolution, the bourgeois machinery must be smashed and proletariat dictatorship should be proclaimed. Proletariats should develop an effective mechanism to crush the remnants of capitalism. They should make the economic situation viable for the growth and sustenance of socialism and the maintenance of global peace and security. It could be possible only through proletariat solidarity at international level raising a powerful army and getting help from the working class from outside. Lenin was in favour of national liberation movement as he was thinking socialism is the only way to maintain security all over the world. For achieving this objective, he stressed on proletariat internationalism. The amalgamation of the workers of different nationalities in a single organization would enable the proletariat to wage a victorious war against the bourgeois, which would establish democracy not only by treating nations equally but also by realizing the right of the oppressed nations to self-determination.[5]

Spirited by the ideals of 'world revolution' and proletariat internationalism, Bolsheviks after capturing power in Russia tried to spread the revolution all over the world, but failed miserably. On the other hand, capitalist powers helped the white guards in the civil war. Lenin realized that it was not the right time for world revolution, so, he dropped the idea till the revolution in other countries could take place and join hands with Russia. As Soviet Union was the only socialist country surrounded by capitalist bloc and security was primary need of the State, so he enunciated the concept of peaceful co-existence among all States with different social system.[6] Lenin staunchly advocated peace with Germany as it was most important for Soviet Union to save its revolution. Lenin was a pragmatist who gave importance to national considerations over the international revolutionary priorities, but he was not a pacifist who could abandon the principles of arm struggle. He struggled seriously to search out a programme of cohabitation, a plan to learn to live with the capitalists. His main motive was to defeat capitalism peacefully by producing superior social and economic system and supremacy of Soviet Union over capitalism. This was revealed from his address to 8th Party Congress held in March 1919, when he said:

"We are living not merely in a State, but in a system of States; and it is inconceivable that the Soviet republic should continue to exist for a long period side by side with imperialist States. Ultimately one or the other must conquer. Until this end occurs, a number of terrible clashes between the Soviet republic and the bourgeois States are inevitable".[7]

Even in the struggle between socialism and capitalism, co-existence between the two antagonistic ideologies was not ruled out. Lenin tried his best to avert world war and secure peace for which he developed good and cordial political and economic relations with other countries of the world. As he pointed out "the Russian Socialist Federation Soviet Republic wishes to life in peace with all people and devote all its efforts to internal development".[8] Lenin stressed on New Economic Policy for rebuilding war devastated economy and safeguarding the economic viability of the Soviet Union. Thus, under the dynamic leadership of Lenin, Soviet Union ensured both internal and external security. Lenin realized that socialism was the only panacea to reduce and redress the sufferings of the people and maintain peace and security in Soviet Union and rest of the world. Keeping this in mind, he developed friendly and warm relationship with other countries on the basis of respect for their independence and equality. He supported the struggle of these countries against colonial atrocities and neo-colonial imperialism and for universal peace and security.[9]

2.3. Stalin's Approach to Security

Stalin's views on security were based on his attitudes towards West, which was greatly influenced by experimental and circumstantial evidences. During the World War II, Soviet Union under the leadership of Stalin collaborated with capitalist block, of course changing its initial stand of supporting fascist power for the protection of its national security. But after the World War II, the situation took a different twist as USA changed its stand, which created a sense of suspicion and hatred for them and marred the smooth and cordial relationship between two powers. Stalin in February 1946 speech referred to the inevitability of conflict with Western power as he thought it was the right way for maintaining Soviet security. Stalin's views on security was based on the proposition that Soviet Union was confronted by implacable enemies with whom no friendship could be possible as they were dedicated to the destruction of the world's first socialist State.[10]

Soviet Union was an infant socialist country surrounded by capitalist countries. Those were bent upon utilizing every means at this disposal to undermine and weaken it. So the need for vigilance was over-emphasized as Soviet security was in danger and the most importance was given to the survival of socialism by Stalin for which he stuck to offence than defence as the security measure. As Sonnefeldt and Hyland write:

"Stalin had increased substantially the sphere of dominant Soviet power and had thereby seemingly strengthened the physical security of the USSR. Yet he never lost the siege mentality that had marked Soviet revolution in 1920s and 1930s. 'Capitalist encirclement' remained for him a reality, both in terms of military threat to the Soviet Union that he envisaged and in terms of potential connections between internal opposition to the regime and external enemies. Internal repression was, therefore, as necessary an expedient for him as defence against external aggression".[11]

Soviet insecurity was further heightened as the hectic environment continued and it was not possible on the part of the Soviet Union to alter it. It was further asserted that world wars remained an inescapable feature in international politics under capitalism. During Stalin's period international relations was depicted as zero sum game where there were two players – socialist camp and capitalist camp involved in direct conflict. The gains of the one side were inevitably the loss of the other. The easing out of the international tension was viewed as dangerous from Soviet security point of view. Stalin's concern was to preserve the tension as it would be vigilant towards its enemies and could easily spot them out. Stalin was against 'détente' as it was not possible to detect enemies from its sudden attack, hence, weaken the security of a nation.

From the above analysis, it is clearly reflected that the objective condition of the Soviet Union moulded the security policies of Stalin. His prime task was the safeguard of the security of the Soviet Union and its territorial unity and integrity for which he stressed the military potential of Soviet Union to deter or ward off the potential invader. His military theory was greatly influenced by Clausewitzian themes – an anti-thesis to the Western deterrence theory based on the rejection of "both the optimism and dogmatism of 18th century theory that war was neither a scientific game nor an international sport but an act of violence". Clausewitz did not appreciate the victory of a nation without bloodshed as it undermines the terrible nature of war and might lead to a condition whereby "we allow our swords to grow blunt ... until some steps taken with a sharp sword and cuts our arms off our body".[12] Some of the Clausewitzian military ideas are used by Soviet strategic thinkers, for the justification of the offensive mobility theatre warfare with or without the use of nuclear weapons.[13] Trotsky, the founder of the Red Army also expressed the similar view that "war bases itself on many a science; but was itself is no science; it is a peaceful art, a skill, a savage bloody one".[14]

Stalin realized that offence is the best defence for ensuring the security of a nation, as it was the viable technique to face the challenges of the enemies effectively. During later stage of his tenure when USA was rated as the most powerful nation of the world after acquiring nuclear capability and dictated terms and conditions to other nations. Stalin challenged the hegemonistic tendency and imperialistic design of USA for preserving global peace and security. For this purpose, he renovated the Soviet military set up and expanded the Soviet military power beyond the borders of the Soviet Union incorporating nuclear weapons in the Soviet forces. Thus, he laid the economic and technological foundation of the Soviet forces.

The World War II put Soviet Union in an advantageous position as a result of which it extended its influence over its bordering nations and finally it had militarily occupied Eastern Europe. Thus, the post World War security arrangements got a new shape after the installment of communist regime. These satellite States of Soviet Union strengthened its security militarily and otherwise. When Soviet Union consolidated its hold over Eastern Europe, it expected some reaction from Western powers as they harmed western values. USA also reacted sharply and developed a belligerent attitude towards Soviet Union. It further aggravated when USSR supported communist parties for coming to power in Western Europe and Asian countries like Manchuria, outer Mangolia and North Korea. Thus, in late forties, Soviet Union dominated the 'global society' and it appeared as if capitalism had been camouflaged under the neon light of socialism. The Stalin's famous slogan for communism in one country that was pronounced in 1920s was no more relevant. The security of the Soviet Union and its friends was strengthened through military alliances and they desperately tried to weaken the non-Communist regime of the world. It was clearly reflected in the Soviet perception of security – "that the politburo ... believes that its very life remains acutely threatened as long as major enemies exist. Their utter defeat is a sheer necessity of survival".[15] George Kennan also mentioned that Russia's age-old sense of insecurity was the main cause for its expansion move. In late 40's and 50's the hostile relationship between Soviet Union and the West got widened when Soviet Union reinterpreted its national interest from security angle and over-stressed its policy of isolationism, non-cooperation and consolidation of communist regime. The Soviet attitude towards the West compelled USA to take counter measures to check the influence of the communist power. Thus, in 1949, North Atlantic Treaty Organization (NATO) was created under the leadership of USA, comprising of countries lying on the Atlantic coast to prevent the aggression of Soviet Union in Western Europe. In a counter move to this military alliance, Warsaw Treaty was formed in 1955 with the leadership of Soviet Union taking its allies to defend its national interest and that of its allies in terms of security. During this period, military security was the prime concern of the Soviet Union for which Stalin stressed on modern warfare. Although in Stalin's scheme of things, political and economic aspects of security did not play any significant role, still, he tried his best for the expansion of communism as that would strengthen his position as the leader of the communist block.

It is interesting to note that he had developed very good relationship with the West during the early phase of his career. His decision to cultivate the West was conditioned by economic considerations as Soviet Union was facing terrible economic crisis during the days of the two World Wars. Stalin was desperately trying to strengthen its economy and he stressed on campaign for peace and tried to whip up anti-American feelings in Western Europe. Malenkov offered peaceful co-existence with the West and co-operation on the basis of equality and non-interference.[16] After the Second World War, Soviet Union developed a sisterly relationship with its Satellite States and cultivated a strong and stable relationship. It sought to boost its economy through Council of Mutual Economic Assistance (CMEA). Soviet Union also revived Communist International by forging together all the anti-imperialist forces, "COMINFORM"[17] in September 1947 for the coordination of the work of the Communist parties of various nations. The primary task of this organization was to popularise Communist ideology.

In the mid 1950s, Soviet Union also tried to win over Middle East and South Asian regions as it carried relative weight in security calculations. Even though few observers claimed that Soviet Union's position was secure in early 50's, his successor Khrushchev expressed his dissatisfaction. In his memoirs, he gives a summary of this period: 'We had our own doubts about Stalin's foreign policy'. He overemphasized the importance of military might and consequently put too much faith in armed forces. After Stalin, the most important task before his successor was to broaden their horizons and grope for definitions more suited to the emerging situation.[18]

2.4. Khruschev's Period

Soviet security policy during the subsequent days under Khruschev was the reflection of this notion as he was the first Soviet leader who intertwined his peace proposal and military strategy for ensuring Soviet security. He realized that offence was the best defence but at the same time he stressed on peaceful means for the settlement of international crisis. In fact, the transition from Stalin to Khrushchev was a shift from the regional conception of security to a global one, from basically defensive orientation to an offensive and from the era of World War II to the nuclear rocket age.[19] His defence strategy in the 1950s was to avert the possibility of any nuclear war. He had realized by then that a nuclear war could never be won.

This motive of Khrushchev was clearly reflected in 20th CPSU Congress when he said that war was not inevitable and could be prevented. Thus he rejected Stalin's statement that advocated the inevitability of conflict with capitalist block. It was held that though future conflict could not just be postponed, nevertheless, any internal crisis could be settled by peaceful means and not by war.[20] So, he stressed on 'peaceful co-existence as it was the objective necessity for the maintenance of peace and security'. Khrushchev also succeeded in persuading American President Eisenhower to acknowledge in principle the necessity of renouncing war between their two countries. Like Khrushchev he also condemned nuclear war which he saw as no less than 'the possibility of civilization destroyed ... and the condemnation of mankind to begin all over, the age-old struggle, upward from savagery'.[21] In the 21st Congress, in 1959, Khrushchev came forward with a proposal of ban on testing, production and use of atomic weapons but at the same time glorified Soviet's military achievement – USSR could launch 'powerful rockets with pinpoint accuracy to any place in the Globe'. It was clear that though disarmament got priority but Khrushchev was not in favour of complete disarmament. It was widely recognized that nuclear weapons have little political utility, they remain weapons nonetheless they are to be used if deterrence fails and military organizations of both sides develop plans for their use.[22] He was also influenced by another consideration for which he did not reject nuclear weapons and rightly, though nuclear weapons unusable as military instruments, are paradoxically important political symbols, which confer certain advantage on their possessors. These advantages, moreover, seem to accrue not merely in a general way, but rather precisely in proportion to the size and sophistication of the various national arsenals. Conditions like inferiority, superiority, parity have become politically significant, even though the sheer unusability of nuclear weapons would seem to argue against the political relevance (indeed the military relevance also, assuming that deterrence holds) of even quite large disparities between the various national arsenals.[23] The attitude of the Khrushchev was further reflected in his apprehension of World War. If there were another World War, he said, 'it would begin with missile strikes deep into the enemy interior and end with the victory of socialism'. In 1962, V.D. Sokolovskii, Chief of General Staff from 1952-60 put forward the military strategy of Soviet Union described by Khrushchev. Sokolovskii argued about the importance of the initial period of the war, the main problem was to master "methods of reliably repulsing a surprise nuclear attack and also methods of frustrating the aggressive plans of enemy, by means of a timely shattering blow against him".[24]

Thus, Khrushchev's 'offensive détente' was a strategic ideology that served to legitimize the outcome of political logrolling. His offensive détente relied on nuclear technology and especially on the Inter-Continental Ballistic Missile (ICBM). Khrushchev believed that it would change the equation with the West by paving the way for a political settlement in Europe, and it would lower the cost of security and contribute to the rise in Soviet living standards.[25] Despite his fascination for high quality nuclear and other weapons, he also recognized that these nuclear weapons alone could not guarantee security and that the arms race and high military expenditure could economically undermine the prospects of socialism in USSR. No doubt, Khrushchev's proposal on defence cuts in January, 1960 was motivated by this recognition. In the 21st CPSU Congress, he stressed on the 'prevention of thermo-nuclear war and establishment of 'everlasting peace' to save the mankind from the scourge of war. His speech in UN General Assembly amply proved it –"With the present nature of international relations and the present level of military technology, when any military conflict can lend to a Nuclear-Missile war, a radical solution of the problem of security for all states involves precluding the very possibility of wards being started. So long as there exist large armies, air forces and navies, nuclear and missile weapons, so long as young men on the threshold of life are first of all taught the art of warfare and general staffs are busy working out plans for future military operations, there is and can be no secure peace among nations in the present situation".[26]

Both internal and external situations compelled Khrushchev to take this confusing stand on security. The emergence of United

States as a powerful nation and the nuclear competitor of USSR, the Suez crisis of 1956, Berlin question and the final settlement of the German problem were the motivating factors behind his security policy. The problem of adjusting to the nuclear age was no doubt a cardinal security issue in the 1950s, which also influenced his concept of security. Besides external issues, internal developments like the initial 'thaw', the subsequent de-Stalinization and the disappearance of mass terror had a bearing on security problems. Khrushchev continued to see Stalinists as his principal opponents and tried his best to drive them to extremes. Even he went to the extent of reversing Stalin's policy to prove that his anti-Stalinism would be successful: where Stalin ignored the third world, Khrushchev courted it; where Stalin insisted on iron rule, Khrushchev proclaimed relaxations; where Stalin rule Eastern Europe through the army and KGB, Khrushchev hoped for loyalty to principles; where Stalin sought security in Red Army, Khrushchev sought it in the strategic rocket forces (though he bluffed about the strength).[27]

As Khrushchev defined Soviet interests broadly, the area of the security concern obviously expanded. By 1964, national security of Soviet Union took a complex turn. It involved calculations concerning the internal repercussion of foreign policies, cost of the fulfillment of the political and economic commitments made to Eastern Europe and other areas, the burden of armaments to challenge the hegemony of Western powers.

2.5. Brezhnev's Period

The emergence of Brezhnev in this critical juncture twisted the Soviet approach to security. Of course, like Khrushchev in late 60's, his emphasis was on the accumulation of military force and the extension of its reach beyond the Eurasian landmass. The main purpose behind this was to equate Soviet Union with United States in nuclear capability for which it took steps like modernizing ground and air forces, increasing and diversifying the navy and updating technology to improve these forces. As power grew so did the definition of security. The safety of the home land was no doubt the prime consideration, the inviolability of Soviet pre-dominance in Eastern Europe was a close second; finding power elsewhere on the Soviet periphery were next; and entitlement to a role at least equal to that of the United States elsewhere came last.[28] The implementation of such plan was problematic. With the increase in forces, the home-land was safe from land attack, but it could not be protected from a nuclear war. Secondly, the Eastern Europe which was under Soviet control fluctuated in his stand. Other countries on the periphery were not hostile towards Soviet Union but not friendly and were not deterred from maintaining and building military forces and alliances that enabled them to resist Soviet pressures. China was hostile, an active rival of Soviet Union and Japan was not also that much friendly.

Though Brezhnev proceeded methodically to build Soviet military power in all dimensions but failed to change the attitude of China and the surrounding that were negative at that time.[29] He realized that the pace at which nuclear stock piles were built in the name of equal security was feverish. This was the paradox of the nuclear arms race, nuclear weapons did not provide additional security and yet they were built in the name of the security.[30] So, he changed his approach to security in early 70's. He stressed on 'détente' for the security of the Soviet Union, when the entire world was on the brink of nuclear war. Thus, he broadened the concept of security and tried to secure Soviet Union through the security of the entire world. He developed new and friendly equation with Europe, China and other Asian countries. His motive of maintaining world peace and security was clearly reflected in 24th CPSU Congress 1971. In this Congress he highlighted on the 'peaceful co-existence' and normal mutual co-operation in the fields of human endeavor. This peace programme regarded the following as the set of objectives for ensuring peace and security: –

- To extirpate the hot-beds of war in South-east Asia and Middle East and to promote a political settlement in the regions on the basis of respect for the lawful rights and people's suffering from aggression;
- To discourage belligerent States and the acts of violence by promoting peace and security and for this purpose the UN must be used to the fullest extent;

- To solve political problems through mutual friendship and cooperation for which it proposed to conclude bilateral and regional treaties.[31]

This programme further emphasized the need for renouncing the use of force in international relations and banning nuclear, chemical and bacteriological weapons, ending nuclear weapon tests by all countries everywhere including underground tests and establishing nuclear free zones in different regions of the world. In this context Brezhnev said: *"We are for the nuclear disarmament of all states possessing nuclear weapons and for this purpose holding conferences of the five nuclear powers – the Soviet Union, the U.S., the People's Republic of China, France and Britain"*. This 24th Congress of the CPSU stressed on improving the relationship with capitalist countries particularly with the United States adhering to the principle of "peaceful coexistence". This peace programme was further given logical continuation in the 25th CPSU Congress with special emphasis on peace and international cooperation and for the freedom and independence of peoples.[32]

This programme emphasized on the following:

- Consolidation of peace all over the world while strengthening the unity of socialist countries;

- Efforts to end arms race which is endangering peace and steps to reduce accumulated stockpiles of arms;

- To take adequate steps for conducting world conferences on disarmament;

- To work for ensuring security of Asia on the basis of joint efforts by the states of that continent.[33]

It was only in the 25th Party Congress held in 1976, where he seemed to be optimistic about international situation that he began to use *détente* more frequently and often without accompanying 'peaceful coexistence'. No doubt *détente* was confined to easing out of tension particularly military tension from the globe without sacrificing the basic principles and ideology of socialism.[34] His reservations about *détente* clearly reflected when he upheld: "*Détente* does not alter nor can it change the laws of class struggle. It is for creating favorable conditions for the peaceful socialist and communist construction".[35]

With efforts towards disarmament, a new era of friendship and cooperation began in global politics where two opposing social systems created a favorable climate and the Soviet Union joined hands with U.S.A. in signing Nuclear Non-Proliferation Treaty (NPT) in 1968. In the year 1969, Brezhnev came forward with a new doctrine popularly known as 'Brezhnev Doctrine' where Asian security was given importance. He tried to make the continent free from intercontinental tension and conflicts so that it would deter U.S.A. to interfere in the matters of Asian countries with a pretext of sorting out internal conflicts. He tried to ensure the security of Asian countries not only by providing peace and stability but also by solving social and economic problems of that region.[36] In early 70's he seriously tried for maintaining peace and security all over the world. He conferred with American President Richard Nixon in May 1972 and concluded famous Strategic Arms Limitation Talk (SALT-I) treaty, Anti-Ballistic Missile (ABM) treaty and other agreement relating to trades. In 1973, Brezhnev met USA President Nixon in Washington and discussed widely on strategic arms control and trade and technical cooperation. In June-July 1974, he decided to extend SALT-I treaty from five years to permanent one and to take adequate steps for banning underground nuclear tests and for that purpose again he met Nixon in Moscow. With the change in leadership in the United States, Brezhnev continued his peace efforts with redoubled spirit and new vigour and in November 1974, a meeting was arranged between Brezhnev and American President Gerald Ford in Moscow where tentative agreements on limiting strategic nuclear weapons and future strategic arms control were discussed. This principle of 'peaceful coexistence' was further accelerated to such an extent that ultimately it culminated in Helsinki Peace Process where two power blocs decided for social, economic, technological and cultural cooperation. The Soviet Union regarded this as an important stage of *détente*. The principle of inter-state relations to which the Soviet Union agreed in Helsinki Final Act were:

"Sovereign equality, the non-use of force, the inviolability of frontiers, non-interference in international affairs, respect for human rights and the basic freedom, equal rights and the right of people to be their own masters, cooperation between states and the conscientious fulfillment of obligations".[37]

Though the second half of the 1970s witnessed strange relationship between two powers and ultimately SALT-II treaty, which was signed between Brezhnev and the USA President Carter in June 1979, was not ratified by the Senate, yet Brezhnev continued his peace process. It was clearly reflected from his Tula speech, where he stressed on "minimum security and futility of nuclear war". In his speech, he mentioned that the Soviet defence would be guided by the needs of defence sufficiency and Soviet policy would be aimed at the prevention of nuclear war, parity at low levels, balance of interest approach and defensive military doctrine.[38]

Brezhnev's proposal to take several foreign policy initiatives for maintaining global peace and security and to make 1980's renewed success of *détente* by supplementing political *détente* with military *détente* faced terrible set back as it was disrupted by west through escalating arms race. In 26th Party Congress report, 1981, he hardly mentioned *détente* and blamed the USA for infringement of *détente*.[39]

From this analysis, it is clearly reflected that Brezhnev tried his best to ensure global pace and security. For this objective, he not only stressed on political and military aspects of security but also economic aspect of security. The CPSU attached special importance for developing healthy cooperation with communist parties of the fraternal countries. It developed healthy economic relations with the Council of Mutual Economic Assistance (CMEA) countries on a long-term basis. During his tenure, active work was done for organizational structure and technical basis for multilateral economic cooperation. He had done a great deal to promote major advances in the specialization and cooperation of production, trade, finance and scientific-technical research among CMEA countries. During his time, CMEA member states had multiplied their economic potential. The member states of CMEA, Brezhnev stressed, "are active champions of equal and mutually beneficial economic cooperation between countries belonging to different social systems. This basic approach follows from their devotion to peace and is inalienable element of the policy of easing international tension".[40] Chernenko also glorified the peace efforts of Brezhnev:

"The Soviet Union, together with the fraternal socialist countries, is ready to do everything possible to help development in our continent to lead to the elimination of the military threat, and to the creation of an atmosphere of confidence in the inevitability of its peaceful future, as well as to an expansion of all round cooperation between states for the good of the people".[41]

Really, the steps taken by Brezhnev were praiseworthy. He tried to ensure the security of the Soviet Union and socialist countries through the security of the entire world but without deviating from the ideological framework of Soviet Union. In this context, he said:

"That realism in politics and the will for détente, for progress will eventually prevail, and mankind will be able to step into the 21st century in conditions of peace dependable as it has never been in the past and we will do all in our power to make this come true".[42]

After Brezhnev there was no spectacular changes in the concept of security. His successor Andropov restrained himself within the framework of 26th Party Congress resolutions. He continued the same security policies of Brezhnev. He realized the consequence of nuclear war and he took steps to save the world from nuclear threat. He appealed to U.S.A. and other European countries to stretch their hands in fulfilling this mission. In this context he said: *"We are prepared for radical solutions. The ball is in the other side's court. Like all people of good will you must rest assured that the USSR will continue to do everything that depends on it to ease international tension, to curb the arms race – both on earth and in space and to prevent a nuclear blaze".*[43] For maintaining peace and security of Europe and the rest of the world, he favoured approximate balance of military forces including nuclear ones between the states of NATO and Warsaw Treaty states. He opposed to the deployment of American nuclear missiles in Western Europe. In his view, the appearance of Pershing-2s and cruise missiles of U.S.A. in the European continent particularly in the Soviet border was not intended for ensuring security of Europe as USA was already in an advantageous position so far as the military parity between two forces were concerned. So, the only motive behind USA's action was to exhibit its hegemony in Europe. That was the reason in June 28, 1983, Soviet Union declared to take adequate measures to stop the superiority of the NATO bloc over the countries of Warsaw Pact.

It adopted the following four measures. First, since by its actions the United States has torpedoed the possibility of reaching a mutually acceptable accord at the talks on question of limiting nuclear arms in Europe and their continuation in these conditions would only serve as a cover for the actions of the United States and a number of other NATO countries directed at undermining European and international security, the Soviet Union considers its further participation in that talks impossible. Second, being cancelled are the Soviet Union's unilateral obligations, which had the objective of creating more favourable conditions for success at the talks. Thereby the moratorium on the deployment of Soviet medium range nuclear weapons in the European part of the USSR is abrogated. Third, in agreement with the government of the Germany Democratic Republic (GDR, before reunification of Germany), and Czechoslovakia, the announced preparatory work to deploy on the territory of these countries operational-tactical missiles of increased range, that was started some time ago will be accelerated. Fourth, since by deploying its missiles in Europe, the United States increases the nuclear threat to the Soviet Union, the corresponding Soviet systems will be deployed, with due account taken of this circumstance, in ocean areas and seas. By their characteristics these systems of ours will be adequate to the threat which is being created to us and our allies by the American missiles that are being deployed in Europe. It goes without saying that other measures too will be taken to ensure the security of the USSR and other countries of the socialist community.[44]

But he was not in favour of Soviet military superiority over the United States. He expressed his willingness to restore the previous situation if USA stopped from these belligerent activities and responded positively to his desire for maintaining global peace and security. Andropov was convinced that peace could be strengthened and the security of people guaranteed not by way of building up and inventing new types of armaments but on the contrary by way of reducing the existing armaments to lower levels.

2.6. Gorbachev's Period

Gorbachev's concept of security which brought radical changes in the security structure of the world, reorienting the basic components and stressing more on the political and economic aspects than the militaristic side was a novel approach to the concept of security. His ideas, which were enshrined in the 27th, CPSU Congress reflected his pragmatism and vision by combining the philosophy of ensuring security in nuclear age with an agenda for action aimed at creating a peaceful world. His ideas of security were broader in connotation as they offered a comprehensive approach to the future development of international politics, not only by creating a conducive atmosphere for favourable interactions among the international actors in various spheres of their activities, but also by guaranteeing the security through peaceful coexistence and cooperation with the west. His concept of comprehensive universal security had four major dimensions-military, political, economic and humanitarian. The military aspect concerned 'the renunciation by the nuclear powers of war against each other or against any third country with either nuclear or conventional weapons, which reflected that peace could be achieved only by terminating the material preparation of a nuclear war'.[45] When the world was on the brink of nuclear war, Gorbachev took consistent efforts to ease out the tension from the globe for a secured and prosperous world. He took the initiative to bridge up the gap between the two super powers towards which he concluded various treaties with USA. Geneva, Reykjavik, INF, Moscow, Malta and Washington summits were milestones in this regard. The second idea behind the proposal of the 27th CPSU Congress relating to the military aspect of Gorbachev's concept of security was aimed at the "prevention of the arms race in space, cessation of all nuclear weapon tests and total destruction of such weapons, a ban on and the destruction of chemical weapons and renunciation of the development of other means of mass annihilation".[46] To materialize this proposal Gorbachev attended various summits and concluded the famous INF agreement in December 1987. Gorbachev's security concept, which formed the basis of new thinking on security, was the doctrine of 'reasonable sufficiency' or 'non offensive defence'. This doctrine rejects the idea of developing military potentiality of a country to maintain equality with its enemy for safeguarding its security. This doctrine acts like an antidote against nuclear arsenal that destabilizes sound relationship among states.[47] On the other hand it aims at guaranteeing security not by highest possible but by lowest possible level of strategic parity with western bloc.

Gorbachev tried his best to maintain parity between two blocs and to correct the asymmetries existed in both sides. Even he took steps to eliminate the disproportion of military strength between NATO and Warsaw Pact for which he stressed on the approach of reciprocity and cutting down of military weapons from both the sides.[48] His decision for the disbandment of military alliance and the renunciation of their enlargement clearly reflected his inner motive of making a noble world of cooperation and friendship instead of hatred and enmity. Warsaw is no more an active organization. It is a defunct body. His decision to spend money cutting down from the defence budget was a reflection of his slogan 'Disarmament for development'. To sum it up, the provision of Comprehensive Universal Security measure was the real basis of putting an end to the Cold War by reducing armaments and defense expenditure and above all eliminating the nuclear threat from the globe. The implementation of these programmes could free planet from the threat of war.

The political aspect of Gorbachev's concept of security aimed at removing all the factors that led to antagonistic relationships between two power blocs. It was clear that East-West political rivalry included regional conflicts, human rights issues and the totalitarian regime of East European countries etc. On this front the most important proposal was the "strict respect in international practice for the right of each people to choose the ways and forms of its development independently".[49] Gorbachev tried his best to develop peace and cooperation among various countries for which he advocated multilateral cooperation and reliance upon the political process. Security is to be sought through the give and take of international negotiations. In the words of Gorbachev:

> *"The nature of current weaponry leaves no country with any hope of safeguarding itself solely with military and technical means, for example, by building up a defence, even the most powerful. To ensure security is becoming more and more a political task and it can only be resolved by political means".*[50]

He also spelled out an important corollary to this perspective by stressing the need for mutual security and stressed on the need of the deeper understanding of the security considerations of other nations which could refrain a nation from pursuing their policies which other nations found threatening. He acknowledged the intimate connection between Soviet and American security interests. The Soviet Union would not be secured until other nations – especially the U.S.A. truely feel secured.[51] For this reason, he emphasized on the balance of interests rather than balance of forces and underlined the supremacy and imposition of the will of the power blocs over small independent nations.

The second proposal of 27th CPSU Congress on political aspect of security prepared grounds for 'a just political settlement of International crisis and regional conflicts'. Gorbachev took bold steps to solve major international problems. His initiatives for the solution of Middle East problem, Central American problem, Asian and African problems were in the positive direction. He also realized that crises and conflicts, which provide the seed-bed for international terrorism endanger World Peace. All nations should take steps to curb it through cooperation. This problem could be solved by the initiatives of US and USSR and other nations under the leadership of the United Nations.[52] He genuinely tried for the solution of regional conflicts amicably for a better and prosperous world as he realized that it would weaken the security structure of the world.

Soviet Union's decision to withdraw troops from Afghanistan, Hungary, Czechoslovakia and its pressure on Vietnam to withdraw from Kampuchea reflected his inner motive for global peace and security. Gorbachev's decision for creating an all embracing system of international security consisted in the "elaboration of a set of steps aimed at building confidence between states and the creation of effective guarantees against attack from without and inviolability of their frontiers".[53] The proposal along these lines materialized in the Stockholm Conference, which created barriers against the use of force or constant preparations for war, whether on land, sea or air. Gorbachev stressed on the reliable system of international security and inviolability of the borders was the most important element of the security. It could be conceived with effective guarantees for states against outside attack. The American invasion of Grenada and heavy bombardment in Libya revealed the need of it, which could only ensure the security of a nation and the security of the world as a whole. He also condemned the invasion of Kuwait by Iraq. The final proposal relating to the political aspects of Gorbachev's concept of comprehensive universal security deals with "effective method of preventing international terrorism including those ensuring the safety of international land, air and sea communications".[54]

In the 40th Session of UN General Assembly, Soviet Union and other socialist countries stressed on Gorbachev's ideas of preventing international terrorism through effective methods. In his letter to the UN Gorbachev made some proposals for activating and strengthening the world body. These proposals were:

(i) a special humanitarian development/disarmament fund and friendly relationship with NGOs;

(ii) efforts for strengthening environmental agency with power to check transnational ecological degradation;

(iii) protection of human rights;

(iv) a tribunal on international terrorism including state sponsored terrorism;

(v) mandatory jurisdiction for international court;

(vi) More special session of the UN General Assembly.[55]

In his UN speech, Gorbachev underlined three principles of peaceful international relations. First renunciation of force, both nuclear and conventional; freedom of choice and freeing of international relations of ideological bondage. Second, he enumerated the "global task to be taken up by the international community for maintaining peace and security. Third, UN should be treated as an embodiment of interests of various states. It should try to sort out the problems of the world in all the spheres, i.e. military, political, economic, scientific and technical, ecological and humanitarian.[56]

The economic aspect of Gorbachev's concept of security had two main extrapolations. First, to boost up the stagnant Soviet economy through its integration into the emerging global economic order, his concept of comprehensive international security envisaged stable economic relations, mutual trade and aid among socialist and non-socialist countries on equal basis. For achieving this objective, he emphasized on restructuring international economic relations and establishing New International Economic Order (NIEO).[57]

Second, to bridge up the gap between two antagonistic blocs through mutual friendship, cooperation and trade relationship. He tried to better up Soviet economy through trade relationship with western bloc. Unlike his predecessors, he tried for restructuring (*Perestroika*) Soviet economy through opening up new avenues for westerners to invest their money in Soviet Union. His focus was on market oriented economy instead of regimented or closed economy. He was guided by cost-accounting culture and demand supply considerations. His economic reforms could not bring as much change as was expected of them; however it certainly resuscitated a moribund economy. It also helped in improving the economic positions of the people.

On the international front, an important proposal made on this regard aimed at 'exclusion of all forms of discrimination from international practices, renunciation of the policy of economic blockades and sanctions if this is not directly envisaged in the recommendations of the world community'.[58] It also stressed on normalization of international economic relations among various states which was essential for the economic development of the countries whose economic backwardness was the result of exploitation by the capitalist policy of neo-colonialism.

The second proposal relating to the concept of economic security was the call for "joint quest for ways for a just settlement of the problem of debts".[59] The Third World countries and those who were in debt trap were benefited out of that measure. Soviet leader Gorbachev's ideas of 'Common European Home', 'Common Market' and 'Common Currency' for entire Europe were definitely positive steps in this direction.

The most important proposal of the economic aspects of security under *perestroika* was the "establishment of a New World Economic Order guaranteeing equal economic security to all countries".[60] Soviet Union tried seriously within and outside the U.N. framework to cooperate with interested parties to remove all types of discriminatory restrictions and barriers from international economic relations. During this phase, Soviet Union and other socialist countries developed equitable economic relationship with the rest of the world. Soviet leader Gorbachev also emphasized on North-South dialogue and played a decisive role in restructuring of international economic system towards the establishment of NIEO based on sovereign equality, justice, and mutual interest.

The fourth proposal in the economic sphere stressed on the "elaboration of principles for utilizing part of the funds released as a result of reduction of military budgets for the good of the world community, of developing nations in the first place".[61] Soviet Union under *perestroika* emphasized on 'disarmament for development' rejecting the earlier notion of 'armament instead of development'. In this context Abel Aganbegyan has rightly said:

"If the Soviet proposal for disarmament, security and stable peace are accepted, the means and resources liberated from the military sector could augment the rate of growth of the economy".[62]

The last proposal in this sphere dealt with "the pooling of efforts in exploring and making peaceful use of outer space and in resolving global problems on which the destinies of civilization depend".

During this *perestroika* phase, Soviet Union took steps for environmental protection, solution of the problems of food, energy and population, the peaceful exploration of space and resources of the world oceans, the elimination of the economic backwardness of newly independent countries, the eradication of diseases etc. The humanitarian aspects of security had not been underscored in Soviet security plans. From the above discussion, it was quite clear that Soviet security during *perestroika* period was concrete, comprehensive, and holistic in nature. This was the approach the world was clearly in dire need of.

A critical study of Soviet concept of security revealed that there were three important factors or as Geoffrey Roberts would say "grand narrative themes",[63] which moulded the security decisions of the Soviet leaders and strategic experts. First factor was the bi-polarity, which stressed on the polarization of world politics into two opposing camps and contest between Soviet Union and USA for power and position. Second factor was the ideological competition, which was about the struggle between communism *vs.* capitalism. Third factor was about systemic crisis. The focus was on internal weakness, contradictions and conflicts of Soviet and Communist system.

Besides, the above mentioned factors, Roberts pointed out certain "meta-narratives", like particular and local considerations, also influenced perceptions of decision-makers in formulating security policy.[64] As perceptions and objective conditions of USSR changed from time to time, so also did the security policies of Soviet Union. It had traversed a long way from peaceful co-existence to mutual security via confrontation.

But now the USSR no longer exists. Soviet concept of security under *perestroika* did not succeed in ensuring the internal security of Soviet Union, which ultimately broke up into fragments. The operational failure of such a framework would suggest serious theoretical and operational flaws in the Soviet security system during *perestroika*. This is discussed in succeeding chapters and in the conclusion.

But still Gorbachev's approach to security has its own relevance as it brought an end to the second Cold War in the most peaceful manner possible and contributed to global peace. Russia's (true successor of USSR) security system is also based on the broader framework of this security system with very little modifications to meet the exigencies of the time.

References

1. Helmunt Sonnenfeldt and William G. Hyland, "Soviet Perspective on Security", in Alford Jonathan (ed.), *The Soviet Union Security Policies and Constraints*, (London: Gower Publishing Company, 1985), pp.1-2.
2. *Ibid.*, pp.1-2.
3. V. I. Lenin, *War and Peace*, (Peking: Foreign Language Press, 1960), p. 24.
4. V. I. Lenin, *The Foreign Policy of Soviet State*, (Moscow: Progress, 1968).
5. V. I. Lenin, *Collected Works*, Vol. 22, (Moscow: Progress, 1964), pp. 143-46.
6. V. I. Lenin on *Peaceful Co-existence*: *Article and Speeches*, (Moscow: Progress, 1975).
7. Cited in E. H. Carr, *The Bolshevik Revolution (1917-1923)*, Vol. III (London: Penguin, 1977), p.123.
8. V. I. Lenin, *Collected Works*, Vol. 30, (Moscow: Progress, 1964), p. 231.
9. Vadim Zagladin, *Peace the Only Option*, (New Delhi: Allied Publishers, 1987).
10. R.C. Tucker, *The Soviet Political Mind*, (New York:. W.W. Norton, 1963), pp. 20-35.
11. Sonnenfeldt and Hyland, *op.cit.*, p. 9.
12. Quoted in H. Rothfels "Clausewitz", in Edward Mead Earle (ed.), *Makers of Modern Strategy*: *Military Thought from Machiavelli to Hitler*, (New York: Atheneum, 1966), p.100.

13. C.V. Clausewitz, *On War*, (Combat Forces Press, 1953), p.16.
14. Quoted in Issac Deutscher, *The Prophet Armed*, (Oxford: Oxford University Press, 1976), p. 482.
15. Nathan Leites, *A Study of Bolshevism*, *Glencoe, III*, (New York: Free Press, 1953), p. 31.
16. Neil Malcom, "De-Stalinisation and Soviet Foreign Policy: The Roots of New Thinking", in Tsuyoshi Hasegawa, et. al., *Perestroika*: *Soviet Domestic and Foreign Policies*, (London: Sage Publication, 1990), pp.182-183.
17. Communist Information Bureau (COMINFORM) – The purpose of COMINFORM was to tighten the Soviet control over Eastern Europe. It might be Stalin's practice or due to cold war. It published a journal for transmitting directives to its members. COMINFORM was dissolved by Khrushchev in April 1956 as he felt it was no more relevant.
18. See Sonnenfeldt and Hyland, "Soviet Perspective on Security", *op.cit.*
19. *Ibid.*, p.10.
20. Summarized on 20th CPSU Congress Documents, (Moscow: Novosti Press, 1956).
21. Quoted in Herbert S. Dinerstein, *War and the Soviet Union*, (New York: Praeger Publishers, 1959), p. 69.
22. John Van Oudenaren, *Deterrence, War Fighting and Soviet Military Doctrine*, *Adelphi Papers*, (London: International Institute for Strategic Studies, 1986), p. 7.
23. *Ibid.*, p. 8.
24. V. D. Sokolovskii (ed.), *Voennaia Strategiia*, (Moscow: Voenizdat, 1962), pp. 238-239. Quoted in Kurt Gotfried and Bruce G. Blair (eds.), *Crisis Stability and Nuclear War*, (New York: Oxford University Press, 1988) p.128.
25. See Jack Snyder, "The Gorbachev Revolution: A Waning of Soviet Expansionism", in Sean M. Lynn, Jones Steven E. Millar and Stephen Van Evera (eds.), *Soviet Military Policy*: *An International Security Reader*, (Cambridge: The MIT Press, 1989).
26. Speech by N. S. Khrushchev at the 14th Session of UN General Assembly, *To Live in Peace and Friendship*, (New Delhi: Soviet Land Booklet, 1959), p. 91.
27. Sonnenfeldt and Hyland, *op.cit.*, pp.12-13.
28. *Ibid*, p.16.
29. *Ibid*, p.16.

30. Arvind Gupta, "Soviet perspective on security and military doctrine", *Strategic Analysis*, Vol. XII. No. XII, (February 1990), pp.1151-52.
31. Leonid I. Brezhnev, *Pages from his Life*, Written under the auspices of the Academy of Science of the USSR, (New Delhi: Allied Publishers, 1979), p. 154.
32. *Ibid.,* p. 157.
33. *Ibid.,* p. 159.
34. Margot Light, *The Soviet Theory of International Relations*, (Great Britain: Wheatsheaf Books, 1958), p. 63.
35. L. I. Brezhnev, "Reports of the CPSU Central Committee and the Immediate Tasks of the Party in Home and Foreign Policy", *Socialism Theory and Practice*, No. 3, (March 1976), pp. 39-40.
36. *Soviet Review*, December 6, 1973, p. 90.
37. A. Valentinov, "One Year After Helsinki", *International Affairs*, No. 9, (1976), p. 24. Quoted in Arvind Gupta, *Ideology and Soviet Foreign Policy: Lenin to Gorbachev*, (New Delhi: A.V. Genus Publishing House, 1993), p. 88.
38. Arvind Gupta, "Soviet Perspective on Security and Military Doctrine", *Strategic Analysis*, Vol. XII, No. XII, (February 1990), p. 1152.
39. *The Report of the 26th Congress of CPSU*, (Moscow: Novosti Press, 1981), p. 6.
40. Brezhnev, *Pages from His Life*, *op.cit.,* p. 104.
41. V. Chernenko, *Selected Speeches and Articles*, (New Delhi: Allied Publishers, 1984), p. 104.
42. Quoted in K. V. Cherenenko (ed.), *Selected Speeches and Writings*, (Oxford: Pergamon Press, 1980) p. 248.
43. Y.V. Andropov, *Speeches, Articles, Interviews – A Selection*, (New Delhi: Allied Publishers, 1984), p. 295.
44. Ibid., pp. 298-299.
45. *Report of the 27th Congress of the CPSU*, (Moscow: Novosti Press, 1986), p. 71.
46. Mikhail S. Gorbachev, *Perestroika*: *New thinking for Our Country and the World*, (London: Fontana/Collins, 1988), p. 231.
47. Alexi Arbatov, "Reasonable Sufficiency", *International Affairs*, (October 1988), p. 77.
48. Gerhard Wettig, "New Thinking on Security and East West Relation", *Problems of Communism*, (March-April, 1988), p. 3.
49. Gorbachev, *Perestroika*, *op.cit.,* p. 231.

50. Quoted in Carl G. Jacobsen (ed.), *Soviet Foreign Policy New Dynamics: New Themes*, (London: Macmillan, 1989), p. 20.
51. *Ibid.*, p. 21.
52. Gorbachev, *Perestroika*, *op.cit.*, p. 173.
53. *Ibid.*, p. 231.
54. *Ibid.*, p. 231.
55. Sashi Kant Jha, "Perestroika and International Relations", in Sushil Kumar (ed.), *Gorbachev's Reforms and International Change*, (New Delhi: Lancer Books, 1993), pp. 25-26.
56. Sashi Kanta Jha, *op. cit.*, p. 26. See *Soviet Review Documents*, of Mikhail Gorbachev's Address to the 43rd Session of the U.N. General Assembly, December 7, 1988, (New Delhi: New Age Printing Press, 1988), pp. 15-20.
57. Evenest Obninsky and Andrei Bugrov, *International Economic Security: A Major Factor of Peace*, (New Delhi: Allied Publishers, 1988), p. 82.
58. Gorbachev, *Perestroika*, *op.cit.*, 231.
59. *Ibid.*, p. 231.
60. *Ibid.*
61. *Ibid.*
62. Abel Aganbegyan, *The Challenge: Economics of Perestroika*, (London: Hutchinson, 1988), p. 219.
63. See Geoffrey Roberts, *The Soviet Union in World Politics: Co-existence, Revolution, and Cold War, 1945-91*, (London: Routledge, 1999).
64. *Ibid.*, pp. 101-102.

3

Military Aspects of Security During Perestroika

3.1. Origin of Military Security During Perestroika

Military aspects of security played a subdued role in Gorbachev's concept of common security, which was enshrined, in the 27th CPSU Congress of 1986. He tried to ensure the security of the Soviet Union through the security of the entire world. Security under *perestroika* stressed more on 'comprehensive universal security' i.e. common security, than on national security. Changes had to be brought in the national military policies and strategies for materialising this dream and under Gorbachev's leadership, Soviet national security was intertwined with the concept of 'comprehensive universal security'. Though during this phase, concept of security bore the stamp of political and economic colour but military aspects of security could not be underrated. He brought radical changes in the military thinking on security. Unlike his predecessors, he de-emphasized on defence build up and the development of nuclear capability of the Soviet Union. He realized that the entire world was on the brink of nuclear war. The only panacea to save the world was to reduce the defence build up of the Soviet Union and the West.

The 27th Party Congress became a watershed in Soviet defence agenda after which one doctrinal principle after another was subject to review, discussion and revision. From that point on Gorbachev's *New Political Thinking* on security grew by accretion. What compelled to revise Soviet military doctrine and to go for a new military doctrine and strategy? Some Western scholars argued that Soviet leadership since 1966 had systematically been altering doctrine to reduce the likelihood of nuclear war. Soviet security changed under *perestroika* was nothing but a logical extension of Soviet military strategic trends spanning the last twenty years.[1] Others had suggested that deterministic forces within Soviet society produced an inevitable and irreversible shift in doctrine. In particular, a shift from extensive economic growth to intensive growth, and the expansion of the Soviet "intellectual class" – for whom defense occupied lower priority were seen as important engine of change. Besides this factor, his personality factor particularly his perceptions, impressions, recollects, biases and above all interest to change for a better world affected significantly the Soviet defence agenda.

Of the many factors contributing to change in the Soviet security under *perestroika*, those had the most important impact, were of course the mix of economic reforms and institutional changes that had been occurring over the past several years. The nature of defense burden and its weight in the Soviet economy compelled Gorbachev to change and innovate new military policy that would satisfy the need to change the economy and satisfy the military at the same time. Gorbachev further realized that in building the political, economic and social bases underlying Soviet super power status were intimately tied to economic reform that in turn had important implications for defense.[2] Seen in this light, security of Soviet Union under *perestroika* was perceived more as a product of instrumental necessity than of military strategic enlightenment.

3. 2. Components of Military Security During Perestroika

Given its instrumental origin, it was not surprising that the defence agenda under *perestroika* had emerged in a piecemeal fashion rather than as a master blue-print, designed once and for all times to come. Nevertheless, by 1987, Gorbachev's new political thinking on security had been clearly expressed. In the military sphere, the concept of security stressed:

- *Renunciation of War*: No war including nuclear war could be considered a rational continuation of politics; and inadvertent paths to nuclear war were as likely as, if not more likely than, deliberate paths.
- *Prevention of Arms Race and Destruction of Chemical Weapons* was a fundamental component of Soviet military doctrine.
- *Security is Mutual*: Soviet security could not be enhanced by increasing other State's insecurity.
- *Reasonable Sufficiency* should be the basis for the future development of the combat capabilities of the Soviet armed forces.
- *Defensive Defense*: Soviet military thinking should give priority to defensive (non-provocative) defence, not offensive capabilities and operations.
- *Disbandment of Military Alliance*.
- *Reduction of Military Budget*.[3]

3. 2. (i). Renunciation of War

Soviet security, under *perestroika*, stressed on the idea of renunciation of war as the then Soviet leader Gorbachev was the first political leader who realized the futility of nuclear war and tried his best to renounce war for the survival of humanity. In his words: *"We want a world free of war, without arms race; nuclear weapons and violence; not only because this is an optimal condition for our internal development. It is an objective global requirement that stems from the realities of the present day"*.[4] As the world was living in an atmosphere of nuclear threat, stockpiling of weapons especially missiles made the situation more precarious and the war might breakout for a slight human error, so steps for renouncing war was inevitable. In this context Gorbachev said:

"Everyone seems to agree that there would be neither winners nor losers in such a war. There would be no survivors. It is a mortal

threat for all. Although the prospect of death in a nuclear war is undoubtedly the most appalling scenario possible, the issue is broader than that. The spiraling arms race, coupled with the military political realities of the world and the persistent traditions of pro-nuclear political thinking impedes cooperation between countries and people – which East and West agree- is indispensable if the world's nations want to preserve nature intact, to ensure the rational use of and reproduction of her resources and, consequently, to survive as benefits human beings".[5]

Gorbachev's efforts for a nuclear free and safe world were positive direction in this regard. On January 15, 1986, the Soviet Union announced programme for the stage by stage elimination of nuclear weapons and other means of mass destruction.

At the first stage, Soviet Union and USA would reduce half of the nuclear weapons from their stockpiles, while complete ban would be imposed on the development, testing and deployment of space strike weapons. The intermediate-range missiles of the USSR and USA located in Europe would be scrapped.[6] At the second stage, the other nuclear powers would join the disarmament process initially by freezing their arsenals and agreeing not to transfer nuclear weapons to other countries. Secondly, the Soviet Union and the United States froze their tactical arsenals and move to eliminate remaining medium range forces, while all other froze their tactical arsenals. Thirdly, he took steps for banning nuclear testing by all countries and banning space strike weapons by leading industrial nations. At the third stage, Gorbachev tried for abolishing remaining nuclear weapons. Thus he mapped out a stage by stage plan for nuclear disarmament.[7]

From Gorbachev's approach to disarmament, arms control and peace Initiatives, it was revealed that he was genuinely interested in the renunciation of war. He felt that "security can no longer be assured by military means – neither by the use of arms or deterrence nor by continued perfection of the "sword" and the "shield". Attempts to achieve military superiority are preposterous. Now such attempts are made in space. It is an astonishing anachronism, which persists due to the inflated role played by the militarists in politics. From the security point of view the arms race has become an absurdity because its very logic leads to the destabilization of international relations and eventually to a nuclear conflict. Diverting huge resources from other priorities, the arms race is lowering the level of security, impairing it. It is in itself an enemy of peace. The only way to security is through political decisions and disarmament. In our age genuine and equal security can be guaranteed by constantly lowering the level of strategic balance from which nuclear and other weapons of mass destruction should be completely eliminated".[8]

3.2. (ii). Prevention of Arms Race and Destruction of Chemical Weapons

The second idea behind the proposal of 27th CPSU Congress in the military sphere stressed on it. Before Gorbachev, this idea was also mooted. As long as June 19, 1946, the Soviet Union proposed a convention prohibiting the production and use of atomic weapons at a session of the International Atomic Energy Commission which had been created in accordance with the resolution of the General Assembly of UN. But this plan was rejected, as the United States did not favour it.

After that Soviet Union also submitted several proposals to avert the danger of nuclear war; but the proposals were not accepted as imperialist powers turned cold shoulders to such recommendations. But when Gorbachev came to power, he consistently tried to implement it.[9] His new political thinking on security was the formal shift in emphasis in military doctrine to prevent war. The inclusion of war-prevention, as a strategic goal, in Soviet military doctrine during the *perestroika* phase changed the military aspect of security by giving greater weightage to politico-military consideration (such as strategic stability) and politico-diplomatic efforts such as arms control and actions that reduced regional and international tension.[10] As far as strategic stability was concerned, his efforts for disarmament and arms control were positive in this direction. He concluded several treaties and agreements with USA and other European powers for preventing arms race and maintaining global peace and security. In this *perestroika* phase, international treaties, and legal documents like Helsinki Final Act, Geneva, Reykjavik, INF treaties played a decisive role in the military sphere of security. Gorbachev not only tried for implementation of the security proposals but also made it a code of conduct for all practical purposes. Gorbachev's security doctrine was the manifestation of his deep understanding of the security issues of the world and keen desire to share responsibility with other powers.[11]

His efforts to reduce the threat of nuclear war, to prevent a race in space strike arms and to stop the arms race on earth got a practical touch in Geneva Summit concluded on November 19-21, 1985 by both the super powers. But ultimately it did not yield any concrete result as USA decided not to stop its Strategic Defence Initiative (SDI) programme. No doubt the spirit of this Summit played an important role for easing out tension from Europe and the world.[12]

The next important Summit was concluded at Reykjavik on 11-12 October 1986 between Reagan and Gorbachev. Gorbachev submitted several proposals to American President Reagan for making a nuclear free world possible. The first proposal was on strategic offensive weapons. He declared his readiness to have these cut by fifty per cent in the course of the next five years. He also proposed that the strategic weapons on land, water and in the air i.e. ballistic land based missiles, sea-launched missiles and aircraft would be halved, fairly and equally. The second proposal of Gorbachev at the Reykjavik Summit meeting was dealt with medium-range nuclear missiles. He suggested to Reagan that both Soviet and American missiles of this class in Europe be completely eliminated. Since Britain and France opposed inclusion of their nuclear weapons in the general count during the negotiations between USA and Soviet Union, Gorbachev accepted this position at Reykjavik. Soviet Union also agreed to freeze missiles with a range of less than 1000 km and to begin talks on their future. Soviet Union also accepted the American proposal to limit the number of medium range missiles deployed in the Asian part of the Soviet Union. The third proposal was to strengthen the regime of the Anti-Ballistic Missile Treaty and achieved a nuclear test ban. USA did not give a positive response to Gorbachev's defence proposal as it did not want to limit its SDI programme because of its commitment to the ABM. But the Soviet Union wanted the 'Star Wars' programme of US to somehow not be allowed to proceed on planned. This meeting was useful as it paved new ways for further discussion between two powers on the important issues of security and disarmament of the Europe and the world.[13]

Another important area where he tried for solution was Euro-missiles issue. Gorbachev spoke about "reduction and eventual elimination of the tactical nuclear weapons, to be coupled with a drastic reduction of the armed forces and conventional weapons; withdrawal of offensive weapons from direct contact in order to rule out the possibility of a surprise attack; and a change in the entire pattern of armed forces with a view to imparting an exclusively defensive character to them at a meeting in Prague. Proposals on that score were detailed in Budapest programme of the Warsaw Treaty organization".[14]

Soviet Union and other Warsaw Treaty countries announced a major confidence building measure in the spirit of 'New Thinking' concerning their military doctrine, which was strictly defensive in all its components at a meeting of their political consultative committee in Berlin in May 1987. Soviet Union also took efforts for creating Nuclear Weapons Free Zone (NWFZ) and zone free from chemical weapons as they would help in strengthening the security of Europe. He also accepted gladly the offer of the GDR, Czechoslovakian and West German government to create a nuclear free corridor in Central Europe. Another important milestone in the area of nuclear disarmament was the historic visit of Gorbachev to Washington where he signed famous INF Treaty with USA in December 1987.

As far as military aspect of security under *perestroika* was concerned, the Intermediate Nuclear Force (INF) treaty was essentially a unique document. It was unique in the sense that the agreements concluded between the USSR and USA in this field in the past dealt with the limitation of arms, but the new treaty provided for the actual reduction and physical destruction of part of the nuclear arsenals possessed by both the super powers.

Following were the important decisions taken in INF agreement :–

- INF forces comprising of two categories of land-based, intermediate and shorter-range missiles stationed in nine European countries were to be destroyed. It included SS-20, SS-4 and 387 shorter-range missiles (SS23s, SS22s and SS12s deployed by USSR and 429 US Pershing II and ground launched cruise missiles.

- This treaty also provided for cutting down of 50% of their conventional weapons and to abandon secrecy by setting a new standard for rigorous intensive verification of nuclear arms reduction agreement.[15] The President of US paid return visit to Moscow in May 1988 and Gorbachev went to USA again in December 1988. The decisions of this important treaty were implemented and the destruction of those missiles actually took place in early summer 1988 under mutual supervision which indeed ushered a new era in global peace and security.[16]

George Bush also responded positively to the peace initiatives from the side of the Soviet Union. In September 1989, he agreed to a Summit meeting with the leader of Soviet Union and signed a joint agreement with the USSR for substantial destruction of chemical weapons. This important decision was taken after USSR dropped its insistence to link up joint initiative for Strategic Arms Reduction Talk (START) with the scrapping of Strategic Arms Defence Initiative (SDI) programme.[17] Gorbachev met Bush in December 1989 at a short notice in a ship off the Coast of Island State of Malta. Though there was no fixed agenda but it was significant in a sense Gorbachev declared that Cold War was over. Malta Summit was followed by Washington Summit which was held in June 1990. Important decision relating to the destruction of chemical weapons was taken in this Summit.

On October 5, 1991, Soviet President Gorbachev responded positively to the nuclear reduction initiative of Bush with his own initiative. He agreed to match US demands. He destroyed Soviet nuclear artillery, short-range missiles and landmines and also shifted war-heads for air-defence missile from deployment areas and stored or destroyed them and removed bombers from alert duty and stored their nuclear weapons at storage depots. Moreover, he removed from alert duty all those ICBMs slated for retirement under the START treaty and removed tactical nuclear weapons like ships, submarines and land based air craft from naval forces. He created a single unified strategic command and removed 6 SSBN with 92 SLBMs from operational duty (Five Yankee-I vessels and the only Yankee-II submarine were included). Gorbachev declared that the USSR would reduce its strategic forces to a level of 5000, i.e., 1000 fewer than required by the START treaty and challenged the USA to match this additional reduction. He announced that 503 ICBMs including 137 MIR ved missiles, would be removed from operational alert duty, thus eliminating 1094 warheads from the available force.[18] This included 366 SS-11 and SS-13 missiles, 47 SS-17s and 90 SS-19 missiles, all of which were slated for retirement under the START treaty.[19]

Gorbachev agreed to remove all tactical naval nuclear weapons from ships, submarines and land-based aircraft bases, but suggested elimination of them altogether unlike Bush's idea of storing them. Gorbachev proposed removing tactical air delivered bombs and missiles from forward deployed units and storing the warheads at separate bases. In addition to announcing Soviet strategic cuts to 1000 accountable warheads below the START Treaty limits, he proposed that both powers proceed to negotiate additional cuts of one-half in their strategic weapons. Soviet Union and USA also agreed to stop the production of fissile materials for nuclear weapons. Finally, Soviet Union announced a one-year moratorium on nuclear testing and proposed that other nations should do likewise. In this phase, Gorbachev announced the cancellation of several modernization and deployment programmes. He said that Research and Development (R&D) would cease for a new short-range missile for the bomber fleet and for a new mobile SICBM. The rail mobile SS-24 was frozen at the existing level and no R&D would continue for a follow on missile. Gorbachev announced that the SS-24 would be confined to its three permanent garrison and not deployed in a dispersed manner.[20]

The United States and the Soviet Union had been negotiating since 1973 for the reduction of conventional forces in central Europe but this negotiation known as the Mutual and Balanced Force (MBFR) talks had made little progress. The major disagreement was over verification measures that impeded this process. But when Gorbachev came to power, Soviet officials had publicly indicated greater flexibility on the verification issues, called for major reduction in forces and urged the expansion of the geographic area covered by the talks and claimed that asymmetries should be corrected. On December 7, 1988, Gorbachev announced for unilateral reduction of 500,000 men and 10,000 tanks from Soviet forces.[21] After four rounds of talks on Conventional Forces in Europe (CFE) the two leaders exhibited their desire for the reduction of these forces.

The first round lasted until 23 March 1989 and Gorbachev gave figures for total Soviet force levels. He said that on 1 January 1989 they numbered 4. 25 million and after the completion of the unilateral reduction would be down to 3.76 million, at which time those would be approximate parity with NATO. Before the beginning of the 2nd round talk on CFE, Gorbachev had given a public version of the reductions being sought by the Warsaw Pact by 1996-97 at a meeting in Moscow with the U.S. Secretary of State, James Baker. A rough account for aircraft trade off was implicit in the figures he gave: 1,350,000 men should remain on each side along with 1,500 strike aircraft, 1,700 combat helicopters, 20,000 tanks, 24,000 assorted artillery system and 28,000 assorted vehicles.[22] On May 25, the Warsaw Pact gave a proposal incorporating Gorbachev's figures into sub-ceilings of troops and equipment for single countries and foreign deployments as well as alliance totals, and ceiling for three geographical sub-zones as well as for the entire Atlantic to the Urals (ATTU) region. In subsequent round of talks with USA he took efforts for the reduction of the troops, helicopters, air-crafts and combat air-crafts from both the sides. He also took steps for reducing troops from GDR, Czechoslovakia, Hungary and Poland.[23]

The second part of the programme for the creation of all-embracing system of international security proposed by 27th CPSU Congress dealt with the problem of chemical weapons. After World War I, there was lot of discussions to ban chemical weapons. Even on 28 March 1972, the socialist countries submitted to the Committcc on Disarmament the draft convention on the prohibition of the development, production and stockpiling of chemical weapons and on their destruction. In 1976, the USSR and USA started bilateral talks concerning the prohibition of chemical weapons. But no concrete progress has been achieved till mid-80s. Touching upon this issue, Gorbachev in his speech on 15th January 1986 stated that the task of eliminating chemical weapons in this century is feasible. In April 1986, the USSR advanced a set of proposed on the elimination of the industrial base for the production of chemical weapons, and these proposals made it possible to unite one of the tightest knots at the negotiation. During summer of this year at the

40 Nations' Conference on Disarmament, the Soviets agreed in principle to allow foreign inspectors to witness dismantling of chemical arms factories by accepting the proposal of U.S.A. In November of the same year, the Soviet side came up with a proposal for preventing the production of chemical weapons in the commercial (civilian) industry.

In the year 1987, the Soviet Union offered new proposals relating to the chemical disarmament. In February of that year, the Soviet Union announced its willingness to declare the location of all the chemical weapon stockpiles shortly after a treaty is signed and a willingness to accept inspections on short notice of suspected chemical weapon facilities, except in case where supreme national interest would be jeopardized. On April 1987, Gorbachev announced that the Soviet Union had stopped the production of chemical weapons and had no such weapons beyond its borders. At the same time he declared that a special plant was being constructed to destroy such weapons.[24] In October Western officials visited Soviet chemical weapons production facility at Shikhary but the progress was not upto mark as controlling and eliminating chemical weapons was not an easy task as it needed the involvement of many other nations in the process of negotiation.

3.2. (iii). Security is Mutual

Since the end of the Second World War, Soviet military doctrine was based on the principle of deterrence by defence. Soviet leaders and strategic experts realized that Soviet security could be ensured by increasing the insecurity of its neighbours and other nations. So, the defence policy was designed to carry out this objective. But Gorbachev who was inspired by the work of Palme Commission redefined Soviet perceptions of national security by introducing his new thinking in Soviet defence and foreign policy calculation. He viewed that Soviet security must be intertwined with American and global security. It was clearly revealed when he answered to questions "You asked me what is the primary thing that defines Soviet-American relations. I think it is the immutable fact that whether we like one another or not, we can either survive or perish only together".[25] Soviet strategic experts also adopted Gorbachev's line of thought.

The editorial of a leading confidential military journal assessed his defence policy positively:

"Security in the nuclear age must be evaluated differently. Assessing security is more and more becoming a political task. It can only be resolved by political means through *détente*, disarmament, strengthening confidence, and developing international cooperation. It is unthinkable and even criminal to seek to resolve the problems of security in an arms race, perfecting the 'shield' and the 'sword'.[26]

Thus, his approach of mutual security, which was an antithesis of unilateral security, was based on the premise that meaningful, stable and psychologically reassuring security could never be possible through the efforts of individual states. Mutual security considered both sides hostages to the nuclear arms race. The only way out of this relationship was to strengthen security through cooperation and mutual friendship. Mutual security accepted on a fact that in the nuclear era security of a nation could not be achieved at the expense of the other.[27] If one side felt its security was threatened or damaged by the actions of other, such is the threat perceived by the United States from Soviet heavy missiles and by Europe from Soviet SS20 or by the Soviet Union from America's Pershing II intermediate range or MX ICBM, then it would take compensatory actions that in turn might be perceived by the other side as reducing its own security.[28] In the words of Gorbachev:

"In the context of the relations between the USSR and the USA, security can only be mutual and if we take international relations as a whole it can only be universal... it is vital that all should feel equally secure, for the fears and anxieties of the nuclear age generate on the predictability in politics".[29]

The implications of mutual security for the military policy and the conduct of US-Soviet relations were profound. The idea of mutual security tried to lessen the threats by mutual actions. Gorbachev and Reagan outrightly rejected the deterrence theory and agreed to reduce the nuclear weapons from both sides as they realized it could only increase the sense of security. They took steps for the reduction of nuclear weapons, conventional forces from Europe and destination of chemical weapons as explored earlier. So, the steps taken by USSR and USA for disarmament clearly expressed the significance of interdependence in ensuring security. According to Gorbachev: "Today, world nations are interdependent, like mountain climbers attached to one rope. They can either climb together to the summit or all fall into the abyss".[30]

Both the leaders realized that earlier military doctrine which viewed security dilemma as a zero-sum game was no more relevant; rather the mutual efforts and joint initiatives were the only way for the solution of the global problems. In this context, Gorbachev further said:

"The Soviet Union alone cannot resolve all these issues. And we are not ashamed to repeat this, calling for international cooperation. We say with full responsibility casting away the false considerations of 'prestige' that all of us in the present day world are coming to depend more and more on one another and are becoming increasingly necessary to one another".[31]

3.2. (iv). Doctrine of Reasonable Sufficiency: Its Relevance

Doctrine of reasonable sufficiency, which was a new doctrine in Soviet strategic thinking first, appeared in 27th CPSU Congress when Gorbachev endorsed a military strategy of rational sufficient defence. In May 1987, the meaning of sufficiency was elaborated in Warsaw Pact meeting where he unveiled this new doctrine of reasonable sufficiency characterizing the pact policy. Gorbachev asserted that "Warsaw Treaty signatories have clearly stated their military doctrine, one that is subordinated to the task of preventing both nuclear and conventional war, is oriented on reasonable sufficiency in both volume and nature of arms and armed forces, and is exclusively defensive in nature".[32] The objective of this military doctrine is to maintain global peace and security through minimum defence arrangement by keeping strategic parity with USA at low level. The principal difference between the old and new version of Soviet military doctrine was summarized by Colonel General M.A. Gareyev, a Deputy Chief of the Soviet General staff and a leading military theorist at a press briefing this way: "What is new here is the fact that, whereas military doctrine used to be defined as a system of views of the preparation for war and the waging of war, its substance is now based on the prevention of war. The task of preventing war is becoming the supreme goal, the nucleus of military doctrine, the basic function of the state and the armed forces. Of course, a world war must be prevented chiefly by political means, but this must also be reflected in defensive activity. The chief essence of the political aspect of our military doctrine is that socialism unconditionally rejects war as a means of resolving inter-state political, economic and ideological differences".[33]

The clearest elaboration of this doctrine of reasonable sufficiency was written by Lev Semeyko, a senior researcher at the Institute for the study of USA and Canada, in the newspaper *Izvestia* in August of 1987. He argued that old strategic thinking "more is better" in security affairs which stressed on the military dominance over opponent was the necessary condition for victory in a war. But this new doctrine outrightly rejected this notion and recognized that it was no more relevant in the present world. According to Semeyko, it had three dimensions: political, military-technical and economic.

The political aspect, which dealt with the non-aggressive orientation of Soviet military doctrine, tried to solve security issues through political means i.e. through arms control, disarmament etc. The military dimension of reasonable sufficiency was linked with several other principles of the new political thinking on security. The military potentiality of the Soviet Union must be sufficient to face any attack under the worst imaginable conditions and to reliably rebuff the aggression unleashed by the West, but it must not be so great as to threaten the security of other nations. There should not be unreasonable surplus of military potential. It should also be manifested in the structure, character composition and deployment of the Soviet forces.[34] Marshall Akhromeyev also highlighted on this dimension of reasonable sufficiency. According to him, in the event of aggression, the main type of military operation by our armed forces would be defensive in nature. He also emphasized on the defensive way to challenge the enemy.[35]

The economic dimension of reasonable sufficiency recognized that there was a law of diminishing returns in the arms race. Marginal increase of military power came at ever-greater cost. However, those increments of military power added very less to the military capability of the state.

So, the strategic experts who were supporters of the doctrine of *reasonable sufficiency* argued that Soviet Union should not go for huge expenditure on defence as compelled by USA to maintain parity with USA as it would wreck the Soviet economy and threaten the security of the world. Thus, the doctrine of *reasonable sufficiency* highlighted the lowest possible level of strategic parity for maintaining genuine security. Gorbachev mentioned that strategic parity had already been achieved and the existing correlation of military forces had to be maintained. Of course, he admitted the existence of asymmetries between two forces for which steps had to be taken to correct it. This doctrine also tried to maintain parity between NATO and Warsaw. According to the Defence Minister of Soviet Union, Yazov, it could be possible only through the reduction of defence potential of the West.[36] Soviet Union solely relied on reciprocity for reducing military weapons and they assumed that NATO should cut its military forces to meet the sacrifices made by Warsaw countries in order to maintain strategic parity at lower level. It could be only possible through diplomacy of disarmament.[37] This conclusion fitted well with the repeated Soviet statement that the internal security must be preserved through arms reduction from both the sides and reorganization of the inter-state system that would cease the confrontational postures of the West and the East.[38] This doctrine also tried to ensure the security of the Soviet Union and other Warsaw countries in case of a sudden attack by the West for which they must have enough potential to face this eventuality.

So, the Kremlinologist had highlighted on the three basic requirements:

- The enemy forces who played the role of an aggressor must be stopped at the border of the Soviet empire and instantly be thrown back to its territory;
- The Soviet homeland must be protected from the external aggression which would cause damage to its political, economic stability and territorial integrity;
- The belligerent attitude of the enemy must be dealt with a heavy hand by destroying the aggression; hence Soviet military superiority was required in the European theatre.[39]

Vladimir Lobov of Soviet Union clearly elaborated this idea of 'defensive sufficiency', "What we mean by reasonable or defensive sufficiency is not simply a reduction in troops and armaments but a thorough revision of modernization program and redeployment of forces, primarily with the aim of greatly strengthening country's defence on a long-term basis".[40] Another important aspect of this defensive sufficiency was counter-offensive in case of extreme situation. In this context, General Yazov said:

"The defence cannot defeat an aggressor on its own. Therefore, after repulsing the attack, troops and naval forces must be capable of carrying out a decisive offensive. The transition to the offensive will take the form of counter offensive, which must be carried out in a complex and tense situation or combat with well armed opponent".[41]

The writings of the scholar of the Institute of World Economy and International Relations (IMEMO) and IUSAC threw enough light on the several aspects of this doctrine. This doctrine stressed on minimum deterrence; it would accelerate the process of arms control talks by creating a favourable atmosphere; it would be helpful for strengthening the economic situation of Soviet Union by reducing nuclear and other weapons through negotiation; and it favoured qualitative improvement of weapons by rejecting the old approach of quantitative parity.[42]

The operational aspect of this doctrine largely depended on the response of the West. But this response was not up to Soviet expectation. It was slow and even some times Americans were not ready to reduce their weapons and missiles from the sides of the Soviet Union. No doubt the hawkish attitudes of the Americans compelled Gorbachev to think about the ways to strengthen the defence mechanism of Soviet Union. But he was not at all in favour of offensive operation and his only intention was to safeguard Soviet Union by repelling the aggressor in case of attack. In this context, Mikhail Moiseyev said:

"Hundreds of American military bases surrounding the territory of Soviet Union, US carrier task forces, carrier based air craft and naval forces, in which the US has substantial advantage over the

Soviet navy are constant source of anxiety to us. The sea launched Cruise missile which the US is unwilling to reduce and the deployment of Stealth air launched Cruise missiles, which are undoubtedly a first strike weapon, represent a growing danger. Can all this be qualified within the category of peaceful intentions?".[43]

Whatever might be the intentions of Americans, he was ready to convince them to go for arms control. Even he was prepared for unilateral cuts in defence expenditure and withdrawal of equipment's and troops from the Soviet periphery in conjunction with achieving reasonable sufficiency. As Moiseyev stated:

"The reductions will be made on a unilateral basis. By agreement with our allies in the WTO we have made the decision to withdraw six tank divisions from the GDR, Czechoslovakia and Hungary and to disband them by 1991.The Soviet forces in those countries will be cut by 50,000 persons and their arms by 5,000 tanks. In addition, in the Europe part of our country and on the territory of our European allies, the Soviet armed forces will be reduced by 10,000 tanks, 8,500 artillery and 800 combat air craft".[44]

It is important to note that the doctrine of reasonable sufficiency envisioned the most finite deterrence on both the nuclear and conventional level: a parity in defence potential. This doctrine on the nuclear level aimed at reducing nuclear weapons to a minimum level for which he signed several treaties with USA. The INF treaty was of course a radical shift in Soviet arms control policy. For the first time, Soviets had not only accepted asymmetrical reduction in missiles and warheads but also relinquished weapons system in which they were in advantageous position over the US. In addition the concept of reasonable sufficiency also envisioned reductions on the conventional level. The genesis of reasonable sufficiency, like that of the New Thinking is rooted in a decision by the political leadership to achieve foreign and domestic reforms.

In summary, the increasing proliferation and lethality of the super power's nuclear arsenals helped Gorbachev in conceiving the doctrine of reasonable sufficiency in national defence. A careful analysis of Soviet doctrinal writings revealed that two decades of Soviet military thought had led logically to reasonable sufficiency on both nuclear and conventional level.

3.2.(v). Disbandment of Military Alliances

Before the introduction of *perestroika,* both the military alliances i.e. Warsaw Pact and NATO were very active. Like NATO, Warsaw Pact played also an active role in defending the security of the territorial integrity of the Soviet Union and East European countries. But in the beginning of 1970s when Europe started moving towards institutionalization of the territories of the European States including East Europe, Warsaw took the initiative for proportional reduction of arms in Europe with NATO. After the mid 80s when Gorbachev assumed power, he drastically changed the concept of security by introducing changes in military strategy and defence policies. No doubt his reform policies posed a challenge to both the alliance systems.[45]

The 27th Congress of CPSU dealt with "the disbandment of military alliances and as a stage towards this, renunciation of their enlargement and of the formation of new ones".[46] This proposal on disbanding military organizations and military blocs had been repeatedly put forth by the Soviet Union separately and Warsaw Pact member States together. It was clearly revealed in one of the important proposals of the Berlin Declaration on May 31, 1987.

Eventual liquidation of the Warsaw Pact and NATO as an extension of the view that the "continuing division of Europe into opposing military blocs is abnormal", and supplanting them with an all embracing system of international security".[47] But the West had ignored this proposal. In fact, it took steps in the other direction by expanding its sphere of action. Washington proposed various schemes for strengthening NATO. Even NATO countries went to the extent of claiming its responsibility for the situation in the Middle East and South Atlantic etc. Though it was opposed by some of its European members. When Soviet Union did not succeed in the dissolution of both NATO and Warsaw Pact; it decided with other Warsaw members to disband Warsaw Pact in 1991 as it lost its relevance under the impact of Gorbachev's grand design of new thinking.[48]

No doubt, the disbandment of Warsaw Pact has tremendous impact on both West European and East European nations. Not only it has military implications, but also far reaching political and economic implications. It has drastically changed the political and economic equations of Russia (claimant of erstwhile Soviet Union) with East European countries. It has also replaced bipolar world for a uni-polar world order. Though it seems to be a New World Order but it is really not a New World Order, rather a world to be ordered.

3.2. (vi). Reduction of Military Budget

The crisis of the 'militarized economy' coupled with the ideas of global peace and security forced Gorbachev to go for reduction in military budget. No doubt, before Gorbachev, several proposals were tabled by Soviet Union and its allies before UN General Assembly in 1973, 1976, 1978, 1982 to this effect. The Warsaw Pact countries also came forth with proposals for reducing military budget on a collective basis, even at the beginning of 1984, the Warsaw Pact countries came forth with detailed proposal on freezing and reducing military expenditure of States. But there had been no progress in this sphere due to opposition put up by NATO countries. But Gorbachev thought seriously in this direction and took concrete steps to solve this problem as he feared that unless his idea of 'balanced proportional reduction of military budget' materialized, there was risk of 'serious destabilization of society'[49] as it would shatter the Soviet economy. In October 1988, the then Finance Minister, Boris Gostev, published an assessment that Soviet budget deficit stood at 38 billion roubles. By the following year this figure had risen to 100 billion roubles. The defence budget was considered as one of the most important area where some inroads might be made into the deficit. Gorbachev in his UN speech promised a cut of 14.2% in the military budget, although at this stage the size of that budget had not been announced. Gorbachev and other leaders also promised further military budget cuts.

There was unanimous official opinion for reducing defence spending though it was opposed non-officially by few military leaders. In February 1989, General Moiseev said, "To be blunt, we must also find ways of economising on defence".[50] Of course in early 1990 some strategic experts even Moiseev himself expressed his discontent on this issue. At the Congress of People's Deputies Gorbachev announced 77.3 billion roubles figure for the military budget and proposal for a 14% cut in 1990-91. Prime Minister Nikolai Ryzkov also expressed his intention to cut the burden of military spending on national income by 33 to 50% by 1995. He further said that the USSR would press ahead with the conversion to civilian production of the defence industry. In late 1980s particularly after INF treaty, many military production plants in the USSR made civilian products. In this phase, funds were also cut for military research and development. This reduction of military budget had impact on the military budget of USA and other European nations. Though they did not come up to the expectation of Gorbachev, but the West, particularly USA decided to reduce their military expenditure in half in relation to GNP – i.e. to three per cent. No doubt the cut in defence expenditure helped in strengthening his idea of 'Comprehensive Universal Security' and paved the way for the solution of economic problems faced by numerous countries and peoples.

3.3. Internal Changes in Military Thinking Under Perestroika

Soviet concept of security under *perestroika* focussed its attention on 'Comprehensive Universal Security'. For attaining 'universal' or 'common security' changes were brought in both external and internal aspects of military thinking. Internal changes were made in military thinking to cater the needs of 'universal security'. There was a need for new institutions and ideas. The days of military-industrial complexes, the reigning ideas of old style ideologues and autarkic interests had begun to eclipse. Civilian defence intellectual reformists and supporters of liberalized trade policies among the intelligentsia gained influence and tried to institutionalize the policy. During this phase Gorbachev brought drastic changes in Soviet armed forces and personnel, a drastic cut in resources aimed at slimming down the corpulent military bureaucracy. Unilateral reduction of Soviet troops coupled with proposal of further military troops cut through an agreement of CFE. The emphasis was on the training programme for officers and higher military education to defence personnel. Those were in top positions. There were proposals for adopting small voluntary army instead of universal military service. In the institutional level, he brought changes in the politburo, Defence Council and Central Committee Secretariat. His supporters occupied central position in military set up. He increased party's control over the military leadership in the politburo and defence council.

At the 27th Party Congress and at the successive Central Committee plenums, Sokolov, the institutional representative of the military, failed to attain voting membership in politburo and Marshall Ogarkov was sidelined. Gorbachev also replaced Sokolov with a relatively unknown army General Dimitri Yazov. During this time, Gorbachev occupied a key position by tightening his personal control over the entire military set up. He brought Anatolii Lukianev, Chief of the Central Committee (CC) General Department into CC Secretariat and gave him defence task to supervise the work of the CC administrative organs department, which dealt with appointments, promotion in the Ministry of Defence, the KGB and in the Ministry of Internal Affairs.[51] He also set up two departments for arms control, one in the MFA– the Administration for problems of Arms Reduction and Disarmament headed by Viktor Karpov– and the other, an Arms Control Sector in International Department (ID) of the CPSU Central Committee led by LT. General Viktor Starodabov.

As the emphasis was on quality rather than on quantitative factor in defence, so steps were taken to scrap majority of old ships and submarines for navy those needed special attention and more money for maintenance. Most of the 'New Thinkers' felt that there was the need of scientific and technological base rather than outdated technological base for strengthening Soviet defence. In this context, Shevardnadze said "any advantage enjoyed by the aggressor can be reduced to naught if the state possesses a developed industrial and scientific and technological base".[52] For resuscitating the moribund economy of Soviet Union and also for maintaining global peace, arms control measure and reduction of military troops were carried out unilaterally in an effective way without waiting for the response of the West.

During this phase of *perestroika*, not only Soviet Union but the members of Warsaw Pact also stretched their cooperation to accelerate the process of disarmament changing their offensive military doctrine and posture.[53] Soviet and East European force reductions in Europe would amount to nearly 300,000 troops, 12,000 tanks, 9,130 artillery systems and 930 combat aircraft.[54] In this stage decision was also taken to reduce Soviet military personnel by 500,000 men including roughly 400,000 conscripts and 1,000 officers.

Another important military reforms was renewed emphasis on training. Many military officials and civilians occupied the fact that there was incompetent and useless people in Soviet defence. "It is no secret" commented one high ranking official, "that we have people that don't meet today's high requirements, they bring discredit to Soviet officers uniform."[55] Akhromeyev also expressed similar opinion about the incompetence of junior officers due to lack of skill and proper training. Corruption and drug addiction among officials made the situation even worse.

Yazov also introduced reforms, including reorganizing higher military schools, improving instruction through stricter certification of teachers and modifying the course structure. Some schools those lacked proper facilities and competitive environment were decided to be closed. There was also emphasis on higher military schools, which would produce skilled and intelligent officers.[56]

In 1988, the most controversial matter relating to conscription and universal military service system was approved when restructuring in Soviet Armed Forces was going on. Various proposals were tabled for adopting a smaller, volunteer army, a conscripted territorial militia or combined cadre-militia system. There was much hue and cry inside the Soviet army against it. Military personnel opposed it with an apprehension that they might lose their jobs. Most of the senior officials saw this move as threatening to undermine the power and prestige of the military and exacerbating the already complicated recruiting problem.

The most realistic alternative for replacing conscription was a compromise cadre-militia system– "a relatively high-tech equipped, professionally trained and manned, predominantly volunteer cadre military organization, supported by a broad network of territorial-militia formations".[57]

But Soviet military officials opposed any move towards professional army as the threat of war had not vanished and the response of the USA to the peace initiatives of Soviet Union was also not upto mark. So, the conscription could provide adequate pool of reserves in case of war.[58] Secondly, the expense of moving towards voluntary army was exorbitant. Akhromeyev and Moiseyev both agreed on this point. Moiseyev declared that it would cost 'five to eight times' as much as the present system and later on he lowered his estimate to 'three to four times'.[59] Another small change related to the internal security forces was the creation of "special purpose detachments" in several cities to check mob and demonstrations. They were recruited mainly from former paratroopers and Spetsnaz soldiers with an average age above 30. They were well trained to curb mob with little physical force.[60]

From the above analysis, it was clearly revealed that Soviet concepts of security, particularly its military aspects, underwent a radical change under *perestroika*. Perestroika changed both internal and external dimensions of security too. It was a fact that domestic, social and economic compulsion coupled with Gorbachev's ambition for a better world was the driving force behind such a change.

New Thinkers (Vitaly Zhurkin, Sergei Karaganov, Andrei Kortunov, Zhillin, etc.), Old Thinkers (Yazov, Kostev, Varenikov, etc.) and even Western scholars studying Soviet security, accepted the inevitability of change, but there were differences of opinion among the scholars about the ways and means of achieving this desired objective. There was a debate between the New Thinkers and the Old Thinkers about the military aspects of security. On the other hand, most of the Western scholars were skeptical about the changes in the military field during this phase. New Thinkers considered nuclear war as accidental whereas the Old Thinkers considered it deliberate. For them, the cold rational decision to initiate a nuclear strike was a remote possibility.[61]

In the New Thinking, therefore, nuclear war was portrayed as a threat in its own right – irrespective of its political content. The greater danger, as one of the central committee consultant of that time put it (in most un-Marxist terms) was that "nuclear war could begin and without political decision".[62] In other words, technology, not politics might be the cause of nuclear war. They tried to minimize the chance of nuclear war through maintaining strategic parity with

USA at lower level. But the old thinkers disagreed with this notion as USA did not stop its belligerent attitudes even after Soviet leaders took peace initiatives.[63] Secondly, New Thinkers considered security as mutual and inter-dependent as no country could defend itself by military technical means alone, national and international security were intertwined, the other side's security concerns must be taken into account.[64] So, they expected a cordial response from the West. But the Old Thinkers rejected this premise that Soviet Union's effort to reduce military weapons and expectations of USA's cooperation in this regard would be interpreted as threatening to the security of the Soviet Union.

The most controversial idea relating to security was the 'doctrine of reasonable sufficiency'. Of course, there was general agreement among New and Old Thinkers that the Soviet defence posture should be based on sufficiency.[65] But differences appeared when the issues of "What is sufficient?" and "how is sufficiency to be determined?" were addressed. As this doctrine was confusing, it served Gorbachev's best interests by making it a wild card, which could be applied according to the need of the time, so far as the operational aspect of this doctrine was concerned. The New Thinkers favoured unilateral restructuring of Soviet forces without waiting for the West to agree to bring about mutual change in the number of forces, as they thought it would represent a net increase in Soviet security.[66] Even they argued unilateral reduction in combination with bilateral and multilateral action would strengthen Soviet security by reducing the overall level of the East-West military confrontation.[67] They thought there was no harm in resorting to asymmetric responses as it could neutralize the Western strategy of wrecking Soviet economy by compelling Soviet Union to buy inappropriate military products.

In contrast to New Thinkers, Old Thinkers stressed on strict parity. This involved careful analysis, forecasting of Western military trends and timely procurement of forces needed to compensate for any deviations from strict parity.[68] Skeptics preferred to use the term, "defensive sufficiency" or "just sufficiency" instead of "reasonable sufficiency". They emphasized importance of possessing every type of weapons, which could only make Soviet Union defensively sufficient to face any attack from the West. They argued that asymmetries in the European theatre needed to be corrected and unilateral reductions should be stopped, as such actions would not improve the security and rather they would magnify the threat.[69]

Internal military reforms during *perestroika* phase were also not free from contradictions. Military officials opposed the dominance of civilians on the military matters and criticized the ideas contained in a draft paper prepared by Supreme Soviet Committee on defence pointing out that Soviet army were already a "professional army working on the basis of a mix of voluntary and compulsory service. They also expressed their apprehensions about the material cost of the reforms suggested by the deputies group and opposed armed formations on national ethnic basis as it would do untold harm to the nation".[70] Military officials, particularly Old Thinkers argued to moderate the pace of the military reforms; otherwise it might unsettle the military which was already worried by the internal changes in the military.[71] Even they expressed their dissatisfaction about the defence budget cuts and reduction of military personnel in Soviet army. They founded an union named 'Shield' to defend their rights and tried to make the new model army 'free of bureaucracy, protectionism and nepotism, as well as of barrack-room bullying'.[72]

The Western critics considered the changes in the military sphere as a hoax. 'There was neither a methodology nor a system of criteria for defining security requirements. It was a set of notions that was ex-post-facto could be used by Gorbachev to justify doctrinally and ideologically, his efforts to manipulate the Soviet agenda. The elements of 'New Thinking' could be used to rationalize any force posture and defence policy. Thus, it would be fruitless to use this framework to attempt to predict specifically what Soviet forces might look like in ten years, since neither Soviet Minister of Defence Dimitri Yazov, Chief of the General Staff Akhromeyev, nor Gorbachev himself could do this objectively'.[73] They were also against the defence cuts like military officials of Soviet Union as they argued it would sharply diminish the USSR's ability to launch deep offensive on short notice.[74] Some of them were also skeptic about the intention of Gorbachev for ushering in a new era free from nuclear holocaust. They also argued that Soviet party-military relations were inherently conflict ridden.[75] So, it would put Gorbachev in a critical juncture.

It was a fact that military aspects of security during *perestroika* had some theoretical and operational flaws. The internal military changes that were introduced during this phase had following effects:

- It encouraged the dissatisfaction among military personnel by appeasing civilians through military reforms.

- It reduced the strength of KGB and the intelligence departments, making it almost defunct.

- The military dimension of security was underplayed by Gorbachev as he stressed on political and economic aspects of security. At the same time, international security got priority over national security.

- Gorbachev's broader reform agenda was having paradoxical consequences. The very strategy of *glasnost* and *perestroika* removed the rationale for a large standing military. Thus, military reforms weakened the internal security set-up of Soviet Union. The weakening influence of the military had devastating effect on the internal socio-political scenario. It stimulated divisive forces and led to ethnic assertions in a number of republics. The reliability of the army was put to question too because of the inter-ethnic division with the armed forces. That was dramatically visible during the intervention in Baku in 1990 when Soviet army expressed their unwillingness in this operation.[76]

- The frailty of the internal security set up was quite visible when the Soviet Army, enfeebled by the reduction of the forces, was unable to check the secessionist movement in Tajikistan, Georgia and Baltic republic through military force.[77]

At the operational level, American response and reactions was not upto mark. Unilateral reduction of forces exhibited the weaknesses of the Soviet Union. American penetration in Soviet Union's internal affairs aggravated the situation and ultimately helped in the process of disintegration of Soviet Union.

It was a fact that disintegration of the Soviet Union was inevitable. Gorbachev, through his reforms, was only seeking to stem the tide of an impending doom. Soviet Union was facing crises on all fronts and Gorbachev sought to face them through measures outlined above. But the situation was so bad and the time so inopportune for a reformer that in spite of all his good intentions he could not avert the crisis. This has led many to opine that Gorbachev was responsible for the failure of the Soviet system. However, whatever might be the intentions of Gorbachev in bringing about changes in the military sphere of Soviet security, the steps he took to bring about widespread reforms, could not be underrated as they helped in ushering in a new era.

Gorbachev led the foundation of a more peaceful world by ending the cold war. At the same time he sought to liberate USSR from the conceptual and ideological baggage that had heavily influenced it in the past. Though Soviet Union is no more, but his military reforms have had an enduring impact on Russia and the World. The ideas like renunciation of war, the danger of inadvertent nuclear war, prevention of arms race, interdependence in the sphere of security and acknowledgement of strategic theatre, nuclear sufficiency have eternal significance.

References

1. For some imaginative speculation on this point see Michael Mcc Gwire, *Military Objectives in Soviet Foreign Policy*, (Washington DC: Brookings, 1987). For details see Jack Snyder, "The Gorbachev Revolution: A Waning of Soviet Expansionism", in Sean M. Lynn, et.al., (eds.), *Soviet Military Policy*, (Cambridge: The MIT Press, 1989), p. 112.
2. Snyder, *1* p. 113.
3. Summary of XXVII CPSU Document. see also Mikhail Gorbachev's *Perestroika: New Thinking for Our Country and the World*, (London: Fortana/Collins, 1987), p. 231.
4. *Ibid.,* p. 11.
5. *Ibid.,* p. 12.
6. Mikhail Gorbachev, "Nuclear Disarmament by the Year 2000", *New York Times*, (Feb. 1986), p. A.13.
7. *Ibid,* p. A13. see also Donald M. Snow, *The Necessary Peace*, (Lexington, Mass.: Lexington Books, 1987), pp. 68-69.
8. Gorbachev, *Perestroika*, *op.cit.,* p. 141.

9. Vadim Zagaldin, *Peace the Only Option*, (New Delhi: Allied Publishers, 1987), p. 78.
10. Stephen M. Meyer, "The Sources and Prospects of Gorbachev's New Political Thinking on Security" in Sean M. Lynn Jones et.al., *Soviet Military Policy*, *op.cit.*, p.120.
11. *Pravda*, October 15, 1986.
12. *The Soviet-US Summit, November 1985, Geneva*, (Moscow: Novosti Press, 1985).
13. *The Result and Lessons of Reykjavik*, (Moscow: Novosti Press, 1986), p. 29. see for further details, Gorbachev, *Prestroika*, *op. cit.*, pp. 236-240.
14. Gorbachev, *Perestroika*, *op.cit.*, p. 203.
15. *USSR-US Summit, Washington, December, 7-10, 1987*, (Moscow: Novosti Press, 1987); See also A. S. Chopra, "European Security – INF Treaty Leads the Way", *World Focus*, (May 1988), p.17.
16. *USSR-US Summit, Moscow, May 29-June 2, 1988*, (Moscow: Novosti Press, 1988).
17. Zafar Imam, *Soviet Foreign Policy – 1917 to 1990*, (New Delhi: Sterling Publishers, 1991), pp. 97-99.
18. Gorbachev used the figure of 134 MIR red missile but this was corrected later as 137. see"Nuclear Note Book", *Bulletin of the Atomic Scientist*, (March 1992), p. 49.
19. *Ibid.*
20. Richard Field House, "Nuclear Weapons Development and Unilateral Reduction Initiatives", in *SIPRI Yearbook*, (Stockholm: SIPRI, 1992), pp. 71-72.
21. Robert L. Arnett, "Arms Control in Soviet National Security Policy Under Gorbachev", in George E. Hudson (ed.), *Soviet National Security Policy Under Perestroika*, (London: Unwin Hyman, 1989), pp. 287-288.
22. *Soviet News*, 17 May 1989.
23. Gerard Holden, *Soviet Military Reform*, (London: Pluto Press, 1991), pp. 142-148.
24. Arnett, *op.cit.*, p. 289.
25. "Mikhail Gorbachev's Answers to Questions put by Time Magazine", *Novosti Press Release*, (Moscow, 1985), p. 5
26. "A Concrete Program for Assuring Peace and Security", *Voyennaya Mysl* (Military Thought), No. 6, (June 1986), pp.3-4,

cited in Raymond L. Garthoff, "New Thinking in Soviet Military Doctrine", *Washington Quarterly,* (Summer, 1988), p. 134.

27. *Tass* Press Release, July 28, 1986.
28. Philip D. Stewart and Margaret G. Herman, "The Soviet Debate over 'New Thinking' and the Restructuring of US -Soviet Relations" in George Hudson, (ed.), *op.cit.*, pp. 51-52.
29. *Gorbachev's Politcal Report to 27th CPSU Congress, 1986*, (Moscow: Novosti Press, 1986), p. 74.
30. From Gorbachev's Speech in Prague on April 10, 1987, "For a Common European Home: For a New way of Thinking", (Moscow: Novosti Press, 1987), p. 20.
31. Gorbachev, *Perestroika*, *op.cit.,* p.137.
32. See Steven P. Adragna, "A New Soviet History Doctrine and Strategy", *Orbis*, (Spring 1989), p.165.
33. *Ibid.,* pp.165-166.
34. See Stephen M. Meyer, "The Sources and Prospects of Gorbachev's New Political Thinking on Security", in Sean M. Lynn-Jones et.al., *op.cit.,* p.131.
35. Steven Adragna, *op.cit.,* p.169.
36. Gerhard Wettig, "New Thinking on Security and East West Relations"; *Problems of Communism*, (March-April 1988), p. 3.
37. *Ibid.*
38. *Ibid.*
39. Gerhard Wettig, "Gorbachev Strategies for Disarmament and Security", *Aussen Politik*, Vol. 38. No.1, (1987), pp. 3-10.
40. Alexi Arbatov, "How much defence is sufficient", *International Affairs*, (April 1989), pp. 31-44.
41. Quoted in Holden, *Soviet Military Reform*, op.cit., p. 80. Similar views are also expressed by Colonel General Gareyev, Lt. General Vladimir Serebryannikov and the Chief of the Staff of the Warsaw Pact General Lobov.
42. Alexi Arbatov, "How much defence is sufficient?", *International Affairs*, (April 1989), pp. 31-44.
43. Mikhail Moiseyev, *The Soviet Military Doctrine: Orientation Towards Defence,* (Moscow: Novosti Press,1989), p. 7.
44. *Pravda*, December 8, 1988, p. 2.
45. *NATO Review*, Vol. 36, No. 5, (1988), p. 28.
46. Gorbachev, *Perestroika, op. cit.*, p. 231.
47. *Izvestia*, May 31, 1987, p.1.
48. Zafar Imam, (ed.), *Restructuring Soviet Society*, (New Delhi: Panchsheel Publications, 1987). see also *M. S. Gorbachev*,

Speeches and Writings, Vol. 2, (Oxford: Oxford University Press, 1987).

49. "Komulyudi doveryaayut" in *Pravda*, 13 April, 1989.

50. *Izvestia*, 4 June 1989.

51. Lukianov headed the General Department from 1985 until May 1987, when Gorbachev's aide for domestic affairs Valery Boldin was given this new assignment. It is important to note that both Lukianov and Georgii Razumovskii, Gorbachev's Secretary for Cadres had close ties with General Secretary and were hand-picked by him for these positions.

52. Report by E. A. Shervardnadze on July 25, 1988, to a Conference of the USSR Ministry of Foreign Affairs on "The 19th All Union CPSU Conference: Foreign Policy and Diplomacy", *International Affairs*, (Moscow), October 1988, p. 16.

53. On December 7, 1988, Gorbachev announced the USSR's intention to cut from the Soviet Armed Forces by the end of 1990: (1) half a million men, including 100,000 officers; (2) 10,000 tanks world wide, including six tank divisions (5,000 tanks) in the German Democratic Republic, Czechoslovakia and Hungary; (3) one air assault brigade and all assault-landing bridging formations forward deployed in Eastern Europe; (4) nearly one-fifth of all Soviet armament production; and (5) the level of defence spending, by 14.2%. Moscow would reduce its troop strength by 12 per cent, including approximately 240,000 from Eastern Europe and the Western USSR, 200,000 Army and Navy personnel in the Far East and 60,000 personnel in the southern USSR. For details see "Restructuring in the USSR Armed Forces Toward Reasonable Sufficiency", *Bratislava Pravda*, February 23, 1989, in FBIS-SOV, March 2, 1989, and "Lebodev's Briefings before the press on Troops Reduction", *TASS,* December 22, 1988 in FBIS-SOV, December 23, 1988.

54. *Izvestia*, February 28, 1989, pp. 1-3.

55. Quoted in Patrik Kronin, "Perestroika and Soviet Military Personnel", in William C. Green and Theodore Krarasik, *Gorbachev and His Generals: The Reforms of Soviet Military Doctrine*, (Boulder, Colo.: Westview Press, 1990), p. 134.

56. *Krasnaia Zvezda*, March 30, 1989, p. 4.

57. *Moscovskie Novosti*, No. 45, November 6, 1988.

58. See M. A. Moiseev, "Unfading Deed", *Sovetaskaia Kirgigizia*, May 9, 1989, p.3 in *JPRS Military Affairs*, June 27, 1989, pp. 23-25.

59. Moscow Tass International Service in Russia, May 3, 1989, translated in *FBIS-SOV*, May 3, 1989, p. 88.
60. Quoted in William E. Odom, "The Soviet Military in Transition", *Strategic Digest*, Vol. XXI, No. 2, (February 1991), p. 287.
61. See Vitaly Zhurkin, Sergei Karaganov and Andrei Kortunov, "Vyzovy bezopasnosti-staryyei novyye", *Kommunist*, No.1 (1988), pp. 43-46. In Fall 1987 Gorbachev speech in Murmansk, noted that if one gauged the threat facing the Soviet Union by the rhetoric and statements of Western leaders, then the treat would not appear to be declining. However, he pointedly observed, such words are always forgotten in a few days.
62. Quoted in Stephen Meyer, *op.cit.,* p. 122.
63. *Ibid.,* p. 124.
64. *Ibid.,* p. 128.
65. Brezhnev first raised the notion of sufficiency for defense in his Tula speech in 1977.
66. See Stephen Meyer, *op.cit.*
67. This was not a widely shared perspective among new thinkers and some openly disagreed with their colleagues who advocated unilateral Soviet reductions in the name of reasonable sufficiency.
68. Stephen Meyer, *op.cit.,* p.133.
69. *Ibid.,* p.135.
70. Article in *Krasnaya Zvezda* (April 14, 1990).
71. *Ibid.*
72. Jonathan Steele, "Perestroika invades Soviet army", *The Guardian* (London), 12th November, 1989.
73. Stephen, Meyer, *op.cit.,* pp.141-142.
74. *New York Times,* January 26, 1989, p.1.
75. See William E. Odom, "The Soviet Military in Transition", *Problems of Communism*, (May-June, 1990).
76. RFE-RL, *Daily Report*, No. 209, November 2, 1989.
77. William Odom, *op.cit.,* p. 291.

4

Political Aspects of Security During Perestroika

4.1. The Nature of Political Security During Perestroika

The political aspects of security, which determined the course of strategic foreign policy of the USSR during the Cold War period, underwent a qualitative change within the conceptual framework of the 'comprehensive universal security', elaborated by the 27th CPSU Congress. It was based on the assumption that military power could not exclusively ensure security for any nation because security was a political problem and the most rational way to achieve security was by political means. As it has already been mentioned, Soviet concept of security during *perestroika* sought to achieve security by reducing nuclear weapons in a phased manner and aimed at complete elimination of nuclear arsenal over a period of time. This approach to security was taken after studying the objective conditions of the world and assessing the threat of nuclear war. As Soviet leader Mikhail Gorbachev said:

"Human thought does not adjust immediately to everything new. This applies to every one. We feel this. We have begun to reassess, are adjusting many customary things, including those in the military and naturally, the political sphere, in full conformity

with new realities. We would like such reassessment also to take place in Western Europe and beyond".[1]

The Central Committee of the CPSU at its plenary meeting critically analyzed the problems of international security and defined the practical steps that could improve the situation. It stressed on the mutual and universal character of security. In this context Gorbachev said:

"The highest wisdom is not in caring exclusively for oneself, especially to the detriment of the other side. It is vital that all should feel equally secure, for the fears and anxieties of the nuclear age generate uncertainty in politics and concrete actions. It is becoming extremely important to take the critical significance of the time factor into account. The appearance of new systems of weapons of mass destruction steadily shortens time and narrows down the possibilities for the adoption of political decisions on questions of war and peace in crisis situation".[2]

The Soviet concept of security ensured peaceful development of the human community and opened up reliable prospects for international cooperation between peoples and states to resolve military, political, economic and other problems facing mankind. The Soviet approach to security sought to address the security needs of the entire world— i.e., "all governments, parties, public organizations and movements and all those who were genuinely concerned about peace". No doubt comprehensive universal security was inseparable from the concept of a nuclear weapons free world and it stemmed logically from the Soviet Union's policy of peaceful co-existence. In this context, the resolution of 27th CPSU Congress stated, "the Congress notes the special significance of the fundamental principles for building an all-embracing system of international security advanced in the political report of the Central Committee. Guided by them, it would be possible to make peaceful co-existence, the highest universal principle of inter-state relations".[3]

The Congress examined the tendencies in the coming world order taking fully into consideration the scientific, technical, military and strategic factors, and made a creative analysis of the correlation and interconnection between universal and national security. An objective analysis showed that national security could be achieved through the system of international security, which could be possible only through balance of interests, mutual friendship, and cooperation.[4] Thus the Soviet concept of security during *perestroika* was comprehensive and universal which tried to ensure security of the Soviet Union and the security of the other nations of the world.

The West also recognized this new concept of security. In this context SPD Chairman Willy Brandt stated:

"Our technological revolution has progressed much faster than our political wisdom. We need to shed the ideas of the pre-nuclear age and formulate a political doctrine for the nuclear age. In my view that means that East and West can feel safe from one another only together with each other. Our aim must be mutual guaranteed security instead of mutual guaranteed destruction".[5]

Similar views were expressed by US Defence Secretary Robert McNamara and Hans Batha, an eminent scientist. As Batha said, "post-Hiroshima history has taught us three lessons that shape the present proposal. First, all our technological genius and economic progress cannot make us secure if they leave the Soviet Union insecure; we can have either mutual security or mutual insecurity. Second, while profound differences and severe competition will surely continue to mark US-Soviet relations, the nuclear arms race is a burden to both sides, and it is in our mutual interest to rid ourselves of its menace. And third no realistic scheme that would rid us of all nuclear weapons has even been formulated".[6]

Nonetheless, the Soviet concept of security during *perestroika* was a realistic scheme and a sincere effort on the part of the Soviet leader Gorbachev to rid humanity of nuclear weapons and create a 'Common Security System' for ensuring security of the world. However, some Western scholars were a bit skeptic about the Soviet concept of security and they considered there was nothing new in Gorbachev's concept of security.

In the Soviet concept of security, the nature of today's world, which is interdependent and largely integrated, was clearly reflected.[7] As it has been mentioned earlier, the different strands of the concept of security— military, political, economic and humanitarian— were woven together into a brilliant tapestry in the Soviet security structure during *perestroika.* The internal coordinates of security were given as much importance as the external ones and together they aimed at an integrated system of "comprehensive security system", which appealed to strategic thinkers all over the world. This, in fact, initiated a new wave of thinking that revolutionized the concept of security and compelled people to re-imagine security as a dynamic concept.

It was a fact that Soviet concept of security during *perestroika* tried to underplay the influence of strategic military doctrine and put equal premium on other aspects of foreign policy.[8] The Soviet Union realized that mutual trust could be possible only through friendship and cooperation. Disarmament talks promoted stronger confidence between the two sides, which made it easier to reach new agreements strengthening mutual security. Thus, there was a positive feed back emerging between the enhancement of mutual trust and strengthening of security.[9] Further, the Soviet concept of security during *perestroika* played a positive role in improving the mutual trust between each other by emphasizing on de-ideologization in inter-state relations which helped to certain extent in loosening up the power bloc system and improving co-operation with capitalist societies. Gorbachev's political opponents, notably Yogor Ligachev, unsuccessfully used the newly defined concept as a symbol in his attack on Gorbachev's entire reform program.[10] It placed all human, moral ethical norms at the foundation of international politics and for the first time it tried to humanize inter-State relations.[11] It stressed on mutually acceptable ways through constructive dialogues for the solutions of the problems faced by nations.

Soviet leader Gorbachev's emphasis on summit diplomacy opened up new ways and created a positive atmosphere for ensuring peace and security in the world. The communiqué of the PCC meeting of the Warsaw Pact countries held in Budapest in June 1986 stressed on the political means for the solutions of the global problems. The communiqué said, "The conference is convinced that only political means and joint efforts of all countries can ensure the reliable security of all countries and peoples, and peaceful conditions for their development and progress. This position corresponds to the realities of the nuclear age and testifies to the high responsibility for the destinies of their own peoples and the whole of mankind".

Political aspects of concept of security tried its best to ensure security of the Soviet Union and the world through the process of de-militarization, democratization and humanization of international relations with a reliance on the prestige and resources of the UN organization.[12] It highlighted on the political legal methods for the solution of global problems and for maintaining peace and security. Soviet leader Gorbachev in his address at the 43rd Session of the UN General Assembly said, "UNO is increasingly manifesting itself as a unique international centre serving the cause of peace and security".[13] He believed that authoritative world organization was needed for strengthening security and submitted proposals at the Session of the UN bodies held in 1989 on building a model of security for ensuring peace and security not through the building of arms as the case in the past but through their reduction and through strengthening confidence, openness and co-operation in all spheres of inter-State relations.[14] Gorbachev's statement, "On the whole, our credo is as follows: political issues shall be resolved only by political means and human problems in human way", clearly revealed his noble intention for solving global problems.

4. 2. The Common European Home

In the analysis of political aspects of security, Gorbachev's ideas of 'Common European Home' appeared as a special feature. It appeared for the first time in December 1984 when Gorbachev delivered his speech in the House of Commons and referred to Europe as 'Our Common Home'.[15] At that time, he considered United States as a Trans-Atlantic power, which had no business in that house. As *Pravda* editorial put it, 'Washington is a stranger to that house',[16] but later on he changed his stand and realized that the concept of 'Common European Home' could be materialized with positive and reciprocal responses from USA. Another implication of the idea was based on the idea of 'Common European Interests', which needed to be safeguarded. Soviet leaders including Gorbachev tried to protect it for strengthening European security.[17] A second theme which supplemented the first was the assertion that in addition to geography, 'Europe' is bound together by historical ties and a 'Common Foundation of European Culture', including a 'Common Political Culture'[18].

The concept of 'Common European Home' assumed a degree of integrity even if its states belonged to different social systems and opposing military political blocs. The concept took due account of burning problems and the ways for settling them. This concept tried to restructure international order by giving priority to European attitudes, orientation and value patterns disposing national chauvinism and bloc-egotism.

The objective of this 'Common European Home' was to develop genuine cooperation and constructive interactions with European power by removing ideological, military and undemocratic factors from international politics but without sacrificing its interests and loosing its identity.[19] This concept gave prominence to non-military factors in the interaction among the actors of the nations and tried to ensure the European security by "Common European Security System" by replacing 'military alliance' system. As Soviet Union realized common European security was impossible without drastic military charges in the military set ups of two super powers, so Soviet Union tried its best to normalize its relation with USA. However, Gorbachev continued, "We are not for a single moment forgetting that the world is not limited to that country alone",[20] but later on he confessed the relations between USSR and USA were extremely important part of international politics but he then added, "we are far from seeing the world through the prism of these relations. We understand the weight which other countries have in international affairs and take this into account in the assessment of the overall situation in the world".[21] This statement of course could be interpreted that Soviet Union had other options, which it could pursue in case of strained relationship with USA.

No doubt, in the concept of 'Common European Home', the emphasis was on European progress or he thought it would contribute to the world's advancement. Europe should not hesitate to help in the battle against hunger, backwardness, and foreign debts or to help in settling armed conflicts. Gorbachev stressed on the good neighbourly atmosphere of confidence, co-existence and cooperation among European powers which he thought essential not only from ethical grounds but also from the interest side of every European nation. He considered that the problems like terrorism, crime, drug addiction could be settled through European and world efforts.[22]

Soviet Union's efforts to make a nuclear free world by dismantling nuclear missiles from Eastern Europe and the Western part of the Soviet Union and talks between NATO and Warsaw Pact created a positive environment, which strengthened this concept. In the beginning of 1989, Warsaw Pact came out with its proposal for cuts in its conventional arms and reduction of army under its command and expected similar measures from NATO. In summer 1989, it withdrew its troops from Hungary, Poland and East Germany. It also proposed dialogues for disbanding both NATO and Warsaw.[23] Though NATO was not disbanded but during this phase it stopped its belligerent and jingoistic postures towards Soviet Union and its allies.

The concept of 'Common European Home' also needed a reliable economic foundation for the realization of it for which Gorbachev chalked out a plan for the formation of a single economic zone from Atlantic to Urals based on interdependence of the national economies of European nations. Though it was not fulfilled but Gorbachev's efforts during this *perestroika* period helped in strengthening the economic relationship between the West and the East. In 1988, an EC CMEA treaty was concluded enabling individual CMEA members to deal directly with EC.[24] Gorbachev also worked hard to establish good bilateral relations with individual European countries. His efforts for strengthening European security by making nuclear-free zones and zones free of chemical weapons were positive in this direction. He also tried to implement the proposals of Rumania, Bulgaria and Greece for establishing in the Balkans a zone free of nuclear and chemical weapons and in the region of Finland and other European countries.[25] Soviet Union also appreciated the initiatives taken by Greece, the Netherlands, Spain, Italy, Finland and many European countries for Euro-missile settlement. Thus Soviet Union placed much importance on Europe for the successful of "New Political Thinking".[26] Though the concept of "Common European Home" seemed to be theoretically sound and a nice idea but it remained as an idea unfulfilled and unmaterialized. The objective conditions of East and West, which was diametrically opposite to each other, the problems relating to the integration of two opposite political and economic systems, unification of Germany, limited success of perestroika were impediments for materializing his cherished idea. As discussed earlier, the proposals relating to the political aspects of security played a decisive role in the concept of "Comprehensive Universal Security" and they expressed the crux of the problem by representing those elements of political inter-state relations without which the entire system was not conceivable. Gorbachev also expressed similar arguments in his speech to the Council of Europe in July 1989. He asserted that "respect for each people's sovereign right to choose a social system as it sees fit represents a most important pre-condition for a normal European process". And he stressed that any interference in internal affairs of whatever kind, 'any attempts to limit the sovereignty of states, both friends and allies, no matter whose, is impermissible'.[27]

4. 3. Political Aspects of Universal Security

In Gorbachev's scheme of things, "strict respect in international practice for the rights of each people to choose the ways and forms of its development independently" formed the core of the universal security doctrine. It did not recognize the supremacy of any state over other nations. Soviet Union opposed the attitude of the West of seeking to influence and interfere in the affairs of the Third World countries for their political and economic benefits. In the words of Gorbachev:

"It is high time to recognize that the Third World nations have the right to be their own bosses. They have attained political independence after many years of hard struggle. They want to be economically independent as well. The leaders of these countries enjoy the support of their people and to do something for them.

They want their countries to be genuinely independent and to be able to cooperate with others on equal terms. The decision of these nations to use their vast natural and human resources for national progress is understandable. They want to live no worse than people in developed countries. What they have now is under-nourishment and disease. Their resources are exploited by developed states and incorporated into the latter's national incomes through the channels of non-equivalent exchange. Developing countries won't put up with the situation for much longer".[28]

He blamed USA for its action against Nicaragua, Afghanistan, Angola and other states. The White House did not even hesitate to intervene in Grenada – the victim of US naked aggression. Imperialist action of subverting unsuitable regimes by fair or foul means reversed their development and made the situation worse.[29] This was confirmed officially by US Secretary of State, George Shultz, who said in his speech in San Francisco as 'moral responsibility of USA'. Though the US doctrine of 'neo-globalism justified it, but it was inhuman and unethical. US News and World Report wrote, "the Administration is increasingly trying to support and find rebel insurgents – democratic resistance forces as Reagan calls them – who wants to fight against Marxist governments forced upon them with outside help".[30]

In majority of cases US either tried to create a favourable public opinion in favour of its actions by resorting to propaganda wars, or else it remained insensitive to democratic values. It was clearly reflected in an article published in *News Week* Magazine, which said, in effect that Reaganisation of foreign policy called for three things. First, sticking to Reagan's doctrine of supporting the resistance movements on the margin of the Soviet empire (Nicaragua, Angola and Afghanistan). Second, use of military force in Libya and Grenada even without agreement of the allies. Third, restoring realism even by halting the arms control process, which created barrier for Soviet-American relations.[31]

However, Soviet Union reacted sharply to US imperialism. The CPSU programme declared, "the threat of war comes chiefly from it. Claiming world domination, it arbitrarily declares whole continents to be zones of its 'vital interests'. The US policy of hegemony, the imposition of its will and unequal relations with other states, support for repressive anti-popular regimes and discrimination against countries that do not suit the US, disorganises inter-state economic and political relations and prevent their normal development".[32]

In the economic sphere, it also exploited the Third World countries through his policy of neo-colonialism. Newly independent nations particularly Afro-Asian countries were exploited by USA. Gorbachev believed that they should not be exploited rather they should be helped to stabilize their economic positions without any strings attached to it. American companies particularly MNCs and TNCs should not be exploitative in the network.

Although Gorbachev was very critical of USA during the early period, later on he took a positive stand and qualitative changes took place in Soviet-US relations. While both sides had sufficient reasons to differ over a number of issues, including important ones, the realities provided the requisite incentives for their joint efforts in solving shared problems.[33] Leaders of both the nations emphasized on balance of interests as the basis for Soviet-American interactions in an inter-dependent world.[34] They realized that the problems of Third World countries would definitely affect the healthy relationship (for which they tried for) between the two powers. So, these problems should be solved sincerely by taking joint efforts and positive involvement by overcoming the syndrome of ideological 'irreconcibility'.

In late 1980s Reagan responded well to the initiatives taken by Gorbachev for the fair political settlement of international crisis and regional conflicts when he was convinced that Soviet leader was genuinely interested for a change. Even Western critics became Gorbachev's silent admirers seeing his sincerity in this direction.[35] Though Soviet leader did not succeed in his mission of making world free of regional wars as regional wars were still continuing and civil wars in some parts of the world had raised its ugly heads, regional conflicts of the third world were regarded as very important. Under the veneer of the ideological confrontation between the two Super Powers, such regional conflicts were passed off as unimportant and inconsequential and not accorded due importance.

4.4. Regional Conflicts: Negotiations of Their Settlement

Here one can draw attention to two problems related closely to the Third World: regional wars and conflicts, and the negotiation of their settlement. Soviet concept of security during *perestroika* tried to ensure the security of the entire world. It believed that without the settlement of regional conflicts, security of the world could not be maintained. History shows that "tension arises more frequently as a result of political conflicts than due to weapons deployment".[36]

This concept of security was based on the assumption that the primary cause of international crisis and large number of regional conflicts was the imperialist policy of *diktat* and interference in the affairs of sovereign states and the settlement of these conflicts could be possible when the imperialist forces would respect each people's right independently to decide its future. Thus, there was a logical relationship between first and second political components of the Soviet security system.[37]

In theory, the Soviet approach for the settlement of regional conflicts under *perestroika* was not confined to the conflicts in the third world. But in practice that was where most conflicts took place and where Soviet leaders applied their security framework. It was a fact that many regional conflicts were originated before the emergence of Gorbachev in Soviet politics and they were called national liberation movement, which the Soviet Union supported. But during this phase (1985-91) there was a substantive changes in the approach of Soviet foreign policy.

Thc priority of Soviet relations with the Third World had been on the Soviet agenda before Gorbachev assuming power, but Soviet leaders were disillusioned about the political reality and economic and social development of most less-developed countries.[38] But there was a general feeling in the Soviet Union that these Third World conflicts could be solved only by political settlement not by military means, which also needed positive response and initiatives from US side. During the Geneva Summit, it was clearly mentioned that Soviet Union believed that these regional wars between different states were also rooted both in the past and their socio-economic conditions were responsible for that. It was wrong to assume that these problems emanated from East-West competition. Here, of course, Soviet Union contradicted its earlier stand and tried to lay the blame at someone else's door; but it can be interpreted as an attempt to involve USA in the settlement of conflicts as it needed 'multilateralist' strategy even hard decisions to implement it as was expressed by US Sovietologists.[39]

In the Middle East, the Arab-Israeli conflicts started five decades back. The United States supported Israel and in most of the cases took anti-Arabian stand and complicated the situation in this region. Of course, in early 1970s Richard Nixon tried to pacify the situation in West Asia through his shuttle diplomacy and Jimmy Carter also convened international conference on West Asian problems; but it did not yield any concrete results. But from 1967 till the advent of the Gorbachev era, the Soviet Union tried either to construct joint peace initiatives with the United States or to oppose US moves by extending helping hands to Arab radicals in the Middle East. Gorbachev, however, initiated two changes in his approach to regional conflicts as part of 'New Thinking'. First, since 1985, Moscow broadened its option by opening a dialogue with the Middle East actors beyond the members of radical club. Second, he expressed his willingness than his predecessors to press traditional allies towards moderation.[40]

These policy changes reflected ideological flexibility in moderation. It advocated stronger relationship with Third World countries having a capitalist leaning.[41] In the Middle East various conciliatory moves were taken towards the Arab states and at the same time Gorbachev initiated greater interactions with Israel. Indeed, these efforts of Gorbachev improved the relationships phenomenally with Arab Gulf states, Egypt, and Jordan and in turn they extended their support for the idea of international conference. At the same time Gorbachev also distanced himself from Syria – supposed to be the closest ally of Soviet Union in the Middle East.

American President Reagan's policy in the Middle East in early 80s was not positive in solving problems. Rather he made the situation complicated by instigating internal conflicts in this region by supporting Israel and taking steps to curb the *intifada* of Arafat, the leader of Palestine. But in the second half of his tenure, he took a soft stand and keen interest in settling the problems through conferences and summits. The situation took a different turn at the time of George Bush. The changes in the Soviet domestic affairs, in Eastern Europe and Soviet politics in third world in 1989-90 helped Bush in changing his stand. It was reflected in Malta Summit in late 1989 where he expressed his near unanimity on the question of Lebanon and West Bank.[42]

During 1989-90, two super powers took a joint action to prevent UN recognition of a declared Palestine State. They exerted pressure on their respective allies to moderate their positions concerning the Israeli initiative to hold elections in the occupied territory and issued a joint declaration in June 1990 Summit in Washington against the settlement of new emigrants (mostly from the Soviet Union) in the territories held by Israel. They also held talks on arms control and non-proliferation of non-conventional weapons in the Middle East.[43]

During summer of 1990, both US and Soviet opposed Iraq's aggression against Kuwait and succeeded in passing UN Security Council resolution seeking to impose economic sanctions and authorizing the use of force against Iraq in late November. The two super powers also agreed that following the resolution of the Gulf crisis, a major effort should be made to resolve the Arab-Israeli conflict and that they should cooperate in this enterprise.[44] Super powers also played an active role in favour of separate State of Palestine. Of course, the world public opinion, Sadam Hussain's linking of Palestine issue with Gulf problems helped in pressurizing USA to take a soft stand on Palestine.

Finally, with the end of the Cold War, Israel's opposition to the Soviet participation in the peace process died out. The USA also improved its relationship with Egypt and United Arab Emirates. It was quite obvious that Kuwait and its friendly nations developed some sort of obligation towards USA. Syria also improved its ties with USA. No doubt Soviet and US efforts changed the scenario of the Middle East during this phase.

In other parts of the Third World in Cambodia, Ethiopia and the Caribbean region, Soviet policy had a moderating impact. Nicaragua issue was more important for USA than for the Soviet Union. In fact, Moscow did not put Sandinista in power, though Daniel Ortega and Mikhail Gorbachev were good friends for some time. Soviet Union carefully avoided sending Nicaragua heavy arms that would provoke USA.[45] As such it did little to inspire the Sandinista regime to reject free elections and their results. On the other hand, Soviet efforts were directed at encouraging a negotiated settlement of disputes in the Latin American region. During the *perestroika* phase, Soviet relations with Fidel Castro of Cuba were strained. Like North Korea and Iraq, Cuba was treated globally as an outcast and this might have influenced Gorbachev's decision to underplay the communist connection with Cuba.

Soviet policy towards Third World under *perestroika* also changed US attitude towards Moscow as it stopped talking about 'the hand of Moscow' in Central American conflicts. On the other hand, it helped in creating a favourable atmosphere for joint initiatives for the settlement of international crisis and regional conflicts. In East Africa, Moscow was seen to be withdrawing whatever political and military support it had given earlier to Mengistu's efforts to crush the Eritrean and Tigrean rebellions and persuaded the Ethiopian regime to negotiate with rebels.[46] Soviet Union's interest to reduce Moscow's involvement in the conflicts of Africa was clearly revealed when in 1988 Soviet Union took a major role in ending the operation of thirteen years of Cuban expeditionary forces in Angola, the South African presence in Angola and South African administration in Namibia. The United States could not have mediated the agreement signed in 1988, at the UN without Soviet pressure on both Luanda and Havana. The resolution of the Angolan issue became the central point of Soviet-US co-operation aimed at resolving disputes in the Third World.[47]

In 1990, Soviet and US persuaded the Luanda regime and UNITA for cease-fire and free election. In the same year, Ethiopian-Eritrea agreement was possible due to Soviet-US pressure, which also helped to re-open the Red Sea port of Massawa and permit food deliveries to the millions of refugees.[48] Against this backdrop, high power dignitaries like Soviet foreign minister Shevardnadze and US Secretary of State James Baker made their first visit to South Africa in March 1990 to participate in the independence celebrations in Namibia as well as Angola, Mozambique, Zambia and Zimbabwe. Namibia's independence was no doubt an achievement of Soviet-US successful joint venture in the field of resolution of regional conflicts.

In early 1990s, Moscow supported Nelson Mandela's conciliatory approach rather than that of the ANC party which was confrontational. In Asia, Soviet Union also took constructive measures in this direction. In 1979, Soviet Union intervened in Afghanistan, the cold war situation resumed. A policy of national 'reconciliation' was adopted in Afghanistan following the Summit meeting in Tashkent in April, 1988 which sought to put an end to the war in Afghanistan. The joint declaration by Gorbachev and Najibullah also urged the interested States to search for settlement of the Afghan problem. Soviet troops began to withdraw from Afghanistan as May 15, 1988 and Soviet withdrawal from Afghanistan was completed in February 1989. In the later part of 1989 Soviet Union also put pressure on Vietnam to withdraw from Kampuchea.

In East Asia, Moscow emerged as a multi-dimensional actor and expanded its political economic and diplomatic connections with other actors by renouncing its ideological ambitions and reducing its military presence. The improvement of relations with China, the defusing of the tension along the Sino-Soviet frontier, its rapprochement with South Korea, Moscow's desire to end the stalemate with Japan, co-operation in solving the regional wars in the Peninsula of Indo-China, and the interest in the economic success of Hongkong, Korea, Singapore and Taiwan were all indications of Gorbachev's desire to make Soviet Union a full-fledged member of East Asia 'co-prosperity' sphere. His desire was neither to oppose the dominance of USA nor to marginalise other powers in this region, rather it was only to participate in the prosperity of the two regions (Europe and Asia) of which it has been part geographically.[49] Perhaps this was the reason for stressing the concept of 'Common European Home' and co-operation with Asian countries at the same time, for which he was criticized by Western scholars.[50]

Gorbachev aimed at developing friendly relations with all States, and at the same time he opposed the extension of NATO's activity, particularly in Asia-Pacific region. He laid emphasis on the importance of UN and other international institutions and their sincere efforts in solving the regional problems through 'summitry'. The most important Summit during those days was the Reagan-Gorbachev Summit, which helped the process of negotiation and settlement of the international crises and regional conflicts.

4.5. Peace and Security in Asia and the Pacific

Soviet concept of security, during *perestroika*, emphasised on peace and security of the Asia-Pacific. Gorbachev held that the comprehensive system of international security and world free from conflicts could not be achieved without restoring peace and stability in Asia-Pacific. No doubt, the situation of the Asia-Pacific was affected by the legacy of the past: differences of the historical evolution of nations, territorial disputes and clashes of local interest but, during 1980s the situation became complicated with the direct foreign military presence and spreading nuclear weapons race in the region.[51]

In early 1986, Soviet Union took efforts for eliminating nuclear weapons for ensuring peace and security. In this context, Mikhail Gorbachev said:

"The Soviet programme for eliminating nuclear and chemical weapons by the end of the current century is harmonious with the sentiments of the people of the Asian continent, for whom the problems of peace and security are no less urgent than for the peoples of Europe. The implementation of our programme would fundamentally change the situation in Asia, rid the nations in that part of the globe as well of the fear of nuclear and chemical warfare, and bring security in that region to a qualitatively new level".[52]

Soviet approach to the security of Asia-Pacific was the index of the changes in Soviet Union, both in internal and external sphere. This was based on the assumption that global affairs had reached a new stage, and hence a thorough critical appraisal has to be made in the field of security in light of this development. As he considered the world as 'interdependent and integral', the security of the world was also deemed to be related to the peace and security of this region. He argued that this "policy can only be effective if the novelty of the situation is taken into account." Hence, peace and security in Asia-Pacific was examined not in the regional context alone. It considered the interests of USA and USSR — two major powers and other actors involved in it.[53]

In addition to above factors, socio-economic and military factors were also taken into consideration. While considering economic factors the importance of Pacific Rim/Basin is worth mentioning as Gorbachev thought it (Pacific Rim) would become the centre of global economic activity, more than any other region of the world.[54]

For the first time Gorbachev's views on Asia-Pacific were expressed in the Vladivostok speech on 26th July 1986 where he stressed on five-point plan of action for ensuring security in this region.

- settlement of regional conflicts by political, not military means;
- the prevention of the proliferation and building up of nuclear weapons in Asia and Pacific;
- reduction of naval activities on the Pacific;
- radical cuts in armed forces and conventional weapons in Asia;
- confidence building measures and the non-use of force in the region.[55]

Most of the nations like India, Indonesia, Philippines, Thailand and Australia responded positively to this proposal. This proposal was extended further during Mikhail Gorbachev's visit to India in November 1986. In his address to the Indian Parliament, the Soviet leader elaborated the above mentioned proposals for strengthening military and political stability of the Indian Ocean. The main outcome of this visit was the signing of the Delhi

Declaration. The two leaders, Gorbachev and Rajiv Gandhi took important decisions relating to the security of Asia and the world. The ten basic principles enshrined in the Declaration sought to usher the world into a nuclear weapons free and non-violent world. The principles included a mature renunciation of nuclear weapons upon which an equitable international order could be built. "It aims at ending nuclear syndrome and move away from the dubious doctrine of 'mutually assured destruction' as the corner stone of deterrence" on which was predicted for decades the hope of *détente* and peace".[56]

In July 1987, Gorbachev gave an interview to the Indonesian newspaper *Merdeka* where he reaffirmed the Vladivostok plan and came out with new clear-cut proposals. The most important among them was the proposal for scrapping Soviet intermediate range missiles in the Asian part of the USSR in conformity with the aspirations of China, Japan and other Asia Pacific nations.[57] His other suggestions were:

- to take steps to reduce Soviet-US naval activities in the Pacific and Indian Ocean;
- to restrict the anti-submarine rivalry in this region;
- to restrict the anti-submarine movement in certain agreed areas;
- to abstain from using combat weapons at the time of naval movements in the zone of traditional sea lanes.[58]

Besides military security, Soviet Union stressed on economic security for which it expanded trade and economic links between all members of Asia-Pacific community on both bilateral and multilateral basis. Soviet National Committee for Asia-Pacific Cooperation was formed in March 1988 for expanding Soviet economic contacts in the region.

For promoting peace and security in Asia, Gorbachev submitted new proposals, which were formulated in his speech delivered in Krasnoyarsk, Siberia on September 16, 1988. First,

Soviet Union decided not to increase the amount of any nuclear weapons in the region. It also called upon the United States and other nuclear powers not to deploy them additionally in the region. Second, Soviet Union invited the Asian naval powers of the region to hold consultations on non-increase in naval forces in the region. Third, the USSR suggested that the question of lowering military confrontation in the areas where the coasts of the USSR, China, Japan, North and South Koreas converge be discussed on a multilateral basis with a view to freezing and commensurately lowering the levels of naval and air forces and limiting their activity. Fourth, Soviet Union expressed its readiness to give up the fleet's material and technical supply station in Cam Ranh Bay, formally assented by the Vietnamese government too, provided the US agrees to eliminate the military bases in Philippines. Fifth, USSR suggested joint measures for the prevention of incidents in the open sea and air space over it. Sixth, the Soviet Union proposed that an international conference on making the Indian Ocean as a zone of peace be held not later than 1990. Seventh, the USSR suggested discussing with any interested country at any level the question of creating a negotiating mechanism to consider Soviet and any other proposals relating to the security of the Asia-Pacific region.[59]

Though Gorbachev's Krasnoyarsk proposals were supported by large number of nations including the nations of Asia-Pacific, but, American and Japanese scholars were bit critical about it. Indian scholars non-officially supported it, but some of them differed on two points –

1. Though they backed the third proposal of Krasnoyarsk* meeting, they had certain reservations. India's response, they said, should consider the concrete reality in view of growing naval and air forces of certain countries in this region;

2. Secondly the proposal that security dialogue on Asia and Pacific region could start between the Soviet Union, China and US, was also not accepted by the Indian scholars. It was suggested that Indonesia, India and Vietnam should also be associated with this dialogue.[60]

In October, 1989 and September, 1990, the international meeting on 'The Asia and Pacific Region: Dialogue for Peace and Co-operation' was held in Vladivostok. The package of Soviet proposals in preventing the militarization of Asia and ensuring co-operation in the region created positive environment. It was a fact that, Soviet Union's efforts in Asia-Pacific were not confined to proposals, it also took concrete measures in late 80's even in 1990 for implementing the proposals for ensuring security in this region.

Though most of the nations expressed their satisfaction over these measures, some scholars particularly the Western writers were bit skeptic about the Soviet military strategic intentions and capabilities relevant to the region.[61] The policies and measures taken by USSR in Asia-Pacific zone did not bear the desired fruits in terms of maintenance of peace and stability, nevertheless it achieved success in lowering the intensity of conflicts and in certain cases even solving it.

4.6. Confidence Building Measures and Zones of Peace

Confidence-building measures, which are based on mutual trust, are essential for eliminating nuclear arms race and creating a secure and peaceful world. Consensus on key issues and closeness of political goals intensify this process. In 1972, during the post-Stalin era, the US administration then in office had a realistic approach to the central issue: the need to avert war and to renounce a course for military supremacy over the USSR (of course it did not mean that it renounced its main ideological views). During that time, the Soviet Union had similar approach to security and thus the political goals of the two sides coincided and confidence developed automatically. But later on the situation took a different turn, the US administration tried to take unilateral advantage over the Soviet Union which ruptured the confidence-building mechanism.[62]

During the *perestroika* phase, however, this idea rose to prominence again in Soviet concept of security. Gorbachev along with the 'New Thinkers' realized that nuclear deterrence strategy would not be effective on the pretext of security parity. They even said: "As long as nuclear weapons exist, strategic parity can be a stabilizing factor with all its negative aspects".[63] Stressing that security should be mutual in the nuclear age, even if it was difficult to eliminate mutual distrust completely, 'New Thinkers' sincerely tried to minimize the dangers of nuclear war through common strategic concepts and efforts at confidence building. In this context, Arbatov said:

"Stability implies an overall balance of the forces of both powers and a symmetrical, mutual confidence in the reliability of their deterrent potentials at, incidentally, the lowest level of these deadly arsenals, with the reduction to the minimum reasonable sufficiency and, ultimately, the complete abolition of strategic potential and nuclear weapons".[64]

He first applied this confidence-building mechanism in the European context through a series of measures that would instill mutual trust among the European states. He believed that once confidence in each other's peaceful intention was established, it would be easier to negotiate on arms reduction. Soon after he came to power, the French proposal for a new round of European negotiations to be labeled the Conference on Confidence and Security-Building Measures (CSBM) and Disarmament in Europe (CDE) was accepted, which resulted in the Stockholm Agreement of 1986. The purpose of this Stockholm Agreement was to establish rules that would prevent from using force without notification, inspection and accountability.[65] Though this process began in Helsinki Final Act, prior to this agreement, it was systematically formulated and elaborated in the Stockholm Conference. Prior to Gorbachev the Soviet scholars focussed on Confidence-Building Measures (CBMs) but they were piecemeal in approach. Such efforts sought to bring about agreements on non-use of force in Europe and no-first-use of nuclear weapons. By then, Soviet Union was not even prepared to open its military activity to public scrutiny.

However, by late 1985, Soviet delegation came out with specific detailed CSBM proposals, which finally led to this agreement, which was promulgated on September 19, 1 986 after months of intense negotiations.[66] Despite some shortcomings and ambiguities, this Stockholm Conference created positive atmosphere for removing mistrust and suspicion that surrounded its military power in Europe. Of course, some Western scholars had expressed their reservations on the issue as they suggested that major concessions on disarmament aimed at avoiding harder concessions on the area of human rights, which was another major component of Helsinki Final Act. Subsequent reforms in the sphere of human rights tended to overshadow these reservations.

Whatever be the motive of Gorbachev, the fact remained that he reversed the Soviet position on military secrecy; and even modified the Brezhnev's 'dual track policy'[67] by incorporating 'public scrutiny of military activity' which strengthened the confidence-building measures.[68] In 1987, it was extended to USA as part of the process of nuclear disarmament. An agreement on 'Risk Reduction Centre' was implemented to lower the possibility of 'inadvertent' nuclear war.[69]

Another important idea in this regard was the creation of 'zones of peace' partially or wholly de-militarized zones and nuclear-free zones in the context of Europe and in the Third World. In June 1988, in an international forum held in Berlin, Gorbachev emphasized on 'nuclear free zones' which could 'help disengage the nuclear forces of confronting alliances, thereby scaling down the risk of nuclear conflict'.[70] He and his officials also supported proposals by regional states for nuclear free zones in such varied locations as the Pacific, South-East Asia, the Korean Peninsula, the Mediterranean, the Balkans and the Nordic region.[71]

Soviet leaders laid emphasis on a proposal adopted by Warsaw Pact in May, 1987 for a 'nuclear weapon free corridor' along the dividing line between Warsaw Pact and NATO.[72]

As said earlier, in the Third World context, Gorbachev employed the zone concept for denuclearization of distinct regions and for naval arms limitations which played a decisive role in strengthening confidence-building measures. A reliable system of 'International Security' during *perestroika* was also inconceivable without effective guarantees for States against outside attack and without guaranteeing the border inviolability. American invasion of Grenada and heavy bombardment in Libya showed that international community was in need of it, which could ensure their own security and the security of the world as a whole. Inviolability of the boarders was considered as the most important element for national and international security. All steps to carve the border of sovereign States created serious consequences for the nations.[73]

What was the most worrisome feature in this regard was that the revanchist forces most notably in the FRG were encouraged even on flimsy pretexts. Consequently Soviet Union and its allies felt that mere demand for the reviewing of boundaries demarcating various European States would severely impair mutual trust and understanding among the European nations.

During this *perestroika* phase, Soviet Union made genuine efforts in this direction and even succeeded in reducing danger from West German revanchism and militarism. USA on its part responded positively. Whatever might be the latent motive of US in the Gulf war, it took steps effectively against the illegal occupation of Kuwait by Iraq. Soviet Union also condemned the invasion of Kuwait by Iraq, which reflected its sincerity in adhering to the principle of 'effective guarantees against attack from without and for inviolability of their frontiers'.

4.7. Prevention of International Terrorism

The political aspects of security under *perestroika* emphasized on the prevention of international terrorism including safe use of land, air and sea communications as it was one of the important political components elaborated in 27th CPSU Congress. Soviet Union sincerely tried to halt State terrorism, nuclear terrorism and terrorism in any other forms which could destabilize the situations of the various regions of the world and undermine the international security. It opposed Imperialist policy of 'State terrorism' which associated the struggle for liberation with terrorism and under the guise of anti-terrorist actions exported counter revolution and suppressed their legitimate rights. USA even tried to justify its aggressive actions and threats against Libya, Syria, Iran, Nicaragua and other countries on the pretext of international terrorism.

In this context, the political report of the CPSU Central Committee to the 27th CPSU Congress said:

"Crisis and conflicts, are fertile soil also for international terrorism. Undeclared wars, the export of counter-revolution in all forms, political assassinations, the taking of hostages, the hijacking of aircraft and bomb explosions in streets, airport and railway stations – such is the hideous face of terrorism, which its instigators try to mask with all sorts of cynical conventions. The USSR rejects terrorism in principle and is prepared to co-operate actively with other States in order to uproot it. The Soviet Union will resolutely safeguard its citizens against acts of violence and do everything to defend their lives, honour and dignity".[74]

Yet another form of terrorism was 'nuclear terrorism' which threatened global peace and security. Soviet Union called for prevention of nuclear terrorism as one aspect of nuclear security, keeping in mind the incidents of sabotage at atomic enterprises in the USA and Western Europe and theft of highly fissionable material.[75] In land, though terrorism was confined to certain sensitive areas, but sometimes it created serious consequences for the security of the nations. In air, terrorists obstructed air communications, hijacked planes and engaged in disruptive activities. In sea, they violated the rules of international law, misused territorial waters and resorted to violence.

In 40th Session of UN General Assembly, the Soviet Union and other countries addressed with a call for resolute measures against international terrorism. In the address at the 43rd Session of UN General Assembly, Soviet leader Gorbachev stressed on joint efforts to end political terrorism.[76] His steps to create Tribunal on international terrorism, treaties between nations including extradition treaties to curb it helped in strengthening international security. USA also responded positively to the effort of Soviet Union to halt terrorism.

4.8. Changes in Eastern Europe: Its Relevance in Security of Soviet Union

Soviet policies towards Eastern Europe underwent radical changes under *perestroika*. On the one side, Soviet leader Gorbachev refrained from applying coercion, which was the binding force between the Soviet and its satellite countries earlier. On the other side, he encouraged reforms in those countries.

First, in late 1986, he privately expressed views to the East European leaders that they could no longer rely on Soviet military intervention to keep them in power if things went wrong.[77] It clearly reflected that he did not want to repeat the military intervention, which took place in 1956 in Hungary, in 1968 in Czechoslovakia, in 1980 in Poland against communist party reformers and/or against popular rebellion. Second, though the Soviet leader did not urge the communist friends to follow the Soviet path of reforms as it was contradictory to the principle of 'freedom of choice', it was amply clear from his speeches and actions that he was not in favour of the old party dominated 'administrative command system'.

Third Gorbachev stressed on 'freedom of choice' for all nations. In his speech, delivered in October 6, 1989, he expressed at the 40th Anniversary of GDR that 'the choice of the form of development is the sovereign affair of each nation'. And 'each nation would introduce its own feature into the particular form of democracy and the various paces of Socialist transformation'. Thus he rejected 'the attempts to unify and standardize social development to copy or impose some mandatory model'.[78]

This changing approach of Soviet Union towards Eastern Europe coupled with liberalization process of Soviet Union helped in accelerating the process of reforms in those countries. In 1989, it started in Poland as the Polish leaders realized that fundamental changes were needed to strengthen their economic and political security. Inflation, debt crisis and political instability made the situation worse. In June 1989 election, solidarity party came to power with a promise to change the situation. As a champion of 'International Security' [79] Gorbachev accepted this change as he thought the security of other nations (political and economic) should be strengthened.[80]

In Hungary, the wind of liberalization, which was started at the time of Imre Nagy, appeared again in a strong form. In September 1989, it broke the Warsaw pact commitment and opened the borders to the West.[81] It also brought about political changes in East Germany. In October 1989, Erich Honecker stepped down and Kenz came to power with a promise of reforms in political and economic fields. The most important development in Eastern Europe was the reunification of Germany. The Soviet stand on German reunification was characterized by its reluctance to agree to complete support for the move in July 1990. Soviet reluctance was guided by its security concerns, but ultimately Soviet Union accepted the reunited Germany as a member of NATO. As Soviet Union relied on USA and Germany as partners for strengthening international security and source of economic assistance for internal development respectively, when two countries joined forces, virtually there was no way out.[82]

Such political reform also reduced the importance of Warsaw Pact and it became irrelevant with the withdrawal of Soviet troops from Hungary, Czechoslovakia and other parts of the world contemplating withdrawal from organization by the end of 1991. By August 1991 it had been formally disbanded. Now the most pertinent question was: "Did the reforms in the Soviet Union lead to the collapse of the 'outer empire' (Communist rule through out the East European countries) of the Soviet Union?". [83]

It is difficult to disagree with Michael MccGwire's assessment that 'the patterns of events in 1987-88 argues strongly that Gorbachev's leadership deliberately set in motion the process that would lead to the collapse of the Communist rule throughout Eastern Europe by the end of 1989'.[84] Whatever might be the consequences of reforms, but probably, he did it for strengthening 'Universal' (international) security with an expectation to get co-operation from USA and the Western powers, which could only be possible by convincing USA by his sincere efforts for a change.

The shift from 'national security' to 'common security' clearly reflected the importance of universal security for which Gorbachev tried for. Even Gorbachev wanted to ensure Soviet security through the 'common security' paradigm with an assumption that Soviet security could be ensured automatically as a logical consequence. That was the reason, why national security policies were oriented towards strengthening universal security.[85] Internal liberalization, which was started at the time of Gorbachev also aimed at it.

The emerging linkage between security policy and internal liberalization made it clear that liberal reformers under *perestroika* were trying for a peaceful world free from nuclear war for which they were seeking friendly relations with rest of the world and particularly permanent alteration in the super power relationship rather than temporary respite.[86]

From the above analysis it was clear that under *perestroika*, Soviet national security was placed under the umbrella of 'common security'. It was obvious that changes in Eastern Europe and unification of Germany had influenced other nations, so also the republics of Soviet Union when they realized that Gorbachev would not resort to 'Stalinian measures' to suppress them. Thus, the liberal atmosphere both internal and external dimensions of liberalization as discussed coupled with Gorbachev's attitude towards non-interference and recognition of the 'right of the people to choose the ways and forms of their development independently' accelerated the process of disintegration and ultimately shattered the fabric of Soviet national security.

Gorbachev committed a mistake in encouraging the process of change without visualizing the intricacies involved in it, with an expectation that it would strengthen the security paradigm but it acted in a reverse way and belied his expectation. Whatever might be the consequences of the changes brought in Soviet Union during *perestroika* phase, but Gorbachev deserves credit for having given completely positive direction and essentially one without resorting to force to or process of change which helped in ending the Cold War, developing the confidence building mechanism between two super powers, settling international conflicts, preventing terrorism, improving an atmosphere of peace and security.

Though Soviet concept of security could not save Soviet Union from disintegration and with the collapse of the Soviet Union, the 'concept of common security' which was the brain child of Gorbachev, lost its relevance for all practical purposes, but the 'noble ideas' elaborated in his concept of 'comprehensive universal security' still hold good.

References

1. *Mikhail Gorbachev*, *Selected Speeches and Articles*, (Moscow: Progress Publishers, 1986) p. 373.

2. "Political Report of the CPSU Central Committee to the 27th Congress of the CPSU", delivered by M. S. Gorbachev, *Soviet Review*, Vol. XXIII, No.10, (March 3, 1986), p. 69.
3. *XXVII CPSU Congress Document and Resolution*, (New Delhi: Allied Publishers, 1986), p.98.
4. N. Kapchenko, "Political Aspects of International Security", *International Affairs* (Moscow), September 1986, p. 85.
5. Quoted in Kapchenko, *op.cit.,* p. 86.
6. *Ibid.,* p.47.
7. M. S. Gorbachev, *A Time for Peace,* (New York: Richardson & Steirman, 1985), pp. 39-46.
8. Walter C. Clemens Jr., *Can Russia Change? The USSR Confronts Global Interdependence*, (London: Unwin Hyman, 1990), p. 170.
9. Igor Malshenko, "Non-Military Aspects of Security", *International Affairs*, No.1. (Moscow, January 1989), p. 44.
10. Alvin Z. and Rubin Stein, *Soviet Foreign Policy since World War II: Imperial and Global*, (New York: Harper Collins, 1992), p. 323.
11. M. S. Gorbachev, *Perestroika: New Thinking for Our Country and The World*, (London: Fontana/Collins, 1987), p.141. see also Tsuyoshi Hasegawa "Perestroika in Historical Perspective", in Tsuyoshi Hasegawa and Alexi Pravda (eds.), *Perestroika: Soviet Domestic and Foreign Policies*, (London: Sage Publications, 1990), p. 49.
12. M. S. Gorbachev, *On Major Directions of the USSR's Domestic and Foreign Policy,* (Moscow: Novosti Press, 1989), p. 28.
13. M. S. Gorbachev's Address at the 43rd Session of the UN General Assembly, December 7, 1988, *Soviet Review Documents*, (New Delhi: New Age Printing Press, 1988), p.3.
14. M. S. Gorbachev, *New Political Thinking*, (Moscow: Novosti Press, 1989), p.32.
15. *Pravda*, December 19, 1984.
16. Literally for Washington it is 'Chuzhoidom', i.e. a house that belongs to others: Europa-nash Obshchiidon', *Pravda*, 13 November, 1985.
17. *Ibid.*
18. Aleksander Bovin, 'Europeiskoe Napravlenie', *Izvestia*, 25 September 1985, cited in Tsuyshi Hasegawa and Alex Pravda (eds.), *Perestroika: Soviet Domestic and Foreign Policies*, (London: Sage Publications, 1990), p. 243.

19. Andrei Kudryautsev and Romil Schechenin, "Common European Home: The Soviet View", *International Relations* (London), Vol. IX. No. 6, (November 1989), p. 525.
20. *Pravda*, February 20, 1985.
21. *Pravda*, April 8, 1985. Similar formulations were used by Gorbachev in his speech to the 27th CPSU Congress in February 1986.
22. *For a 'Common European Home', For a New Way of Thinking*, Speech by the General Secretary of the CPSU CC at the Czechoslovak-Soviet Friendship Meeting, Prague, 10 April 1987, (Moscow: Novosti Press, 1987), p. 30.
23. Zafar Imam, *Soviet Foreign Policy, 1917-1990,* (New Delhi: Sterling Publishers, 1991), p. 164.
24. See Martin McCauley, *Gorbachev and Perestroika*, (London: Macmillan,1990).
25. *Common European Home*, *op.cit.,* pp. 26-27.
26. *Ibid.*
27. N. Kapchenko, *op.cit.,* p. 88.
28. Gorbachev, *Perestroika*, *op.cit.,* p. 178.
29. N. Kapchenko, *op. cit.,* p. 89.
30. *US News and World Report*, November 4, 1985, p. 90.
31. N. Kapchenko, *op. cit.,* p. 89.
32. Vadin Zagaldin, *Peace: The Only Option*, (New Delhi: Allied Publishers, 1987), p. 45.
33. Vadim V. Udalov, "The Concept of Balance of Interests and US-Soviet Relations", *Annals of the American Academy of Political and Social Science*, (Nov. 1991), p. 174.
34. *Ibid.,* p. 176.
35. In this context Collins Gray argued, "It is inconceivable that he (Gorbachev) could direct and oversee the transformation of thc brutal, continental, multinational empire that is the USSR into something so much kinder and gentler that a truly objective basis for a structural improvement in political security relations would be the consequence". Collins S. Gray "Do the changes within the Soviet Union provide a basis for eased Soviet-American relations? A sceptical view" in Robert Jervis and Sewryn Bialer (eds.), *Soviet American Relations After the Cold War,* (London: Duke University Press, 1991), p. 61.
36. V. Giscard d'Estang, Yasuhiro Nakasone, Henry A. Kissinger, "East-West Relations", *Foreign Affairs*, (June 1989), p. 11.

37. N. Kapchenko, *op. cit.*, p. 89.
38. Martin McCauley, *Gorbachev and Perestroika*, (London: Macmillan, 1990), p. 183.
39. This view is expressed by Graham E. Fuller, "Soviet-American Cooperation in the Middle East: The Changing Face of International Conflict", in Steven L. Spiegel (ed.), *Conflict Management*, (Boulder: Westview Press, 1992), p. 24.
40. Benjamin Miller, "A Theoretical Analysis of US-Soviet Conflict Management in the Middle East", in Steven L. Spiegel (ed.), *Conflict Management in the Middle East*, (Boulder: Westview Press,1992), p. 96.
41. Galio Golan, "The Soviet Union and the Palestinian Issue, and Gorbachev Middle East Strategy", in G. Breslauer (ed.), *Soviet Strategy in the Middle East*, (Winchester, M.A.: Unwin Hyman, 1990), pp. 157-158.
42. Benjamin Miller, *op. cit.*, p. 99.
43. *Ibid.*, p. 99.
44. *Ibid.*
45. Joseph L. Nogee and Robert H. Donaldson, *Soviet Foreign Policy since World War II*, (Oxford: Pergamon Press, 1988), p. 350.
46. Roy C. Macridis (ed.), *Foreign Policy in World* Politics, (New York: Prentice Hall, 1992), p.171.
47. Malvin A. Goodman, *Gorbachev's Retreat to the Third World*, (New York: Praeger, 1991), pp.114-115.
48. *Ibid.*
49. Roy Macridis (ed.) *op.cit.*, pp.175-176.
50. Soviet Union has made intense efforts to be accepted as part of the Asia-Pacific region. Nevertheless, despite its enormous Asian territories, the USSR is commonly viewed as outsider. Gorbachev's own emphasis on the theme of a 'Common European House' appears to Asians to reflect Moscow's orientation towards Europe rather than Asia". Valery Giscard d'Estaing, Yasuhiro Nakasone, Henry A. Kissinger, "East-West Relations", *Foreign Affairs*, (June 1989), p.16.
51. Nikolai Nikolsky, *The Philosophy of New Thinking and the Soviet Initiatives*, (New Delhi: Allied Publishers, 1988), p.109.
52. Quoted in *ibid.*, p. 109.
53. R. R. Sharma, "Asia-Pacific Security: From Vladivostok to Krasnoyarsk", in V. D. Chopra (ed.), *Mikhail Gorbachev's New Thinking in Asia-Pacific*, (New Delhi: Continental Publishing House, 1988), pp. 202-203.

54. In fact the beginning of this trend is already evident. This is a change of extraordinary historical proportions. As historically known, the critical matrix was the Mediterranean Basin till the Seventeenth Century. After this, the economic centre shifted to the Atlantic Rim and the Northern European countries. But almost since 1970 the shift has begun towards Pacific. This economic shift cannot leave political security dimensions untouched. K. P. Mishra, "Gorbachev's New Thinking: An Overview" in V. D. Chopra (ed.), *op. cit.,* p.165.
55. Nikolai Nikolsky, *op. cit.,* pp. 111-113.
56. Rasheeduddin Khan, "Perestroika: An Overview: Gorbachev's Reforms", *World Focus*, (Oct-Dec. 1988), p. 6.
57. Nikolai Nikolsky, *op.cit.,* p. 113.
58. R. R. Sharma, *op.cit.,* p. 205.
59. M. S. Gorbachev's speech at Krasnoyarsk, September 16, 1988, *For building new relations in the Asia-Pacific region*, (New Delhi: Allied Publishers, 1988), pp.13-14.

* The third proposal was elaborated in Gorbachev's Krasnoyarsk speech.

60. V. D. Chopra (ed.), *op.cit.,* p.149.
61. They regard these developments as being useful for the relaxation of tension, and at the same time recognize them as flowing from a national calculation about their probable effect, i.e. a Soviet recognition that strictly guarding military secrecy by traditional methods has been rendered virtually useless by orbiting military reconnaissance satellites, and that the political gain to be expected from such apparent openness would far exceed any conceivable military strategic losses which might flow from it. Michio Royama, "The USSR and the Asia-Pacific Region: Paper II", in Francois Heisbourg, (ed.), *The Strategic Implications of Change in Soviet Union*, (London: Macmillan, 1990), p. 157.
62. Vadim Zagladin, *Peace the Only Option*, (New Delhi: Allied Publishers, 1987), p.102.
63. *Pravda*, 10 July, 1987.
64. Alexi Arbatov, '"The illusion of an impenetrable shield", *New Times*, 8 August, 1987, p. 15. Bovin called this shift in strategic concept the one from 'deterrence by threat; the threat of overall retaliation to 'defensive deterrence', based on military parity maintained at every level of nuclear disarmament. see A. Bovin, *Novoe Myshlenie-novaya Politica, Kommunist*, 9 July 1988, p. 120. Cited in Tsuyshi Hasegowa and Alex Pravda (eds.), *Perestroika: Soviet*

Domestic and Foreign Policies, (London: Sage Publications, 1990), p. 168.

65. For an analysis of Stockholm Agreement, see John Borawski, et. al ., "The Stockholm Agreement of 1986", *Orbis* No. 30, (Winter 1987), pp. 643-62.

66. The Central provision of the agreement were :

(i) All signatories agreed to "refrain from the threat or use of force in their relations with other States, regardless of that State's political, social, economic or cultural system and irrespective of whether or not they maintain with that State relations of alliance". The fact that the Soviets accepted this "Anti-Brezhnev Doctrine" provision was a measure of how important the CBM process was to Gorbachev;

(ii) Forty-two-day advance notice of military activities involving land forces in excess of 13,000 amphibious landings or parachute drops involving at least 3,000 troops, and transfers of at least 13,000 troops into the zone of application (Europe to the Urals);

(iii) Observation of military activities and transfers involving at least 17,000 troops or amphibious landings and parachute drops with at least 5,000 troops. This observation must "allow the observers to confirm that the notified activity is non-threatening;

(iv) Annual calenders of military activity;

(v) Military activities involving more than 40,000 troops should have two years notice and if they involve more than 75,000 troops, they cannot take place without such notice;

(vi) Each signatory may request M-site or air inspection, but no more than three inspections begin within 36 hours of request and may last no more than 48 hours and be carried out by no more than four inspectors.

Extracted from Zwick Peter, *Soviet Foreign Relations Process and Policy*, (New Jersey: Prentice Hall, 1990), p. 262.

67. For meaning and analysis of The dual track policy' of Brezhnev, see Bruce Parrot, "Soviet National Security under Gorbachev", *Problems of Communism*, Vol. 37. No .6, (November-December 1988), pp. 2-7.

68. Zwick Peter, *op.cit.*, p. 263.

69. *Ibid*, p. 263.

70. Message of Greetings, *Moscow World Service*, 19 June, 1988 in SU/0183 A1/1.

71. Roy Allison, "Gorbachev's Armed Control Offensive: Unilateral, Bilateral and Multilateral Initiatives", in Carl G. Jacobson, (ed.), *Soviet Foreign Policy: New Dynamics, New Themes*, (London: Macmillan Press, 1989), p. 74.
72. See *Documents of the Meeting of the Political Consultative Committee of the Warsaw Treaty Member States*, Berlin, May 28-29, 1987, (Moscow: Novosti Press, 1987), pp. 9-10.
73. N. Kapchenko, *op.cit.,* p. 91.
74. Quoted in Vadim Zagladin, *op.cit.*, p.104.
75. N. Kapchenko, *op.cit.,* p.92.
76. M. S. Gorbachev, Address at the 43rd Session of UN General Assembly, December 7, 1988, *Soviet Review Documents*, (New Delhi: USSR Embassy in India, 1988,) p. 31.
77. Michael MccGwire, *Perestroika and Soviet National Security*, (Washington DC: The Brookings Institution, 1991), p. 356. See also Rachel Walker, *Six Years that Shook the World: Perestroika – The Impossible Project*, (Manchester: Manchester University Press, 1993), pp. 216-218.
78. Address by M. S. Gorbachev at the meeting to mark the 40th Anniversary of the GDR, Berlin, October 6, 1989, (Moscow: Novosti Press, 1989), p. 7.
79. Comprehensive Universal Security, Common Security, International Security are inter- changeably used
80. Bruce W. Nelan, "The year of people", *Time*, Vol. 135, No. 1, (January 1990), p. 17.
81. Ibid, p.18.
82. Gerhard Wetting, "The Transformation from cold war to today's challenges", *Aussen Politik*, Vol. 11. (1997), p. 114.
83. *Ibid.,* p.114. Wetting has also used 'inner empire' while analysing the collapse of the USSR.
84. MccGwire Michael, *op.cit.,* p. 860.
85. For excellent discussion, see for example, Raymond L. Garthoff, "New Thinking in Soviet Military Doctrine", *The Washington Quarterly*, Vol.11, No. 3 (Summer 1988), pp. 131-158. George E. Hudson (ed.) *Soviet National Security Policy Under Perestroika*, (Boston: Unwin Hyman Inc., 1989); Joseph I. Nogee and Robert H. Donaldson, *Soviet Foreign Policy since World War II*, (New York: Pergamon Press, 1988), p. 337.
86. Bruce Parrot, "Soviet National Security under Gorbachev", *Problems of Communism*, Vol. 37. No. 6, (Nov.-Dec. 1988), p. 35.

5

Economic Security During Perestroika

5.1. The Necessity of Economic Reforms

Economic security played a decisive role under *perestroika*. It had two major dimensions. In the domestic front it aimed at bringing reforms to boost up the stagnant Soviet economy through structural changes and integrating Soviet economy into the global economy. In the international front, it brought several proposals for restructuring international economy. Soviet leader Gorbachev tried seriously for ensuring peace and security of the world by implementing those proposals.

Now the common question comes to mind of a researcher; Why Economic Reforms? A critical analysis of Soviet economic history revealed that the Soviet economy after the Second World War went through three distinct phases. In the first phase Soviet economy grew rapidly during 1950s and 1960s. In the second phase, it dramatically slowed down in the 70's and came to standstill position in the 80's. This phase was called 'Brezhnevite Stagnancy' as it happened during his time.

Before analysing the second phase, which compelled Soviet leader and economists to bring reforms to overcome the economic stagnancy and to revamp the Soviet economy, one would like to know the strategy for economic growth in 50's and 60's. During this phase, abundance of resources supported the strategy for economic growth. High investment rates also helped for rapid development of the industrial infrastructure of Soviet Union. The most important factor in Soviet economic growth during this period was a growing labour force and increase in labour force participation rate. The Soviet economy was also benefited from the general abundance of raw materials and natural resources and their location near the industrial centres in the European part of the Soviet Union.[1] No doubt, favourable global economic conditions, East-West trade and access to Western technology helped for the growth of its economy.

In the 70's the situation changed dramatically. Soviet economy performance decayed to low level and checked growth in consumer welfare development of industrial base. The cause of declining economic growth rates was due to transition from an economic environment of resource abundance to one of resource stringency. During this phase, there was slow down in growth rate of Soviet labour force due to decrease in the growth rate of Soviet working age population. Another important aspect related to this problem was the reluctance of the Soviet Central Asian Muslims those constituted large chunk of labour force to work in the modern industrial environment.[2]

The availability of relatively inexpensive material output went on declining. Soviet Union was forced to spend huge amount of money as operating cost for extracting fossil fuels from the remote sites in the east. Non-energy raw materials were also becoming less accessible and hence costly.[3] Inefficient utilization of resources, over planned and over administered system, target oriented approach to agricultural and industrial production where emphasis was on quantity rather than quality; linking bonus to the fulfillment of target, lack of incentives and independence to workers and managers to work hard freely made the economic situation worse. Other negative features of 70's and early 80's, which accelerated the process of Soviet economic decay were the 'shift from positive to negative factor productivity and the diversion of resources, especially technological from potentially civilian to defence needs.'[4]

By the time Gorbachev came to power, there was standstill position in industry, agriculture and services. In the words of Desai:

"The Soviet economic system that Gorbachev inherited has all the trapping of a rigid institutional structure. Commands from the central planners have left little initiative and even less incentive, for the performing actors and economic agents. The ill-fitting pieces of shortages, bottlenecks, retarded innovation and faltering growth have been the inevitable consequences. Gorbachev has chosen to restructure the jigsaw puzzle and provide incentives to the players to fit the pieces where they belong".[55]

5.2. Restructuring the Economy

Reforms in Soviet Union was not introduced for the first time during Gorbachev period. Since the death of Stalin, there were three periods of reforms in Soviet economy. The first period of reforms started from the 20th CPSU Congress in 1956 and continued till Brezhnev came to power. During the Brezhnev period, reforms were not successful partly because of bureaucratic resistance and partly due to mistakes committed by the central leadership. The second period of reforms was the mid-1960s when serious attempt was made to decentralize the economy to give independent positions to factory managers, to introduce new economic indicators such as profit and to increase the incentives to employees to work hard. But it could not yield any concrete result as it was implemented slowly because of resistance from the bureaucrats and half-hearted attitudes of central leaders. After 1968, these reforms ceased to exist, because of the influence of Prague Spring during which even more far-reaching reforms were proposed in Soviet Union, protestation of anti-reformers that radical reforms would erode the authority of the Communist Party.[6]

The third period of reforms was started during the time of Gorbachev. Although the plan of restructuring or *perestroika* in Soviet Union was set forth in April 1985, just after he assumed power, the foundation of the new reform programme was laid at the 27th CPSU Congress, 1986. The specific elements constituting *perestroika* were not spelt out all at once. It was a gradual process and obviously continued upto December 1991 when Soviet Union finally disintegrated.

The attempts at restructuring Soviet economy had two important characteristics. First was opening up the closed Soviet economy to foreign investments and new technology. Second was the creation of a market for consumer goods and removal of administrative control over this market These changes aimed at both external and internal liberalization. The reform period during *perestroika* could be divided into two phases. The first phase covered up to November 1989 and the second phase was upto December 1991.[7]

5.2. (i). Economic Management

The major attempts at reforms in this first phase were made for an establishment of an integrated, efficient and flexible system of economic management. The objective of this reform was to reduce the role of the State in all major areas of economic activity by allowing an important role for cooperative and individual enterprise. Private enterprises were allowed in the Soviet Union from Ist May 1987, according to the law of individual labour activity,[8] the first time certain types of private enterprises started functioning in USSR. The activity of the new enterprises was concentrated in the consumer goods and service sectors. Individual citizens and members of their families participated and hiring of employees were not allowed. People who had permanent work elsewhere were provided opportunity to work in State enterprise at their free time. It was really a positive step in the direction of reform as the labour market was supplied with large number of new workers which was helpful for overcoming the problem of labour shortage. In the consumer goods sector, a number of areas were opened to individual labour excepting few areas like manufacture of medical equipment, chemical products and copying machines (Articles 12-13). Even the scope of the private enterprises were small but introduction of new law brought important charges in consumer and service sectors.[9]

Another important reform in the direction of economic management was the introduction of new cooperatives. In May 1987, these new cooperatives started functioning in the Soviet Union. The new cooperatives were of different kind and could be labelled workers cooperatives and in some cases industrial cooperatives. In Soviet Union, cooperative restaurants and cafes were set up to provide meals to the people. New cooperatives also started functioning in the clothing manufacture. Most probably Soviet leaders followed Hungarian model when designed these new cooperative enterprises. These cooperatives were oriented to meet the need of the market. They were extremely flexible and modified their production as demand fluctuated. On 8th June 1988, the law of cooperatives was published which acknowledged the role of cooperatives in Soviet Union.[10]

Another important innovation in the law in this direction was the creation of small cooperatives in the field of science and technology which provided services in engineering, construction and other technologically oriented areas. No doubt, the above mentioned reforms ended the monopoly of the State in key areas like foreign trade, where apart from foreign trade organizations which had complete control over all foreign trade hitherto conducted by the USSR, enterprises were also allowed to conduct trade.

The new system of economic management also stressed on the area of joint ventures. A decree of January 13, 1987 allowed for the first time the creation of joint ventures involving foreign capitalist partners including developing countries on the territory of Soviet Union. Another decree of September 17 of the same year officially sanctioned Soviet participation in joint ventures in developing countries on their territory. The joint ventures were allowed to set up their own targets and to set their prices and market their output without the dictates of the State planning authority.

The same independence was also granted to the State enterprises and associations as well through the adoption of the law on State enterprise in June 1987. They were granted freedom to establish their own business contacts in both domestic and international market. This decision also facilitates individual enterprises to retain more than a third of their output for directly selling in the market by changing the earlier decision of placing the entire output at the disposal of the State.

While a free market for the producers to exploit was being created, the price system remained under the control of administrative mechanism and the correction in price system which was essential for transition to market economy were not allowed.[11] Soviet economists stressed on this price reform as important factors in the reform plan like exchange rate charges linked to the price reform. In the words of Nikolai Shmelyov, a leading economist of Soviet Union:

"Today a few people will probably deny the need for a price reform. Without the establishment of objective and rational price ratios and without the transition of the bulk of our economy to market principles of price formation, the new mechanism will not operate".[12]

But price reform was repeatedly deferred and when it was finally initiated in 1991, it simply made the inflation high. In the process of restructuring, key issues like distribution of national products, ownership of property assumed significance, but government did not take up any clear cut policies. Once the State relinquished property over which it had earlier control, the new forms of its involvement had to be clearly mentioned but the phase did not able to solve these complex problems which surfaced in the transitional phase. It lost its momentum within first two years due to lack of a comprehensive framework. In the first half of 1988, the Deputy PM in-charge of reforms, Leonid Abalkin had commented that *perestroika* had failed to bring the real process of structural change.[13]

Hence, Soviet Union searched for new forms and methods of economic management. As Aganbegyan said:

"This search extends not only to the resolution of internal economic problems but to the whole system of external economic and scientific and technological relations. In all these, new approaches, unorthodox solutions and an emphasis on economic cost effectiveness are essential".[14]

5.2. (ii). Structural Reforms

The second phase of economic reforms began when Abalkin himself came out with a new package of economic reforms which aimed at structural change. Its objective was the promotion of a market for consumer goods, the releasing of all administrative control over pricing and distribution and above all restructuring the property relations and encouraging private property ownership.

This reform plan took up four major issues such as changes in ownership of property; financial restructuring; price reform; and modifications of conditions for foreign investment.[15] This reform plan was formulated for five years, starting with 1990 and ending with 1995. The closing of 13th Five Year Plan. The Abalkin programme presented to the Congress of People's Republics by P.M. Nikolai Ryzhkov was definitely a unique document. It was a detailed and coherent blue print for economic reforms. For the first time, it stressed on de-nationalization of State property through *arenda*, use of credit mechanism through banking system, stabilization of money supply and transition to market economy including the introduction of market for labour, capital and foreign exchange.[16]

However, this programme could not bring any changes in the deteriorating performance of Soviet economy. Hence, government commission headed by Prime Minister was asked to prepare a more radical package of reform. Prime Minister presented its conclusion to the Supreme Soviet on 24th May 1990. Those programs involved a gradual transition to a regulated market in three stages until 1995, incorporating changes to be undertaken to correct the imbalances in the existing market system. Emphasis was placed on consumer goods production and shifting of investment in favour of this sector; increase in food production; undertaking specific measures to stabilize the consumer market by diverting the excess demand for consumer goods to other areas; and correcting the growing government budget deficit.[17]

But the legal changes, pricing and tax reform and reduction in the scope of central planning could not bring any positive result rather the price of commodity like bread raised substantially. The Supreme Soviet called for the government to submit a more developed and coherent programme by 1st September 1990. There was much debate and discussions among the economists and political reformers to protect the population from the negative effect of these changes and how to control the price of the bread and tackle the problem of regulations prohibiting the sale of goods to non-residents.[18]

In this critical juncture, a radical plan put forward by a group under the Chairmanship of presidential council member Stanislav Shatalin, advocated five hundred days transition to market based upon transfer of state to other forms of property and a 'hard' rouble.[19] But Government's original proposal remained on the table. Ryzhkov opposed it as it would lead to probably political instability and fall in the living standards of the people.

Another group chaired by Abel Aganbegyan prepared a proposal for moving to market economy with least social and economic costs and its conclusion were presented to Supreme Soviet and republican parliaments. The Supreme Soviet asked Gorbachev to prepare a unified programme combining the best elements of all the three documents and proposals.

The new guidelines were prepared and approved by an overwhelming mandate on October 19, 1990. These guidelines were based on the principle of maximum freedom of economic activity and it envisaged a transition to 'market economy' in four stages within a relatively short time. The first stage was to be devoted mainly to establishing the economy and beginning the commercialisation of the State enterprises. The second stage stressed on the gradual liberalization of prices, the introduction of various forms of social security and the maintenance of the tight fiscal policies. Further structural reforms were to be completed in the third stage, while financial constraints would be eased as market conditions stabilized. In the final stage, the rouble would become fully convertible against other currencies within the Soviet Union and outside it.[20] So far, restructuring of Soviet economy was concerned, Soviet leader Gorbachev also took steps in restructuring Soviet agriculture in March 1986 by allowing farmers to sell their produce privately at market determined prices. He also introduced land leasing system in March 1989 by which land could be leased to individual, groups or families. Still there were lot of problems remained in this sector.

Gorbachev emphasized on several other elements of reform programme in his speeches of late 1990 and in 1991. But the economic situation got worsened in 1991 when people made a long queue to get their daily items. There were even shortages of drinking water. The 'anti crisis' programme could not bring any change in the economic situation of Soviet Union. *Perestroika* of Soviet economy was an successful for several reasons. It was hesitantly perused. Even after the 1987 Enterprise Act, the State-owned enterprises remained shackled by the system of state contracts, the reformers first perceived competition as the motivating force of any market economy at a later stage, price reform which was essential for the success of market economy in Soviet Union was deferred, agricultural reform, accompanied by the acceptance of private ownership of land was not ventured. Instead of receiving support, the cooperative system tended to be defamed. Larger private enterprises were not allowed, Had there been ten to twenty years time left, the shortcomings could have been gradually put right. But the essential pre-condition was missing as political system was not conducive to market reforms and the holders of power particularly ruling upper *nomenklatura* appointed by the party refused to support to reform rather they turned to be breaking mechanism of *perestroika* Gorbachev complained about.[21]

5.3. Integrating to the Global Economy

As discussed, besides structural changes in the Soviet economy, Soviet Union during *perestroika* tried its best to ensure its economic security through integrating Soviet economy into the emerging new liberal international economic order. Soviet leader Gorbachev revised the traditional Soviet approach to the world economy through mutual friendship, economic co-operation and trade relationship. Thus, the world once divided between the two antagonistic blocs had suddenly become united.

Under *perestroika*, Soviet Union emphasized on the increasing exports of manufactured goods to become an economic force at the international level. For achieving this objective, Soviet Union developed warm economic relations with the West. The introduction of Western hard currency investment improved the quality of Soviet manufactured goods. About 70% of exports of the West was made up of four groups of commodities: motor cars, power plant, technical instrument and laboratory equipment, and railway rolling stock, with motor car making up 46% of this figure. In 1987, the proportion of manufactured good in Soviet exports rose to 21.5 per cent. Soviet exports to industrialized capitalist countries had grown by 5 per cent as opposed to 0.1 per cent for total exports.[22]

Gorbachev's sincere efforts and strong determination helped to convert Soviet Union from a 'raw national appendage' to the West (i.e. exporting its primary products for machinery that it cannot produce internally) to an export of high quality and internationally competitive manufactured goods.[23]

Soviet Union expanded its trade under *perestroika* and played a decisive role as a player in world economy. As mentioned, liberalization provided a conducive business environment for the traders of Soviet Union for developing healthy business relationship with developed and developing nations. From 1987 onwards, twenty ministries and seventy enterprises had been authorized to make direct deal with foreign partners and from April 1989, this right was extended to all internationally competitive business.[24] By April 1, 1991, more than 30,000 Soviet organizations were registered for foreign trade activity.

This was the first time western companies dealt directly with the ultimate buyer of the Soviet Union by passing the bureaucratic rigidities. But this liberalization in the economic sphere had some problems. Foreign businessmen had to travel long distance to negotiate with their Soviet counterparts. Many Soviet businessmen also faced problems as they did not have skilled and experienced personnel to handle foreign trade. Firms were even not allowed to dispose of all their foreign income. For example, one quarter of the car manufacturer Volga's foreign currency income was left at the firm's own disposal; even then the permission of Foreign Economic Relations Ministry was needed. Another important problem during *perestroika* was the inability of Soviet businessmen to export more to meet the needs of the people as there was scarcities of materials. The drive to increase export at the expense of domestic consumption increased the dissatisfaction of the Soviet people. They complained that it had become difficult to have good things since things were exported.[25] Exports of machinery and equipment, ores and metals, chemicals, timber and paper and consumer durables increased from 16.2%, 9.5%, 4%, 3.5%, 2.8% respectively of total exports in 1988 to 18.3, 11.2, 4.6, 3.7, 3.6 per cent respectively in 1990.

The final years of Soviet power also saw the growth of complex and difficult system of export licensing, which proved highly vulnerable to hijacking by populist leaders eager to jump on the bandwagon of 'export nothing that we need ourselves' and departmental bosses seeking to neutralize the competition.[26]

The co-operation in the form of joint ventures was one of the important steps taken by Soviet leaders to strengthen the economic security. It included the following: attracting investment capital; acquisition of technological know-how; acquisition of organizational know-how; learning sales marketing through free sales in both the Soviet market and in world market; and multiple function through the "oil slick effect" of the joint venture company on the Soviet farms co-operating with it".[27]

The joint ventures law of 1987 permitted foreign ownership of equity in the Soviet Union for the first time. The maximum foreign share in a joint venture was initially restricted to 49% but in 1988s it was raised to 80 per cent and subsequently 100 per cent foreign ownership was permitted. In principle, joint ventures were subject to both profit tax and repatriation tax, but with a tax holiday for foreign partners from the date on which profits were first generated. In practice, joint ventures were regulated by the laws of the republics and regions as the authorities and even lower level authorities tried to assert their sovereignty by promulgating their own rules and regulations. Individual foreign firms started negotiating the best deal they could with Soviet, republic or local governments, as the case might be. By the middle of 1991 more than 3,000 joint ventures had been agreed with foreign partners, most of them from western countries. Since the disintegration of Soviet Union, there have been no changes in principle except republics replacing the Union, at least one level of legal confusion over joint ventures has been removed.[28]

The measures taken in the year 1986-87 failed to revitalize the pattern of foreign trade of Soviet Union. The disappearance of Soviet Union even did not produce any change in the situation. Though the number of joint ventures increased impressively in the last years of USSR, but the amount of capital and volume of business was not satisfactory. Joint ventures had attracted just 1.5 billion dollars of international equity capital by February 1990 and that figure had not increased much by 1991. They did not play any significant role for technology transfer into Soviet economy or as major stimulators of Soviet exports. The latest available figure shows that the net effect of joint ventures on the Soviet balance of trade was negative.[29] It was due to unattractive tax regime, uncertain repatriation of profits and the question of converting roubles into hard currency confused for everyone involved in foreign trade. Though in principle joint ventures were autonomous of state organs but in practice their activities were obstructed by state organs.

The position of Soviet trading enterprises was even not upto the mark. The administrative set up rather than market mechanism was responsible for this. It is important that Boris Yeltsin's Russian government is still continuing the same regulations by giving priority to state orders. The general absence of joint ventures activity in 1992 was largely a function of uncertainty over political prospects and anxieties about the international payment position rather than about the planning regimes.[30]

There was discussion of Special Economic Zones (SEZ) after seeing its success in China. The Soviet SEZ was thought up for strengthening its economic position based on the market principles and hard currency settlement and allowing for private property. The one proposed SEZ that was actually set up before the disintegration of Soviet Union was at Nakhodka, in the Soviet Far East. But there was war of laws between Russia and local government of the Maritime Province where Nakhodka is situated. By the end of 1992 Kalingrad had joined Nakhodka as a functioning special Economic Zone.[31] The SEZ were also in operation in a number of other Russian Far Eastern region. But they had failed to match their Chinese counterparts.

Soviet Union expressed its desire to become a member of GATT as it would have a good effect on the external economic transformation of USSR by inducing to adjust to the new rules of the game in the world market. Soviet Union's decision to adhere to a multilateral trade system based on GATT rules and principles was to strengthen its stagnant economy and stabilize the political climate.[32] Other important reasons to become a member of GATT were the expansion of manufactured goods export and acquisition of Most Favoured Nation (MFN) status which membership would offer and which would make its export less vulnerable to arbitrary import restrictions.[33]

Though some CMEA countries were the members of GATT during *perestroika* period, but the case of Soviet Union was little bit different and of course more problematic from the point of view of the GATT than those of the small socialist countries. This was due to economic weight of Soviet Union.[34] Its desire to become a member of GATT remain unfulfilled as it was disintegrated on December 1991.

As for IMF Soviet Union became an associate member of IMF on 24th June 1991. The desire to become a member of IMF was to overcome the crisis ridden economy. Though there was no legal provision for an associate member to get IMF loan, yet it was a step forward for entry into IMF. Russia's entry to full membership of IMF in April 1992 could have important medium term implication.

The CMEA Secretariat and EC Commission adopted a joint declaration in June 1988. Soviet Union established official relations with EC. This was followed by signing of the first long term frame agreement in the year 1989 on trade, economic and commercial co-operation. EC also provided technical assistance to Soviet Union for utilizing country's resources effectively. To fulfill these objectives the EC allocated 400 million ECUs (European Currency Unit of the Common Market) in 1991; the same amount was proposed to be given in 1992.[35] These allocations were for developing basic, priority sectors such as power, engineering, transport, the food processing industry, personnel training for state run private sectors, finance servicing. No doubt, EC's assistance was to encourage private investments into the Soviet Economy.

The 1989 agreement which came into force on April 1, 1990 served as a legal foundation of the USSR-EC relations. This agreement accorded each of the sides the MFN status and the waiving of fixed import quotas. It also defined the co-operation in trade and economic fields. USSR-EC Mixed Commission set up to observe the implementation of the agreements, to solve various problems and other important matters arising between two sides for strengthening their relations. Though it did not cover everything, but it was a positive step taken by both the sides.

As discussed, the situation in Europe and Soviet Union went on changing during this *perestroika* period. Hungary, Czechoslovakia concluded treaty with EC and other East European countries were in the process which forced Soviet Union to take steps to integrate itself into the new European space, otherwise it would lead to isolation and threaten the stability and security of Soviet Union in the continent. In December 1990, European Council proposed a grand agreement which would include political dialogue, comprehensive economic co-operation including cultural sphere between EC and Soviet Union. USSR responded positively. Though it covered a wide range of areas but the focus was on economic co-operation as it wanted to integrate Soviet Union into the European economic space.[36] A protocol signed by both sides in June 1990 in this respect which covered wide range of fields including cooperation in information technology, environmental research, biotechnology, power production, nuclear power and engineering, materials and industrial technology etc.[37] Though this proposed agreement did not materialize, yet it had a positive impact for strengthening the security of Europe and the world.

The establishment of official relations between Soviet Union and EC not only played a significant role for the Europe's construction but also cleared the way for bilateral trade and cooperation between individual CMEA countries and EC. Thus it strengthened the trade between East and West and their economic security. The first step taken by EC in this respect was the agreement concluded with Hungary in September 1988 which proposed to drop all national quantitative restriction of EC countries within ten years. Similar agreements were also proposed by EC to cover other East European countries. These developments were no doubt positive steps taken during this *perestroika* period towards closer relations with EC.

In 1990, a mixed commission of the EC and the CMEA discussed the scope of joint activities and identified subjects like Statistics, Forecast, Environment, Standardization, Science and Technology, Electrical and Nuclear Energy and Transport for discussion.[38] During this *perestroika* phase, East-West trade mainly concentrated on the European Continent. Europe accounted for almost 9 per cent of the export and roughly 75 per cent of the imports of the CMEA from Western industrial countries. This clearly reflected the European character and interest in trade ties between West and East. In this respect EC took a lead over European Free Trade Association (EFTA). The EFTA accounted for 5 per cent of the CMEA's foreign trade and vice versa. Though the CMEA countries share in EC's foreign trade volume was less than 3 per cent, yet the EC was the primary partner of the COMECON/CMEA in its trade with the West. The community accounted for 15 per cent of its foreign trade that was three times share of trade with EFTA and for near about 60 per cent of its trade with the West.

The importance of European community for CMEA's foreign trade increased during Eighties.[39] At the same time, individual CMEA members attained greater autonomy through Soviet *perestroika*. Due to differing pace of reforms in Eastern European countries and changes in their economic structures, CMEA showed the signs of disintegration and took interest to integrate with the EC and New International Economic order.[40] In 1988, CMEA countries also decided to have a common market for free flow of goods and to strengthen the economy of Soviet Union and Socialist Bloc but the idea did not materialize as CMEA collapsed in September 1991.

Soviet Union took several measures as discussed above, it could not revitalize the Soviet economy. Soviet Union's borrowing in the financial market went on increasing. The Western banks responded positively to the request of Soviet Union for lending money. In 1988, the Soviet Union achieved a debt service ratio of 21 which was much more lower than the average of 42 for the other East European countries. At the end of 1988, the net debt in convertible currencies was about $23 billion which was more than the double of 1984 figure. At the end of 1991 (before the disintegration of Soviet Union), Soviet debt went up to $81.4 billion.[41] The Central Bank Chief Gerashchenko also cited a figure of $80 billion for 'old' presumably pre-1992 debts. During this economic crisis, Soviet Union even began to issue bonds in Western market. In 1988 they issued bonds for 100 million Swiss Francs and 500 million Deutsche marks. But the foreign borrowing did not able to resuscitate Soviet dying economy as imported goods were wasted, imported plants were not operated effectively and some plants were over staffed in comparison to its western counterparts.[42] Even Soviet administration used foreign currency to import consumer goods instead of using it for overcoming the economic crisis.[43]

Thus, the mismanagement of Soviet economy and misutilization of foreign borrowing dragged Soviet Union into external debt trap by 1990, borrowing largely to service the debts. After the disintegration of Soviet Union, it is not clear how much of the new loan was assigned to each member of CIS, or whether Russia will take up the responsibility to repay, recovering somehow the dues from the latter.[44] Russian debt at end-September 1992 ought to exceed $ 95 billion.

Soviet Union took interest in pan-pacific basin for its vast potential for economic development. It was clearly reflected from the speeches of Gorbachev delivered in Vladivostok in July 1986 and Krasnoyarsk in September 1988. As the economic centre shifted since 1970 towards pacific, so it was expected that during 80's it would become the focus of economic activity.[45] Soviet wanted to gain more political and economic influences from this region for which it took special interest to join PECC (Pacific Economic Cooperation Conference) and Asian Development Bank.

In August 1987, Soviet adopted a programme entitled 'The long-term State Programme for Complex Development of Production Capability in the Far East Area until 2000'. But it could not nationalize as the Soviet Far East lacked proper infrastructure, appropriate institutions and abundant labour force.[46] Even Soviet themselves did not like to invest resources in that region. The capitalist economies in the pacific basin also did not have any interest at that time to take up this project in Siberia. Japan government was also not so keen to support this Siberian project as the territorial dispute over Kurile Islands was not settled.

The country which took interest in this project was South Korea only when Gorbachev expressed his unwillingness and inability to continue supporting the economy and military of the North. So, it was a success of Nord Politik of the South.[47] Though this project step as it paved the way for Russia to become a participant in many of the regional institutions of the Asia-Pacific such as PECC, ARF, etc. Russia may also play an important role for enhancing the security of this region.[48]

5. 4. The Problem of Convertibility

The most important problem of Soviet economy was the question of convertibility of rouble. Absence of unified formula for transacting export earning into domestic purchasing power obstructed the effective implementation of Soviet foreign trade reforms. A convertibility of rouble would have solved this problem easily.[49] Soviet Union implemented several measures from 1988 to early 1991 to brig about convertible of its currency. In October 1989, a new tourist rate fixed at just 10 per cent of the old rate was introduced and old unrealistic parity of around one rouble to the pound sterling was dropped.

The first Soviet foreign exchange auction was held on 3rd November 1989. It generated rates of exchange two to three times lower than the new tourist rate. In 1990, both foreign exchange auction and black market rates inclined to the bottom rate of that range. In April 1991, Soviet authorities devalued the tourist rouble to a rate of around 30 to the pound sterling. The rate had gone to 50 to the pound by the end of June. In the meantime, in late 1990, a commercial rate, for business transactions was introduced at a rate of about three to the pound sterling.[50] In early 1992, Yeltsin's Russian Federation government introduced system for convertibility of rouble. But the full internal convertibility is yet to be achieved.

5.5. Reinforcing the Council of Mutual Economic Assistance (CMEA)

Soviet Union tried its best to improve the efficiency of the CMEA, obviously to get economic benefits out of it. As 60 per cent of Soviet trade was with COMECON countries, so the concern was quite apparent. Soviet Union took efforts to strengthen the CMEA by intensifying the cooperation in the field of science and technology, the establishment of joint ventures; direct links between CMEA enterprises, joint exploitation of energy sources and convertibility of the transferable of rouble. But the COMECON countries were more interested to develop trade with the West as it could only provide them advanced machinery and technology. Their consent to improve the cooperation within CMEA was very formal and out of political obligation rather than economic benefits.[51]

On 18th December, 1985, all the members of the CMEA signed the 'Complex Programme of Scientific and Technological Progress of the Member Countries of the CMEA upto the year 2000',[52] but it did not yield any concrete result. In this context, it was significant that the slow down in economic growth which occurred in all the CMEA countries during mid-70's went on declining further. Soviet relations among CMEA countries were hindered by the issue of price formation, the decision of Soviet Union to reduce oil supply, the economic crisis in Poland and lack of advanced telecommunications equipment.[53]

Again, the broader controversy emanated from growing economic incompatibilities in the region. Economic structures – some changed, some well organized and some partially reformed – were out of Sync; interaction within CMEA was obstructed for this domestic disparities.[54] Even some CMEA members did not like to sell their commodities to their poorer friends as they did not get proper counter offers. Gorbachev's revision of a unified CMEA market could have solved this problem, but it did not materialise.

For the above reasons, the turnover of trade among CMEA members moved downwards. There was also a drastic fall in Soviet trade with the CMEA partners in 1990-91. Its export crashed to less than one-half; and import to almost a third. The turnover in hard currency fell by 13 per cent and barter trade by 19 per cent.[55]

As discussed, Soviet Union tried to play an important role in global economy by integrating itself into New Liberal International Economic Order. Though, it did not succeed in overcoming the economic crisis, yet it was a positive step to revamp its economy. When a systemic change takes place in a economy, it always takes time and the transition period is always traumatic. So, it was quite obvious that Soviet Union faced problem to cope up with the New Economic Order. Of course, there were several problems those obstructed for an effective participation of Soviet Union in global economy. Though Western technology provided relief yet it was constrained by foreign currency reserve on the Coordinating Committee for Mutual Export Controls (COCOM) regulations restricted technology transfer. In such a situation it was too difficult on the part of the Soviet economy to involve seriously in international system. Even Western countries did not come forward to help *perestroika* by extending subsidized credits or allowing Soviet products to be sold in their market.

Several other factors as mentioned like the shortage of skilled and experienced executives to run things in a new way; the rigid bureaucratization, the imbalance between demand and supply of goods; the difficult system of export licensing; the problem relating to internal convertibility of rouble; and the constraints of getting financial help from international institutions stood on its way to engage actively in world economy. Further, the mismanagement of Soviet economy and misutilization of foreign borrowing coupled with the ineffectiveness of CMEA and problems of its CMEA partners pushed Soviet Union into economic crisis.

Whatever might be the consequences of economic reforms of Soviet Union. But to a certain extent, it incorporated into international economy and strengthened East-West relations which moved towards stabilization and rapprochement. This economic reforms also helped Soviet Union in various ways like exporting high quality of manufactured goods; improving trade with EC and West by enjoying MFN status, encouraging private investment in Soviet economy and also favouring the presence of MNCs in the Soviet Union.

The period of hesitation over new forms of organization of production, such as cooperatives, contracts, and lease holding was ended. For the first time, the idea of regional cost accounting was started and considerable positive changes were taken place. No doubt, this reforms also paved the way for new Russia to become a participant in various institutions like IMF, PECC, ARF, etc.

5.6. Soviet Union's Role in International Economic Security

With the introduction of science and technology, qualitative changes have taken place in world economy towards economic development and prosperity. The trend in the economic development of world economy is characterized by comprehensiveness and greater interdependence. This nature of comprehensiveness and interdependence leads to both conflict and cooperation in global economy. When cooperation strengthens economy, conflict impedes economic progress and creates instability and unpredictability in world economy.

The oil crisis of 1970s, the debt crisis of 1980s and 90s, the policy of economic sanction in violation of international law and several other economic problems pose threat to the smooth functioning of international economy.[56] Despite various efforts and initiatives, those problems were not completely solved. Really this global economic problems call for global solution through worldwide cooperation in the interest of all countries. Several status including erstwhile Soviet Union took various measures to normalize the international economic relations by solving the international problems. From the 1920's onwards, USSR came forward with various policies, proposals and measures particularly at the Geneva Conference, at the world economic conferences of 1927 and 1933, at the league of the nations and at the economic bodies of the UN in the post-war period for the solution of the international problems and improvement of the international economic environment.[57]

But under *perestroika*, Soviet Union put special emphasis on this international economic security which was enshrined in 27th CPSU Congress. Soviet leader Gorbachev tried seriously for strengthening the international economic security by taking several proposals and various measures for the solution of the global problems. Further, his efforts were directed towards the removal of hostile attitudes and antagonistic relationship among various states and the establishment of a New World Economic Order based on mutual friendship and cooperation. In May 1985, during the visit of Willy Brand- the President of Socialist International, Gorbachev stressed on the questions of establishing equal international economic relations without any discrimination and of New International Economic Order, including the debt problem of developing countries. Later on, those ideas were converted to concrete proposals in the 27th Congress of Communist Party of Soviet Union (CPSU) that rejected all forms of discrimination and the use of trade, economic, scientific and technical contacts as a means of exerting pressure, and worked to ensure economic security of all states.

The Soviet Union also condemned the policy of economic blockades and sanctions and demanded the abolition of those heinous practices pursued by imperialist powers which aimed at the economic isolation of certain state or group of states. It endorsed the UN move that states could only use collective measures for the purpose of maintaining international peace and security and only by the decision of the UN Security Council in compliance with Article 27 of the UN Charter.[58] In accordance with UN documents, during *perestroika*, the Soviet Union came forward with a draft resolution International Economic Security on the eve of the 40th Session of UN General Assembly. The resolution was adopted by majority of votes which reaffirmed one of the fundamental principles of international contacts and opened up new hope for UN activities in the economic domain. After all the solution of problems relating to the elimination of disproportions in international economic relations faced the resistance of western power which did not like the UN's authority to deal with such problems. The Soviet Union believed that normalization of international economic relations could be possible through the development of those countries whose economic backwardness was the result of long colonial domination followed by the imperialist policy of neo-colonialism.[59]

By sticking to various means like political maneuvering, unequal trade practices, conditions in trade and aid relations, capitalist countries retained their control over newly free states and started exploiting them both in political and economic sphere. This system of neo-colonialist exploitation made the developing countries with more than 2000 million population, a region of poverty.[60] In 1980s, per capita consumption level in developing nations were one eleventh of those developed capitalist states. The problem of malnutrition, child mortality, epidemics, illiteracy made the situation even worse. Most of the third world countries were under debt trap. The total debt of the developing countries was estimated by experts at nearly one trillion dollar. Further the developing countries had to pay enormous sums by way of debt servicing, which were not covered by new loans and credits and were accompanied by further growth in indebtedness. According to official source in 1985 alone, developing countries net payment account to 31 billion dollars, even more than the new borrowings and subsidies they received.[61]

This heavy burden shattered their economy and swallowed up their plans and hopes for overcoming of economic backwardness and poverty and the solution of the most acute social problems. In this context, Soviet Union supported the move taken by NAM, UN and Latin American countries in the Congress held in Havana in Summer 1985 to solve this debt problem in a proper way adhering to the principle of justice and equality. The Soviet Union along with socialist friends also expressed their concern for the debt problem and grave economic situation of South Africa and took a comprehensive view of the situation. In this connection, Warsaw Pact document mentioned: "The Warsaw Pact member states are for putting international currency and finance relations in order, for these relations not to be made a tool for political pressure and interference in internal affairs, and for a just settlement of the debt problem. They view the problem of developing countries' debt as a comprehensive one both for its sources and for its economic, political and social consequences".[62]

Soviet leader Gorbachev favoured NAM appeal for an urgent action to ease the burden of the debt. His announcement of Soviet Union's readiness for a hundred year moratorium on third world debt and proposal for a summit between debtors and creditors to solve the debt problem clearly reflected his genuine interest in this direction. The Soviet Union believed that this problem could be solved only through the economic development of the Third World countries which would enable them to repay the loans taken from other nations and monetary organizations. Further, it could be lessened by the assistance of the developed and other nations to the debtors. Considering the NAM's concern about the grave situation in Sub-Saharan Africa, Soviet Union decided to render assistance to the least developed African countries in a particularly easy terms and it also entered to Africa Fund in 1987 for giving assistance to countries suffering from South Africa's discrimination.[63]

The Soviet Union supported the move of the Third World countries for the establishment of NIEO which aimed at creating cooperation among all states irrespective of their social and economic systems, correction of existing inequalities, elimination of widening gap between developed and developing countries and ensuring economic and social development and peace and justice for the coming generation.

During this *perestroika* phase, Soviet Union expressed its keen desire to cooperate UN and other organizations in order to remove discriminatory restrictions and other artificially created obstacles for international economic relations. In fact, Soviet Union and other socialist countries tried their best to develop equitable approach to international economic ties in their relations with each other and with third world countries and also made efforts for strengthening international economic security. It was clearly reflected from Soviet Union's positive response to the appeal of NAM to join the Common Fund for promoting the implementation of the Integrated Programme for Commodities, which was the key issue at UNCTAD VII. However, the West was bit skeptic about the genuine efforts and intention of Soviet Union but the document submitted by the Soviet delegation to 1987 Summer Session of the ECOSOC and UNCTAD VII contained an impressive overview of Soviet Union's cooperation with developing countries. The ECOSOC document stated that the Soviet Union had inter-governmental agreement on economic and technological cooperation with only 14 developing countries in 1960s which went up to 72 in 1987. During this year of friendship and cooperation with developing countries, 2100 projects of various kinds were also completed. Considering the external debt of Latin America and tropical African countries, Soviet organizations accepted an arrangement for the repayment of their debts which did not disrupt their balance of payment system, on the other hand, it helped in strengthening their economy by increasing the export capability and providing a stable supply of goods they needed. Thus, the principle of mutually advantageous cooperation was attained.[64]

The UNCTAD document pointed out that Soviet Union was a major economic partner of the developing countries during 1980s. It provided them various types of goods, including those essential for the development of their economy. The import-export relations between Soviet Union and developing countries had also a stabilizing effect in their economic situation.

As noted above, Soviet Union also tried to develop stable trade, economic, scientific and technical contacts with capitalist countries on equal terms. During *perestroika*, he not only brought structural changes in Soviet economy, but also tried sincerely for strengthening Soviet economy and International Economic Security by developing friendly economic relations with USA, Europe and Asian powers. The Soviet Union, other Socialist countries and member countries of Non-Aligned Movement considered the solution of international economic problems was very closely connected with the termination of confrontation and arms race. The huge expenditure on defence since the sixties led to lowering of living standards in the developed and western countries and growth of backwardness in the developing world.

The 1987 UN International Conference on Inter-relationship between Disarmament and Development recognized the relationship between disarmament and development and took steps to divert the resources from armaments to other developmental projects. In this context, the joint statement of Warsaw Treaty Member States said:

..... there is a close relationship between disarmament and development and the only disarmament can release vast additional resources for overcoming economic backwardness, the Warsaw

Treaty member states stand with all resoluteness for concrete measures in the field of disarmament to be accompanied by corresponding cuts in military spending....... military, financial, human and scientific resources released in this way should be used to expedite the economic and social progress of the corresponding countries, as well as to abolish economic backwardness in various parts of the world".[65]

Gorbachev also released a statement on 15 January 1986, in which he addressed the issue of connection between disarmament and development. He also pointed out that without serious efforts to stop the arms race, there could be no solution to this problem, which was a major menace to mankind. He argued in favour of 'Disarmament for Development' instead of armament against development. His efforts for nuclear disarmament clearly reflected his concern for the improvement of the well being of the mankind. As mentioned, in 27th CPSU Congress, there was a proposal in the economic aspects of 'Comprehensive Universal Security' concerning the need to use part of the resources released as a result of military budget cuts to improve the living conditions of the people especially in the developing countries.[66]

Soviet Union also raised this question in UN, other forums and in meetings with top leaders of the world. In September 1987, Gorbachev emphasised international security relating to the UN's role in disarmament for development. It was stated that Soviet Union stood for the creation of a Special UN Fund of humanitarian cooperation which could be established with voluntary state and private donations from the, funds released by defence cut.[67]

Gorbachev and late Rajiv Gandhi, the then Prime Minister of India, also stressed on this aspect of security in November 1986 and November 1988. In this connection, their joint statement issued on November 20, 1988, said, "The resources saved as a result of disarmament should be transferred for development purpose. The decision taken by UN Conference on Disarmament and Development should be implemented". As discussed in December 7, 1988, Gorbachev's address to the 43rd Session of UN General Assembly announced the unilateral reduction of armed forces and sizeable quantity of conventional weapons to be completed within two years. He also persuaded USA to cooperate in this regard. Leaders of both the countries took several measures in the direction of reducing armaments.

In last part of his tenure, in November 1990, he signed a treaty with USA on the reduction of Conventional Forces in Europe (CFE) and started serious negotiations on reduction in nuclear weapons. Further, in July 1991, the Strategic Arms Reduction Talks (START), Treaty was signed in Moscow. This provided for significant reductions on the Soviet and American strategic nuclear arsenals (in 1993 START-II Treaty was signed by Russia and the United States) and exhibited his sincere efforts for a transition from the economics of armaments to the economics of disarmament. To materialize this objective, he took steps for cutting down defence budget and diverting resources spent on defence sectors to civilian sectors. A conversion plan was prepared within the framework of its economic reform and worked out for two or three defence enterprises during 1989 on an experimental basis. He firmly believed that the conversion process was needed for strengthening the economy of a nation as it had lot of benefits and at the same time it could be helpful for the development of third world countries. He also stressed on the submission of similar plans particularly by the major military powers to the United Nations and to set up an *ad hoc* panel of scientists to study the problems relating to conversion both for a general point of view and individual countries and regions.[68] His efforts not only brought a change in the Soviet Union but also, the entire world realized the futility of war and the need of disarmament.[69]

The 27th Congress, which dealt with security, contained a provision in its economic sphere concerning peaceful use of outer space and resolving global problems. On June 13, 1986, Soviet Union gave a proposal at the United Nations containing the reasonable alternative to an arms race in outer space – a stage by stage programme for international cooperation in the exploration of outer space for peaceful purposes. It also proposed UN to set up a World Space Organization, which could rationalize the efforts of states in this direction and help the developing countries to enter to rocket age. It stressed on the need of installing a type of an early warning system for the detection of the new problems facing the world economy.

Another important dimension in Soviet concept of 'Comprehensive Universal Security' was 'Ecological Security'. As discussed in the theoretical chapter, it is connected with people and nature rather than the States, peoples and individuals. The sensitive issues of nature protection and rational utilization of natural resources were raised in CPSU Congress before the introduction of *perestroika*. But during this period, new proposals and concrete decisions for the solution of these problems were taken which was highlighted in 27th Congress of CPSU. Considerable funds were also allocated for the protection of the environment – land, lakes, rivers, plants and the animal world. The 27th CPSU Congress contained a special section entitled, 'Environmental Protection and Rational Utilization of Natural Resources' which provided for the need to improve measures for nature protection by introducing production process, and the use in production of natural resources that reduce the harmful effect of nature.[70]

Special steps were taken for protecting water of Lake Baikal and the basins of Baltic, Caspian and Black Seas, and the Sea of Azov. At the same time, attention was paid to the measures for protecting the Arctic basin and the bodies of water in Soviet Central Asia Kazakhstan and improving the state of small rivers and reservoirs. Protective measures specially included the improvement of the operation of purification systems. For protecting air, special plans were taken to improve production process, equipment and transport facilities and quality of raw materials, faults and at the same time modern techniques were introduced for purifying industrial and other types of discharge.

Another major area of environmental protection where special attention was focussed was land protection. There was special provision in 12th Five-Year Plan (1985-90) for proper utilization of land and its protection from corrosion, landslides, desiccation and salination. Works were undertaken for protection of forests and forest products and new harmless methods were also introduced for protection of crops from pests and diseases.

Special measures were carried out to prevent the wastage minerals during their extraction and pressing and the protection of the environment of the economic zone and continental shelf of the Soviet Union.[71] Other important area where attention was directed was the problem of energy resources. In this context, Gorbachev said, "If no arrangement for energy sources are made, the energy crisis will become a catastrophe of global proportions...."[72]. Special care was also taken for the protection of national parks and protected areas and reproduction of flora and fauna.

In 1988, a new state committee on Environmental Protection, merging the responsibilities previously shared by nine different State Committees and seven ministers was created complete with tough powers to tackle the newly acknowledged environmental pollution crisis.[73] A number of measures were planned out to improve the state environment and the use of natural resources effectively. Soviet Union laid emphasis on economic method rather than administrative in managing these activities. Soviet Union and other CMEA members also worked in this direction. Special bodies like – the Council for Environmental Protection and the Council for Improving the Environment were set up within the framework of CMEA to manage and work out measures for environmental protection. Soviet Union also took steps to make developed and developing nations involved for the solution of this issue. It took initiative for arranging symposiums, discussions and joint research on this issue. In this connection, the Indian National Academy of Sciences and USSR Academy of Sciences signed an agreement in New Delhi in April 1985.

Soviet Union and other socialist countries also helped United Nations Environment Programme (UNEP) and World Health Organisation (WHO) those have been working in the direction. It also gave a proposal to European countries to work out a programme jointly for the resolution of this problem. Though the environmental protection movement is very popular in the West, so many organizations and NGOs are working in this direction, yet the efforts of Soviet Union under *perestroika* can never be ignored. The efforts of Soviet Union would have been more effective had the regime not been subjected to complex pressure, together with heightened popular expectations for 'solutions' which in fact taxed the administrative mechanism.

As noted, the economic security of Soviet Union did not yield expected result but the economic aspects of comprehensive universal security (international economic security) helped positively in solving global problems to some extent. But Soviet efforts were not that effective in this direction as USA and other Western powers responded half-heartily being guided by their interest rather than purely humanitarian concern. Even they were not keen to take some benevolent measures like helping the poor nations and spending sizable amount of money for solution of the global problems. Of course, economic consideration determines their approach towards other nations, which also brought obstacles for complete implementation of some proposals. Complete disarmament was not possible, as it required attitudinal changes of international actors, which was too difficult.

It was a fact that Soviet Union did not able to play that much effective role as it was hard pressed with its own problems. Its sinking economy coupled with collapse of CMEA and resistance from Gorbachev opponents impeded in realizing Gorbachev's much-desired dream of a New World. For the easy way of accepting the payment of debts and assistance to Third World countries during the early *perestroika* period aggravated the economic situation. Gorbachev even took some measures at the cost of the Soviet economy only to exhibit his noble desire for a peaceful world, which later on put him into problem. Really, it is difficult to bring a direct linkage between economic security during *perestroika* and the end of the Soviet system. In fact the collapse of the Soviet Union is attributed to various factors, which may not have been that harmful in separation but which are dangerous in sum total. The reasons for the decline of the Soviet system were the renunciation of forces both inward and outwardly as well as the encouragement of the secessionist movement in Soviet republic through *glasnost*.

However, there is a link between internal economic changes and Soviet Union's new policy during *perestrokia* as far as, in Soviet leader Gorbachev's opinion, the success of economic reform needed openness of discussion (Glasnost), and a positive international environment. As discussed, Gorbachev did not visualize properly the effects of internal and external freedom that were suppressed for a long time which ultimately led to fall of Soviet Union. Whatever might be the result of the economic security during *perestrokia*, but the worst critic of Gorbachev must admit that he was not only a pragmatist, but benevolent statesman who genuinely tried to overcome Soviet economy stagnancy by taking several measures as mentioned, and at the same time worked sincerely for strengthening world economy and establishment of New Economic Order.

References

1. John E. Edstorm, "The Soviet Economy: Growth, Decay and Reform", in George E. Houdson, (ed.), *Soviet National Security Policy under Perestroika*, (Boston: Unwin Hyman, 1989), pp. 74-75.
2. *Ibid.*, p. 79.
3. *Ibid.*
4. Michael Kaser, "Economic problems facing Gorbachev and his possible solution", in Christopher Donnelly, (ed.), *Gorbachev's Revolution,* (Coulsdon: Tane Information Group, 1989), p. 36. see also Padma Desai, *Perestroika in Perspective*, (London: I.B. Touris & Co. 1989), pp. 8-25.
5. Padam Desai, *op.cit.,* p. 25.
6. Jan Åke Dellenbrant, "Restructuring the Economy", in Ronald J. Hill and Jan Åke Dellenbrant, (eds.), *Gorbachev and Perestroikia: Towards a New Socialism*, (England: Edward Elgar, 1989), p. 86.
7. Biswajit Dhar " Economic Reforms in the USSR: The Emerging Scenario", in *RIS Digest,* Vol. 7. No. 2-4, (Dec. 1990), p. 40.
8. *Izvestiya,* 21 November, 1986.
9. Jan Dellenbrant, *op .cit.,* p. 94.
10. *Pravda*, 8 June, 1988.
11. *RIS Digest*, Vol. 7. No. 2-4, (1990), p. 41.
12. Nikolai Shmelyov, *Perestroika as seen by an Economist*, (Moscow: Novosti Press, 1989), p. 16.
13. *RIS Digest*, *op.cit.*, p. 41.
14. Abel Aganbegyan, *The Challenge: Economics of Perestroika*, (London: Hutchinson, 1988), p.156.

15. *RIS Digest, op.cit.*, p. 42.
16. Sutela Pekka, *Economic Thought and Economic Reforms in the Soviet Union*, (New York: Cambridge University Press, 1991), p. 164.
17. *RIS Digest*, *op.cit.*, p. 43.
18. *Pravda*, 14 June 1990, p.1, 16 June, 1990, pp.1-2.
19. Stephen White, *Gorbachev and After*, (Cambridge: Cambridge University Press, 1992), p. 134. For Shatalin's presentation of his proposals, see *Pravda*, 18 September, 1990, p. 2 and for the proposals themselves, *Perekhod K-rynku,* (Moscow: Arkh-angel'skoe, 1990).
20. *Ibid.,* p.135.
21. Roland Goetz, "Structural Legacy and Systemic Transformation in the Former USSR: Experience with Perestroika", *Aussen Politic*, No. 11, (1994), pp.171-72.
22. Akio Kawato, "The Soviet Union: A Player in the World Economy?", in Tsuyoshi Hasegawa and Alex Pravda, *Perestroika: Soviet Domestic and Foreign Policies*, (London: Sage Publications, 1990), p. 129.
23. *Moskovskic Novosti*, 1987.
24. Akio Kawato, *op.cit.*, p. 129.
25. *Ibid.,* p. 130.
26. David Dyker, "Economic Relations with the rest of Europe' in Neil Malcolm (ed.), *Russia and Europe: An end to confrontation*, (London: Printer Publishers, 1994), p. 188.
27. Alexi Lebahn, "Political and Economic Effects of *Perestroika* on the Soviet Union and its Relations to Western Europe and the West", *Aussen Politik*, (March 1988), p. 118.
28. David Dyker, *op.cit.*, p. 189.
29. *Ibid.*, p. 190.
30. *Ibid.*, p. 190.
31. *The Baltic Independent* (Riga) 28 February-5 March 1992, p. 2.
32. Vladislav Malkevich, "East West Economic Relations and their Prospects", *Foreign Trade*, (1/1989), p. 27.
33. Akiokawato, "The Soviet Union: A Player in World Economy", *op.cit.*, p. 132.
34. Seppo Ruoho, "Soviet Foreign Trade and Joint Ventures", in Vilho Harle and Jyrki Livonen (eds.), *Gorbachev and Europe*, (London: Printer Publishers, 1990), p. 183.

35. ECU – European Currency Unit of the Common Market, 1.0 ECU=$1.2 in early April 1993.
36. Valeri Gorsky and Daniel Linotie, "Outlook for USSR – EC Future Relations', *Foreign Trade,* (USSR), 7/1991, pp. 14-17.
37. Alexsandir Loshakov, "Information on USSR – European Communities Regular Session of the Commission", *Foreign Trade* (USSR), 7/1991, p.18.
38. Friedrich Levelik, "CMEA Integration: Stagnation or a new beginning?", in Michael Friedl¬nder (ed.), *Foreign Trade in Eastern Europe and the Soviet Union*, (Boulder: Westview Press, 1990), pp. 56-57.
39. Jürgen Nötzold, "Several European Economic Blocks? The Future Significance of the COMECON", *Aussen Politik*, Vol. 3, (1989), pp. 286-287.
40. *Ibid*, p. 278.
41. Gribsch Hetal, "Advanced Reforming Countries might reach end of Recession", *Forschungberichte*, No. 184, (July 1992).
42. *Pravda*, 8 March, 1987.
43. Akio Kawato, *op.cit.,* p.134.
44. Nirmal Kumar Chandran, "Russia's Sinking Economy: External Dimensions", *Economic and Political Weekly*, May 15, (1993), p. 998.
45. K. P. Mishra, "Gorbachev's New Thinking: An Overview", in V. D. Chopra (ed.), *Mikhail Gorbachev's New Thinking in Asia-Pacific*, (New Delhi: Continental Publishing, 1988), p. 165.
46. Michael Yahuda, *The International Politics of the Asia-Pacific, 1945-95*, (London: Routledge, 1996), p. 180.
47. *Ibid,* p.180.
48. *Ibid,*
49. David Dyker, op.cit., p. 191. See also Igor Doronin, "On the way to the currency market", *Foreign Trade* (USSR); 7/1991; pp. 35-37.
50. *Ibid,* p.192.
51. Akio Kawato, *op.cit.*, p.137.
52. Robert F. Miller, *Gorbachev at the Helm*; (London: Croom Helm, 1987), p. 222. See also Vladimir Sobell, "Mikhail Gorbachev takes change of the CMEA", *RFE Research*, RAD Background Report/ 146 (Eastern Europe, 20 December 1985).
53. Peter Knirsch, "Economic Relations between Soviet Union and Eastern Europe and their implications for East West Relations",

in Kinya Nijscki (ed.), *The Soviet Union in Transition*, (Boulder: Westview Press, 1987), pp. 112-118.

54. Charles Gati, *The Bloc that Failed*, (Indian Polis, Bloomington: Indian University Press, 1990), p. 130.
55. *Foreign Trade* 1992/2, p.40; prepared by Goskomstat, with corrections by the Ministry of Foreign Economic Relations (MOFER).
56. Ernest Obminsky and Andrei Bugrov, *InternationalEconomic Security: A Major Factor of Peace*, (New Delhi: Allied Publishers, 1988), p. 3.
57. *Ibid,* p. 5.
58. Article 27 establishes the voting procedure at the UN Security Council.
59. Vadim Zagladin, *Peace the Only Option*, (New Delhi: Allied Publishers, 1987), p. 107.
60. *Ibid.*
61. *Sixth Ministerial Meeting of Group -77*, PC/77(VI)/2, 8 April 1987, p. 10.
62. *Pravda*, 10 June 1987.
63. Ernest Obminsky and Andrei Bugrov, *op.cit.*, p. 93.
64. *UN Document*, A/ 142/386, E/1987/144, 7 July 1987, pp. 2-3.
65. *Pravda*, 10 June 1987.
66. Ivan Kovalenko, "Soviet Proposals", in Ivan Kovalenko and Rais Touzmohammadov, (eds.), *Disarmament for Development*, (New Delhi: Allied Publishers, 1989), p. 134 .
67. *Ibid.*, p. 137.
68. *Ibid.*, p. 138. See also A. Ozhegov, E. Rogovskii and I. Laramenko, "Conversion of the Defence Industry and Transformation of the Economy of the USSR", *Problems of Economics*, Vol. 34. No. 6, (Oct. 1991), pp. 790-94.
69. Nikolai Gnevushv, *Disarmament for Development*, *op.cit.*, p. 171.
70. Nikolai Nikolsky, *The Philosophy of New Thinking and the Soviet Initiatives*, (New Delhi: Allied Publishers, 1988), p. 146.
71. *Ibid.*, p. 147.
72. M. S. Gorbachev, *Perestroika: New Thinking for our Country and the World*, (London: Fonanta/Collins, 1987), p. 131.
73. Martin Couch, *Revolution and Evolution: Gorbachev and Soviet Union*, (New Delhi: Prentice Hall, 1990), p. 203.

6

Humanitarian Aspects of Security

Humanitarian aspect of security was the soul of the concept of security during *Perestroika*. It is a fact that humanitarian concern was one of the important factors which motivated Gorbachev for developing his concept of 'comprehensive universal security' which tried for ensuring peace and security in the world. As already discussed in previous chapters, various aspects of security are inter-related and humanitarian elements are present in all the aspects of security. So this chapter deals with the necessity of humanitarian security; main proposals of the humanitarian dimension of security during *Perestroika* phase; its impact on strengthening the peace and security of the world and particularly the security of the erstwhile Soviet Union.

6.1. The Rationale Behind Humanitarian Security

Humanitarian aspects of security, which stressed on inter-state relations and contact between people as well, believed that normal relations were not possible without mutual trust and understanding. A rational solution to the humanitarian problems, solution of global problems by international laws could be possible only through such relations. It also tried to change the attitude of the West by following a course of all round development of such cooperation on a sound basis, earlier who alleged socialist countries and particularly Soviet Union as the violator of humanitarian principle. Thus, it provided no space to USA and the

West to use this human rights issue against Soviet Union as the interferer in the internal affairs of other countries as it did earlier.

The most important issue relating to this aspect of security was the issue of human rights. The UN Charter has incorporated human rights and fundamental freedom as the basis of Universal international security system. The preamble of the UN Charter stresses "to reaffirm faith in fundamental human rights, in the dignity and worth of the human person, in the equal right of men and women and of nations large and small". Article 1 of the UN Charter proposes "to achieve international co-operation in solving international problems of an economic, social, cultural or humanitarian character, and in promoting and encouraging respect for human rights and for fundamental freedoms for all without distinction as to race, sex, language or religion".[1] These and other provisions in the UN Charter integrate human rights and humanitarian problems with the problem of maintaining peace and security and with economic and social issues.

The Universal Declaration of Human Rights says in this respect that recognition of the inherent dignity of every member of the human family and his equal and inalienable rights is the basis for freedom, justice and universal peace, that disregard of human rights has led to acts of barbarity that outrage the conscience of mankind; that the creation of a world in which man will have the freedom of speech and conviction and be free of fear and need is proclaimed as a lofty aspiration of the people.[2]

The suppression of information, personal dignity and the fundamental human rights and freedoms in Soviet Union and other parts of the world made it necessary to incorporate these humanitarian aspects in the Soviet model of security during *Perestroika*. Gorbachev had rightly said, "The world can't be considered secure if human rights are being violated".

6.2. Major Dimensions of Humanitarian Security

The humanitarian aspects of security concerned with Soviet human rights policy both as a domestic issue and the issue of foreign policy.

6.2. (i). Domestic Dimensions

In the domestic sphere, Gorbachev called for democratisation and *glasnost* (openness). He encouraged people for open debates and discussions in various fields by giving adequate freedom to them. During this *Perestroika* phase, there was radical changes in the internal dimensions of social security which encompassed political, economic and socio-cultural fields. As it was explored in early chapters, these fields had importance since it was key to all other issues and problems including humanitarian ones. Soviet leader Gorbachev realized that economic conditions of human life were the material basis for the solution to the humanitarian problems. Humanitarian issues could hardly be solved if the essential conditions for a decent life were lacking in Soviet Union. So, he took adequate steps for providing a decent living to the people by improving Soviet economy.

An open political culture by introducing multiparty system, freedom to the people to participate in the process of election, open discussions with people and leaders for the solution of the political problems also added a human face to this concept of security.

Human rights reforms which were started by Khrushchev got prominence by Gorbachev who tried seriously for an open democratic society. Thus Stalin's close society where human rights were violated, controversial books were banned, art and literature critical of Communist ideology were suppressed, was replaced by a new open culture free from the violation of human rights, suppression of information. On the other hand, there was dignity of the individuals, respect for socio-cultural diversity and autonomy of nationalities and ethnic groups, promotion of creative and innovative spirit in educational, scientific and intellectual activities, recognition of the democratic rights of trade union and professional groups, in order to sustain the foundation of multi-nationality socialist federation as a moral entity of enlightened and free citizens.[3]

6.2. (ii). External Dimensions

In the foreign policy sphere, the focus was on dealing with human rights issues in USSR and its influence over other countries.

The human rights issue developed in 1975 Helsinki Conference on Security and Cooperation in Europe and its follow-up meetings. But the actual CSCE negotiations took place in Geneva between September 1973 and July 1975. The Conference approved the Final Act on August 1975. The Final Act was not a treaty and the signatories were not bound to comply with the provisions but it helped in improving the relations between East and West and set the agenda for the next decade of East-West relations, particularly in the sphere of human rights.

Besides the political provisions, Basket I also contained a general human rights provision which included "respect for human rights and fundamental freedoms including the freedom of thought, conscience, religion or belief for all without distinction as to race, sex, language or religion". Basket III also contained numerous humanitarian provisions including "freer movement and contacts" among the people of Europe, "contacts on the basis of family ties", "reunification of families", interactions between citizens of different States for the purpose of marriage, expansion of tourism and cultural contacts.[4] It also covered "freer and wider dissemination of information of all kinds" including wider circulation of printed information, films and broadcasts. As discussed, Soviets had come to Helsinki for an agreement on the Commission. But the US linked up it with human rights agenda. Though the USSR accepted the 'trade off' of the human rights provision of this Act for several reasons but the Soviet and American leaders characterized the Final Act's impact on human rights in different terms.[5]

In the post Helsinki period, Soviet Union changed its defensive position on human rights to offensive in Belgrade (1977), Madrid (1980-83), Ottawa (1985) and Vienna (1986-89) Conferences and started blaming the West for violating human rights by ignoring the right to speak of the commoners by the people those in power. Again the Soviet Union considered the political freedoms of the West was meaningless as there was no social and economic rights like employment, housing and healthcare for the people which was stressed by the socialist systems. The Soviets insisted that any review of compliance with Basket III that enquired Soviet treatment of national minorities, freedom of religion, emigration policy and political dissident must be linked up with the racial discrimination prevalent in USA, the treatment of the American Indians, restriction on immigration into US and the situation in northern Ireland including imprisonment for political reasons.[6]

However, under Gorbachev, real changes were brought in the humanitarian sphere of Soviet policy, which weakened the human rights campaign of the West. The 27th CPSU Congress which dealt with the concept of 'Comprehensive Universal Security' contained specific proposals on the subject. The first proposal concerned "co-operation in the dissemination of the ideas of peace, disarmament and international security; greater flow of general objective information and broader contact among peoples for the purpose of learning more about one another, reinforcement of the spirit of mutual understanding and concord in relations between them".[7]

This proposal was elaborated in numerous UN documents on human rights. It considered the 'enemy image' was one of the chief obstacles in the way of dialogue and contact between Soviet Union and US. It ruled out the possibility of peaceful co-existence, with an enemy which it considered impossible and incorrect without changes in the attitudes of the people. In fact, the 'enemy image' did not promote restraint and civilized behaviour in international relations, but instead hampered international contacts and co-operation.[8]

The 'enemy image' was created by the mass media of both the countries. The US media deliberately created distorted, outrageous pictures of the Soviet People which was reported by the American TV network ABC on February, 1986. The editor in chief of *Die Zeit* – Marion Donhoff said that "US cultivated vulgar anti-communism and blamed Russians for all ills".[9] In this context, Gorbachev wrote:

"Some people in the United States, it turns out, 'need' the Soviet Union as an enemy image. Otherwise it is hard to understand some films, the inflammatory American broadcasts from Munich, the spate of articles and programs full of insults and hatred toward the Soviet people. All this dates back to the forties, if not earlier".[10]

George Kennan, a well-known diplomat of US also expressed his irritation in the same way:

"This endless series of distortions and over-simplifications; this systematic dehumanization of the leadership of another great country, this routine exaggeration of Moscow's military capability and of the supposed inequity of Soviet intention, this momentous misrepresentation of the nature and the attitudes of another great people- and long suffering people at that, surely tried by the vissitudes of this past century, this ignoring of their plight, their hopes- yes, even after their illusion (for they have their illusion, just as we have ours, an illusion too deserve respect). This reckless application of the double standard to the judgment of the Soviet conduct and our own, this failure to recognize, finally the community of the many of their problems and ours as we both move inexorably in to the modern technological age, and this corresponding tendency to view all aspects of the relationships in terms of a suppose total and irreconcilable conflict of concerns and of aim. these, believe me, are not the marks of the maturity and discrimination one expects of the diplomacy of a great power; they are the marks of an intellectual primitivism and naivity unpardonable in a great government".[11]

The Soviet media were also not free from campaign against the USA. It potrayed US as an 'imperialist wolf'. It considered capitalist system as a rotten system which only produced unemployed people, oppressed national minority and greedy capitalist. This attitude of Soviet Union twined with ideological biases also fuelled mutual acquisition, suspicion and hostility. But during Gorbachev, under *perestroika*, there were dramatic changes in the traditional image that was formed over the decades in American public opinion of the Soviet Union, Soviet society and culture.[12]

As discussed, Soviet Union and America took adequate steps for maintaining peace and security of the globe. Both the powers realized that there must be maximum truth in depicting the other side and oneself, that full information be made available and that its deliberate distortion and concealment not be allowed. They also prepared mentally and gathered the courage to picturise the other side and oneself in a proper manner.

Under *Perestroika*, direct personal contacts in the field of culture on both individual and collective basis, as well as contacts between cultural institutions, associations of creative and performing artists and other organizations were encouraged in order to increase the opportunities for their citizens to acquaint themselves directly with creative works with other countries.[13]

During this phase, Soviet Union also developed healthy relationship with other powers like Great Britain, France, Germany, etc. In 1989, Soviet Union and Britain held conferences on humanitarian questions and human rights which produced a major breakthrough towards new frontiers in the European process. These problems were also addressed in Moscow Conference in 1991. Soviet Union and Britain took joint efforts for the solution of the global problems particularly economic and environmental issues. Soviet Union expressed its willingness to faithfully abide by existing agreements and cooperation in international programmes.[14]

Gorbachev's visit to France, Germany, other European powers and Eastern Europe and talks on various issues for maintaining peace and international security were positive in this direction. There was the second proposal in the humanitarian sphere dealt with the "extirpation of genocide, apartheid, advocacy of fascism and every other form of racial, national or religious exclusiveness and also discrimination against people on this basis."

The above mentioned facts were instruments for creating hatred and confrontation. Soviet Union believed that there was no place in civilized society for racism, nationalism and chauvinism. USSR opposed racism in South Africa where black majority was suppressed.

As discussed earlier, Soviet Union championed the cause of Palestine liberation movement and raised voice against the attacks and oppression of Indians, Turks and other Asians in Western Europe.[15] Soviet Union also took steps for doing away with revanchism and terrorism which was common during 70's and 80's. As far as Soviet progress on these aspects of security were concerned, Soviet Union under *perestroika* took adequate steps in this respect. Restriction on the study and practice of religion were being removed. Citizens of Soviet Union were allowed to go through the Bibles and in the Fall of 1988, Moscow ended the Soviet ban on the teaching of Hebrew.[16]

During this phase, citizens including Jews were allowed to leave the Soviet Union to settle abroad. In 1986, during Gorbachev period, a new procedure for considering application for leaving the country to reunify with family members were enacted. Gorbachev in December 1988 speech to the United Nations pledged that in 1989, laws would be enacted for guaranteeing freedom of expression and freedom from religious persecution. He added that laws prohibiting emigration of a person with knowledge relating to the secrets of the Soviet security would be modified to include 'strictly warranted time limitations'.[17]

The response of the United States was positive during Gorbachev's time. Soviet Union tried its best to involve US in solving the above mentioned problems and suggested to USA not to support fascism and revanchist forces of Germany as it would destabilize the peace and security of the world. US approval for participating in Moscow Conference of 1991 amply proved it.

The third proposal of the humanitarian aspects of security dealt with "extension while respecting the laws of each country – of international co-operation in the implementation of the political, social and personal rights of people. This proposal was also closely linked up with the fourth proposal, "The decision in a humane and positive spirit of questions related to the reuniting of families, marriage and the promotion of contacts between people and between organizations".[18]

6.3. Impacts of Humanitarian Security

As discussed, the incorporation of these principles of human rights and freedom into the Soviet security system during *perestroika* phase stemmed from the UN Charter. Soviet scholars during 80's argued that Soviet Union tried its best to observe the principles of the universal declaration of Human Rights but it was deliberately violated by USA and the West. Soviet Union also guaranteed socio-economic and personal rights to the people and ensured equalities of all nations and nationalities by law. But USA and West interfered in the internal affairs of Soviet Union taking the plea of the violation of human rights which was the prime cause of the bitter relationship between the two power blocs.

In this context, Victor Chebrikov, a member of the politburo of the CPSU Central Committee and the chairman of the Committee of State Security said:

"Lately, certain quarters in the West have been repeated by bring up the subject of alleged violations of political and personal rights and freedom in the Soviet Union, and put forward groundless demands and claims. All this is designed to fire up the anti-social ambitions of some renegades among the Soviet citizens, to push them towards openly hostile activities. All those who oppose socialism are revered; things have gone so far that even hardened criminals are now taken under protection. What are the rights demanded for these people by their Western advocates? The right to break the laws of our socialist state with impunity. We shall never give such right to any one".[19]

Whatever might be the claims of the Soviet Union pertaining to the achievements in the direction of humanitarian aspects of security, but in actual practice, there was suppression of political and personal rights of the people of the Soviet Union and other parts of the world. During this *perestroika* phase, Soviet Union genuinely tried to ensure socio-economic rights such as right to work and right to housing for its citizens. The provisions of the international covenant on economic, social and cultural rights were formalised not only in the constitution of USSR, but also in the fundamentals of labour legislation. Soviet Union concluded bi-lateral agreement with most socialist countries for ensuring their social security and social insurance.

The international legal terms relating to the political and personal rights of citizens were also manifested in the legislation of Soviet Union.[20] A Commission for humanitarian cooperation and human rights were set up in 1987 within the framework of Soviet Committee for security and cooperation in Europe for ensuring the implementations of the Helsinki Final Act. In 1988, a delegation of the international Helsinki Human Rights Committee visited the Soviet Union for exchanging experiences in the field of observance of human rights. There was exchange of ideas between the Western delegates and the representatives of Ministries and departments of USSR. As discussed, Soviet Union revisioned certain norms of internal legislation in order to promote the process of democratization and to provide political, social and personal rights to the people.[21]

During Gorbachev period, Yelena Bonner, Andrei Sakarov's wife, was permitted to go to the West for eye and heart treatment. Sakarovs were released from the exile in Gorky and permitted to return to Moscow. He was also allowed to address an international conference on disarmament where he expressed his viewpoints and appreciated Gorbachev's reforms and initiatives taken in this field.[22]

Criminal codes were revised to eliminate the crimes of "anti-Soviet defamation" (Article 190-191 of the RSFSR Criminal Code). A new glasnost law was drafted. Anatoli Shcharansky – the symbol of human rights and religious repression in the former USSR along with other prisoners were released from the prison under *perestroika*. Abuses of psychiatric treatment to political dissidents were exposed and stopped. Amnesty International started playing a significant role in Moscow. Soviet Union took genuine steps for reuniting of families, marriage and the promotion of contacts between people. Many Soviet-American married couples were permitted to re-unite in the West who were separated for years by Soviet policy. Marriages took place between the people of Soviet Union with Europeans and Americans.[23]

Soviet Union's relationship with socialist countries was cordial. Interaction with the leaders and parties of socialist countries was taken a new form. Inter-party meetings became frequent. Soviet leader Gorbachev gave importance to the cooperation for promotion of scientific and technological progress. The relationship with China was normalized. During this phase, equitable friendly relations with newly freed countries were developed. Soviet Union put adequate efforts for the solution of their debts and abolished the unfair international economic relations.

As was discussed, it maintained and developed relations with capitalist countries on the basis of peaceful co-existence. The fifth provision of the programme of the 27th CPSU Congress in the humanitarian aspects of security was the "strengthening of and quest for new forms of cooperation in culture, art, science, education and medicine". It was a fact as most of the Soviet experts argued that cultural cooperation was given importance before '*perestroika*'. Inter-governmental agreement on cultural cooperation was signed. There was also exchanges of artistic groups between Soviet Union and other nations.

After the Bolshevik revolution, books by authors from nearly one hundred and fifty nations had been published on Soviet Union. International film festivals were organized in Moscow and Tashkent. Soviet citizens were allowed to go on tourist trips to abroad; the same was true of the number of tourists who were coming to USSR. But in actual practice, it was bit different as ideological interpretation was the motivating factor for cultural cooperation. As discussed that was the reason for banning controversial books, art and literature critical of communist ideology.

State suppression in the cultural sphere was very much there in the pre-*perestroika* phase. But under *perestroika*, Soviet Union had undergone a tremendous change. *Glasnost*, i.e., openness, was introduced even for the purpose of cooperation. Soviet leaders tried to improve relationship with Western countries through cultural exchanges which led to 'cross cultural fertilization'. Soviet Union invited Westerners as juries to 15th Moscow International Film Festival, which took place in July 1987. Robert de Niro was named as the Chairman of the Jury in the feature film category.

Soviet Union embarked on a bold and sweeping campaign of Westernisation, not because like Peter the Great, they believed that appropriation of western technology and to a certain extent, western mentality was needed for the prosperity and survival of Soviet Union. Soviet Union also stressed on the changes in cultural leadership to get the support of 'intelligentsia', which was badly needed for the success of *perestroika*.[24]

A revitalized culture was also considered as an important instrument for indoctrinating the alienated youth to the existing mainstream ideas of Soviet Union, i.e. *perestroika*. In this context, Vladimir Maslov, a Central Committee lecturer and supporter of Gorbachev put it, "We have lost those who are now between the age of fifteen and thirty. We have to win them back, because there is no one besides them to carry out *perestroika*".[25]

Cooperation in the sphere of art, literature, science, education and medicine was given importance. People of USSR were given chance to meet the artists. Talent of Kandensky was recognized. Unexpected materials were available in print and electronic media. Controversial books were published. Writers, who could not publish their poetry two or three years ago – Semen Lipkin,[26] Aleksandr Kushner,[27] Inna Lisnyanskaya,[28] Yergeniy Reyn,[29] and Boris Chichibabin[30] - shared pages with controversial poets of various eras, from the 1920s émigré Don Aminado[31] to émigrés of the 1970's like Naum Korzhavin[32] and Joseph Brodsky.[33] Movies were being screened in theatres and aired on television and paintings were being exhibited that even five years ago would not have been reached their intended audiences.[34]

In the sphere of science and medicine, western technology and scientific innovation were introduced. There were joint efforts and exchange of ideas between Soviet Union European countries and America to develop science, technology and education, which could provide better living standard to the people of the world. There were also attempts for inventing new medicines for saving the valuable lives of the people from diseases like AIDS.

Under *perestroika*, Western response to the humanitarian changes in the Soviet Union seemed to be positive, but in reality they were bit skeptical and cautious. Even Western scholars interpreted it as a master game by Soviet leader Gorbachev to overcome its crisis and to strengthen its security and finally to dominate American and European nations. But whatever the interpretation of the West may be, Soviet leader under *perestroika* genuinely tried for a secured world where they thought the security of the Soviet Union would be automatically secured.

As discussed, humanitarian aspects of security tried to guarantee human rights to the people of Soviet Union and the world. It also explored the possibilities for cooperation in various spheres like culture, art, science, technology and medicine. So far as exchange of cultures and imitation of western value patterns were concerned, Prokhanov rightly argued that Soviet Union lost its identity by blindly copying Western models, scientific apparatus, rock groups, methods of conducting interviews in the press, administrative and scientific models. Such a copying deprived us of a sovereign path and gave to an inferiority complex.[35]

While formulating Soviet security policies, peculiarities of Soviet social structure, history and culture were not taken into consideration. On the other hand, '*glasnost*' in Soviet culture, art, literature and emphasis on human rights give enough liberty to the people. The Western press also emphasized on these aspects of security and considered Gorbachev as the torchbearer of the world by declaring him "Man of the Decade". In such a situation people those were suppressed for a long time started revolting against the state mechanism and tried to secede from the Soviet Union. Baltic Republic was first to follow this path. Had Gorbachev maintained slow pace so far as '*Glasnost*' was concerned in comparison to his *perestroika*, the people would not be so assertive and Soviet Union might not be disintegrated.

Third and fourth proposals as we discussed helped in developing good relations with the West. But compromising attitudes of Soviet Union, imitation of West, relying on western science and technology provided enough space to USA and other European powers to penetrate into the internal security of the Soviet Union which ultimately helped in the process of disintegration.

Though Soviet Union is no more and Soviet concept of security did not able to save Soviet Union from the disintegration, but the humanitarian aspects of security has relevance in Russia (the true successor of the USSR) and the world. Russia is determined to take steps to further human rights both at the international and national levels. Russia is trying its best to uphold personal rights and freedoms inside Russia and other parts of the world.[36] In the words of Foreign Minister Andrei V. Kozyrev:

"The Supreme Soviet of the Russian Federation has held for the first time hearings on international human rights and we will show persistent and keen interest in the strict, legal observance of the rights of our compatriots, including Russians and other nationalities. We cannot allow the consolidation of nations with the CIS (or those that did not become members of the commonwealth) to be accompanied by any infringement of minority rights. As participants of the CSCE and members of the United Nations, newly created states must assume a very concerned and responsible attitude towards minority populations. Otherwise – and this has already occurred – no alternative exists but to use the mechanism of U.N. or the CSCE for the settlement of national, ethnic and for religious conflicts. If minority rights are not maintained, Europe may face a stream of military conflicts and refugees that will not only disrupt the Helsinki process, so important to the cause of peace and stability, but will also drown human rights under its wake".[37]

So far as economic and cultural interests are concerned, the people's Congress of Deputies ratified the federal treaty for safeguarding the economic and cultural interests of every nationality in the territory of the Russian Federation, in accordance with national identity.[38]

Russia is also trying its best to keep friendly relations with West and other countries including East European countries. Andrei V. Kozyrev has rightly mentioned:

"The distinctive feature of our new era is that humanity is acquiring new dimensions in its developmental values common to all mankind dominate the century. Personal freedom and prosperity and the protection and development of the human being will be one of the cornerstones of international security. The "human dimension" of international relations reflects a transformation of the global international and political system toward the humanization of international politics".[39]

References

1. *Charter of the United Nations*, (New York: United Nations, 1996), p.1.

2. See for example, Nikolai Nikolsky, *The Philosophy of New Thinking and the Soviet Initiatives*, (New Delhi: Allied Publishers, 1988), p. 40.
3. Rashid-ud-din Khan, "*Perestroika*: An Overview", *World Focus*, (October-December 1988), pp. 3-4.
4. Zwick Peter, *Soviet Foreign Relations Process and Policy*, (New Jersey: Prentice Hall, 1990), p. 278.
5. Ibid, p. 279. For more details, see Vojtech Mastny, Helsinki, *Human Rights and European Security: Analysis and Documentation*, (Durham, NC: Duke University Press, 1986), pp. 9, 88, 89.
6. *Ibid*, p. 280.
7. M. S. Gorbachev, *Perestroika*: *New Thinking for Our Country and the World*, (London: Fontana/ Collins, 1987), p. 31.
8. Andrei Mellville, *How We View Each Other. The Enemy Image and New Political Thinking*, (Moscow: Novosti Press, 1988), p. 10.
9. Vadin Zagladin, *Peace, the Only Option*, (New Delhi: Allied Publishers, 1987), p.116.
10. Gorbachev, *Perestroika*, p. 217.
11. George F. Kennan, *The Nuclear Delusion: Soviet-American Relations in the Atomic Age*, (New York: Pantheon Books, 1982), p. 197.
12. Andrei Mellville, *op.cit.*, p. 23
13. "Soviet Culture in the World", *International Affairs*, No. 2, (February 1990). Report of a discussion at the Guest Club of the Journal by a panel of experts which included Chinghiz Aitmatov, Oleg Chernyshev, Nikolai Gubenko, Yuri Khilchevsky, Vladmir Lazarev, Naslediye, Nikolai Petrov, Igor Vinogradov and Galina Volchek, p. 12.
14. Visit of Mikhail Gorbachev to Great *Britain,* (Moscow: Novosti Press, 1989), pp. 24- 29.
15. Vadim Zagladin, *op.cit.,* p. 118.
16. Esther, B. Fein, "Hebrew teaching in Russia seen as means to win West", *New York Times*, November 4, 1988, p. A 8.
17. Robert S. McNamara, *Out of the Cold*, (New York: Simon and Schuster, 1989), p. 126.
18. Gorbachev, *Perestroika*, *op.cit.*, p. 231.
19. Quoted in Vadim Zagladin, *op.cit.*, p.121.
20. *Geneva, Reykjavik, Washington Moscow Summits*, (Moscow: Novosti Press, 1988), p. 93.

21. *Ibid.,* pp. 93-94.
22. Zwick Peter, *op.cit.,* p. 280.
23. *Ibid.,* p. 280.
24. John Dunlop, "Soviet Cultural Politics", *Problems of Communism,* (Nov-Dec. 1987), pp. 34-56.
25. Quoted in *Ibid.,* p.35.
26. In for instance, *Oktyabr'*, No. 8, 1988, pp. 118-120.
27. *Ibid.*, no. 6, 1988, pp. 82-85.
28. *Ibid.*, no. 11, 1988, pp. 130-32, in *Novyy Mir*, no. 6, 1988, pp. 6-7.
29. In *Novy Mir*, no. 2, 1988, pp. 93-95.
30. In *Druzhba Narodov*, no. 11, 1988, pp. 197-219.
31. In *Oktyabr,* no. 9, 1988, pp. 143-46.
32. *Ibid*, no. 8, 1988, pp. 143-50.
33. *Druzhba Naradov*, no. 8, 1988, pp. 226-236.
34. Josephine Woll, "Glassnost and Soviet Culture", *Problems of Communism*, Vol. 38. No. 6, (November-December 1989), p. 40.
35. John Dunlop, *op. cit.*, pp. 34-56.
36. Andrei V. Kozyrev, "Russia and Human Rights", *Slavik Review*, Vol. 5. No. 2,(Summer 1992), p. 291.
37. *Ibid.,* p. 293.bid., pp. 291-292.
38. *Ibid.,* p. 288.
39. *Ibid.,* p. 293.

7

Security in New Russia

After the disintegration of Soviet Union in 1991, the Russian Federation (RF) became the true successor of Soviet Union. At the beginning, Russian military and political leadership was convinced that Common Wealth of Independent States (CIS) would develop into a powerful organization like former Soviet Union under the leadership of Russia. But it could not materialize as the CIS states decided their course of action according to their own political expediency, and developed their own security policies. With the Marxist and Leninist ideology in the trashcan of history, the RF drafted its own security concept. In May 1992, the RF consistently described its NSC (National Security Concept) as the highest security document. But after five and half years NSC was published. This NSC aimed at safeguarding national interests against external and internal threats. It includes not only military threats, but also political, economics, social, environmental threats. Current Russian thinking on National Security is that the state has military, diplomatic, legal, secret information, economic and other means at its disposal for achieving its objectives.[1] In the NSC, Russia's grand strategy, political, social, economic, environmental aspects of security are not neglected. Initially, Yeltsin and his government did not have a clear view of the direction of Russia's security policy because of lack of clarity and indecision. But on 5 March 1992, a decree 'On National Security' was issued, establishing Security Council of the Russian Federation (SCRF), an organ to deal with problems of internal and external security. Sergei Rogov, Deputy

Director of the Institution for American and Russian Studies of the Russian Academy of Sciences argued to form security policy, as there were differences with Ukraine on nuclear arms, the Crimea on energy deliveries. Apparently, there was an urgent need to establish a mechanism for military-political decision-making. Therefore a National Security Council was formed in order to develop a security strategy. In May 1992, Colonel-General Igor Rodinov, Head of the General Staff of Academy presented an alternative to the official military doctrine that was published earlier that month. But all other members of the military leadership did not share his view. Marshal of Aviation Yevgeny Shaposhnikov who until recently served as Secretary of the SCRF (Security Council of the Russian Federation) criticised it saying that this doctrine was premature. First, a national security concept should be developed, which would include national interests and threats against national security. After that other subordinate documents related to the concept like military, foreign policy doctrines could be drafted.[2] Ultimately, in July 1994, the SCRF installed a commission in drafting the National Security Concept. The purpose of the NSC was to fill up the gap in the political vacuum that was created after the eclipse of the communist ideology to provide social, economic and environmental security to the people of Russia and all round development of the nation. Though in the present constitutional setup president has the power to decide the security policy of the Russia, yet it was delayed and finally President signed the first NSC on December 1997. The reason for its belated enactment could be traced to the long debate by the Russian elites about the course to follow in foreign and security policies; power struggle in the security organs; instability both in internal and external matters. After 1997, the external and internal situation of Russia went on changing after NATO's (North Atlantic Treaty Organisation) new strategic concept of 1999 and military intervention of this alliance in Kosovo of March-July of that year.[3] Western security policy was now considered to be a threat to Russia. Besides external threats, internal threats such as the conflict in Chechnya warranted a change in NSC. With much discussion, most of the amendments to the security policy that Gareyev, Army-General proposed were implemented in the new (draft) editions of the NSC on 10 January 2000. President Putin authorized the revised Russian security policy. In the 1999/2000 editions of the NSC, external threats were given priority but internal threats like socio-economic condition of Russia, political instability, religious extremism, ethno separatism, and their consequences were also given importance as they need immediate attention. In this changed situation, Russia was forced to change its objectives from international cooperation at global level as declared in 1997 NSC, to an emphasis on economic, political and military cooperation and integration with the CIS. It is due to the disappointment with the lack of cooperation from the West and its desire to protect its national interests and regain its super power status.

7. The Evolution of the National Security Concept in Russia

After the disintegration of Soviet Union, New Russia faced the problem in the field of security, as Marxist-Leninist ideological was no more relevant for providing a theoretical foundation for security strategy. In due course Russian security experts are guided by pragmatic thinking, and realized that a National Security Concept (NSC) would replace the jettisoned ideology. The NSC wider in conception includes military, political, economic and human security. From the NSC, Russia's grand strategy, concept of foreign, military and other policies would be derived. The National Security Concept of Russia came to the present stage through gradual development. Initially President Yeltsin and his advisors had no clear vision about the security policy of Russia. Hence, there was no hurry to draft a security concept for New Russia. In May 1992, Yeltsin issued decrees, which founded RF Ministry of Defence (MOD) and RF Armed Forces, as well as SCRF (Security Council of Russian Federation). In fact, this security structure opened the way for drafting the NSC. But the first issue of the document appeared at the end of 1997 as the period 1992-1997 was infested by political instability such as conflict between the executive and legislature and the first Chechen war, followed by civil wars in Tajikistan and Moldova within CIS and in the Balkans. The NSC of 1997 provided a positive view of Russia in international development and stressed on non-military socio-economic interests like security against terrorism, disasters, slow economic growth, and acts of war as threats to Russia. To improve these circumstances, Yelstin gave priority to cordial relationship with the

West; and Russia's policy was directed towards achieving international cooperation. But within two years the situation was changed as NATO's expansion posed a great threat to Russia and took a leading role in international security and started dictating terms to other nations using military force.[4] This belligerent attitude of NATO under the leadership of US forced Russia to change its security policy that receives an anti Western slant and puts importance on economic, political and military cooperation within the CIS. This perception was the result of pragmatism, which at the end of 1990's had become the leading trend in RF security thinking. This external development and internal problems were reflected in the NSC (draft) of 1999 and 2000, which aimed at reinforcing central authority and vesting power to the President of Russia to take final decision in guaranteeing national security.

7. Themes of Russian Security

Russia, in search for its security seemed to be more practical as the leaders and strategic experts of Russia tried to explore the destabilizing factors for the military, political and economic situation that were responsible for weakening Russia's security and tried to overcome these by formulating appropriate policies. The leaders of Russia have realized that national interest cannot be compromised on any situation and the prime task of national security is to protect this interest. Russian president, Yeltsin, in the second half of his tenure and present president Putin felt the need of a new security setup for Russia as Gorbachev's concept of 'Common Security' where the importance of power politics was marginalized was no more an answer for the present situation in Russia and global politics where US is spreading its hegemony by violating the norms of civilized society and fixing up the global agenda.

In the National security concept of January 2000, it was reflected that Russia's national interests are the sum total of the balanced interest of the individuals, society and the state in the political, social, economic, domestic, international and information spheres and in the military border, ecological and other fields; they are long term in nature, and determine the principal aims of the state, strategic and current tasks in its domestic and foreign policy[5].

In the military sphere, Russia's interest lies in defending its independence, its sovereignty and its state and territorial integrity preventing military aggression against Russia and its allies handling the dangers arising from wartime military operations and their consequences. For ensuring military security, Russia tries its best to raise the military potential of the state and maintain it at a sufficiently high level. It aims at the prevention of war and armed conflicts; the RF gives preference to political, diplomatic, economic and other non-military action if necessary to repel armed aggression, if all other means are exhausted. It keeps up a deterrence capability in the interest of preventing aggression on whatever scale, including when nuclear arms are used against Russia and its allies. It ensures that the Russian Federation must have nuclear forces for use against any aggressor state or coalition of states if its security is threatened. One of the most important strategic objectives of military security is the interaction and cooperation with the member states of CIS (Common Wealth of Independent States) for strengthening its security. For fulfilling strategic objectives, Russia introduced various reforms in the military field like modernization of its armed forces and command system; reorganization and large cuts in force structure. It also tried to improve the quality of its tactical and operational planning and thinking in order to meet the need of the 21st century.

In the political sphere, particularly in the domestic field, Russia's interests lie in upholding the stability of the constitutional system; eliminating the causes and conditions which contributes to political and religious extremism, ethno separatism, and their consequences by improving the poor system of organization of state power and civil society.

In the international field, Russia's interests lie in strengthening its position as a great power and as one of the centers of influence in the multipolar world; developing mutually advantageous relations, especially with the member states of the CIS and Russia's traditional partners.

At present Russia's prime task is to strengthen its political security both at domestic and international level. At domestic level, by improving the system of state power of the RF, federal relations, its local self-government, maintaining law and order and reinforcing political stability of the society; guaranteeing strict observance of laws by citizens, public servants, state institutions, political parties and social and religious organizations. At international level by reinforcing important machinery for multilateral management of world political processes, above all under the jurisdiction of the UN Security council; defending the legal rights and interests of Russian citizens residing abroad; developing cordial relations with the members of the CIS and developing integration processes within the CIS in Russia's interest; creating a conducive atmosphere for making healthy relations with European states;adapting of existing arms control and arms reduction agreements to new conditions in international relations and if necessary concluding new agreements, primarily concerning confidence and security building measures[6].

With the drastic geo-political changes in Russia in 1990s, political scientists and experts put utmost importance on economic security, as it is essential for a nation's all round development, and also other aspects of security largely dependent on it. Russia's economic interests can be realized only on the basis of stable economic development by guaranteeing the population a high standard of living; reducing the gap between rich and an overwhelming under privileged majority; overcoming its scientific, technical and technological dependence on external sources; creating favourable external conditions for the steady development of Russia[7] Russia is trying seriously to strength its economic security through economic reforms by creating a favourable condition of its economy where by external and internal negative impacts can be neutralized by the viability of its socio-economic system as well as the availability of national economic reserves that can also ensure military and human security. For achieving its objective, the process of privatization and liberalization has been accelerated in Russia. Special emphasis has been given on market reforms, reforms in banking sector and systematization in the internal labour market. Russian leaders and economists have realized that stable economic development could be possible only by saving Russian economy from corrupt oligarchs close to government. Hence, appropriate steps are being taken to keep them out of power. Besides the internal changes in the economic sphere, Russia is moving fast to integrate into Liberal International

Economic Order (LIEO) to strengthen its economic position and to occupy an important place in the global economy. For ensuring it, Russia stresses more on economic cooperation with West, particularly with European Union. The decision taken by Russia to become a member of WTO (World Trade Organization) G8 and APEC(Asia Pacific Economic Co-operation) and to participate in G7 economic deliberations at Kananaski is an appropriate step in this direction. Efforts are also being made for organizing a common economic area with the member states of CIS, exporting human capital and natural resources like natural gas, huge amount of timber and paper, and ferrous and non-ferrous metals for generating revenues. The historic task of the present generation is to find a way to reinvest revenues from the export of raw materials and energy in machine building, metalworking and science-intensive products

With the eclipse of cold war the concept of security has increasingly come under scrutiny from scholars and practitioners alike. Security is no more restricted to well-being of the state; it is more concerned with welfare of the individual citizens or human beings. A conception of security centered on the sanctity of the individual may be called human security. In Russia's security framework, this human security has not been neglected. The localized threats* to human security in Russia are criminalization of social relations; the growth of organized crime; the rising scale of terrorism; ethno-centrism and chauvinism that lead to ethno-separatism and ethnic violence; the threat to physical health of the nation as seen in the rise in alcohol consumption and drug use and in the dramatic reduction in the country's birthrate and in average life expectancy; problem of the homeless and neglected children in Russia particularly refugees and displaced persons from the countries of the former Soviet Union. And one of the most important threats is violation of human rights and freedom of the people of Russia.

In addition to the above mentioned threats, global or international threats that affect the human security of Russia are the growth of ethnic nationalist and religious extremist; the growth of international terrorism, transnational organized crime, as well as illegal trafficking in drugs and weapons; and the rights and interests of Russian citizens and compatriots abroad.

At present, Russia is moving in a positive direction by handling local threats properly and putting adequate efforts to guarantee human security. Appropriate steps are being taken by governmental mechanism and police authorities to prevent crimes in any form by tightening security arrangement and giving punishment to criminals; curbing terrorism by shooting terrorists, destroying their hide outs and freezing their accounts; controlling ethno-separatism and ethnic violence by deploying military forces and dealing with them hard handedly. In Russia, Government, NGOs (Non Governmental Organizations) and voluntary organizations are trying seriously to improve health care of the people through medical facilities and proper controlling mechanism to reduce alcohol consumption and drug use that can increase birthrate and improve the life expectancy. The biggest and difficult task for Russia is how to solve the problem of homeless and neglected children. Efforts are being channelized for improving parents-children relations; removing physical abuse of children by parents through counseling and applying forceful method if necessary; providing helps like schooling facilities, houses from the state and charitable organizations; improving social relations in a broken family through imparting right education and bringing them to social mainstream through proper socialization. This needs constant efforts for systematic prevention of deviation in the home that give rise to the phenomenon of homeless and neglected youngsters on a mass scale. In case of human rights violations and freedom of the people of Russia, steps are being taken not to use extreme violent method in treating people of anti-social background if not necessary, and to provide freedom to the people for which various institutions concerned with it are getting rationalized and demoralized. For managing global or transnational threats, Russia is making sincere efforts like extending co-operation with other states concerned to interdict the export of terrorism and extremism; constructive co-operation with USA and West to chalk out a strategy for combating international terrorism; making collaboration with other states and intensifying search out operations inside and outside the country to combat illegal drug trafficking and the growth of organized crime; taking appropriate steps to protect the rights and interests of Russian citizens and compatriots abroad on the basis of international law and operative bilateral agreements[8].

From the above analysis, it is clear that for a proper understanding of the security of Russia, one needs to know its national interests, threat perceptions both internal and external, various problems and issues relating to it and measures taken and going to be taken for their solution. Hence, I would like to divide this chapter into four parts like Military Security, Political Security, Economic Security and Human Security for giving a fair treatment to it.

7.1. Military Security

At present, the problem of Russia's military security has been receiving much attention in the print and electronics media. Strategic experts and scholars are worried about the situation in the sphere. They argue in favour of increasing military capabilities of Russia to defend its present national interest and to meet the requirements of the future. A .I.Nikolaev, a famous author points out that Russia's military security needs a revolution not only for military security but also for the security existence, and development of Russia as a modern state.[9] In the present day troubled world that relies heavily on military security coupled with various other methods to resolve problems and disputes ranging from economic and political enslavement to direct armed aggression, military security is a major problem for Russia.

Russian Federation is in the ordeal of trouble, as external forces want to exploit its internal weakness, as it is not capable enough to ensure its security in case of external aggression. Further, Russia is also exposed to the impact of various negative process that are occurring in Europe, the Asia Pacific region and the middle and near East due to its unique geo-political position. One distinguished feature of Russia's situations is that many of the international troubled spots are located close to its border. Hence, its security assumes importance. To ensure it, Russia needs not only a modern, highly technological economy and a credible military organization, but also maximum use of the material, technical, intellectual moral and psychological resources of entire society. [10] But Russia was unable to meet this requirement as it inherited from the Soviet Union a poorly equipped large army, obsolete strategic concept, totalitarian military and above all a poor economy to sustain it. Hence, from the beginning Russia faced the tough task of military reform. Further Russia's primitive approach to first Chechen war and use of outdated military technologies demonstrated that Russia's armed forces were deeply troubled and completely ineffective. Of course, Russia did slightly well in the second Chechen war, which commenced in 1999, but it still has got to achieve victory. As viewed, there appears to be compelling factors that propelled Russia to accelerate the process of reforms. At the session of the Russian Security Council, on 9th November 2000, Russian President, Vladimir Putin said,

"Today we must place a full stop and take a final decision on Russian military reforms. On this depend the fate of the army and the security of Russia. Time has runout."[11] The Russian Security Council on 9th November was unanimous in its vote for the reform of the Russian military forces. But it was a huge task especially for the country that experienced the turmoil of changes for more than two decades. However, by the end of 2003, Russian military tried seriously to overcome it and entered the stage of systemic development. The first step in this direction was to adjust to domestic development. Steps were taken to reform the administrative system within the framework of military reform. 'On the military administrative division of the Russian Federation', signed by President Yeltsin on 27th July 1998, the military districts were transformed and got the status of strategic operational districts. This transformation was completed by January 2000. In the summer 1998, the 'Basics of State Military Build up Policy until 2005', was signed and the Military Doctrine of RF in April 2000, after this the role of coordinating body of the country's defence capability was given to the General Staff and territorial operational strategic commands. The MoD (Ministry of Defence) was to coordinate defence related relations between federal and regional authorities.[12] In the new power structure, the problems of federal–regional, civil- military relationship will be solved through the Security Council, its branches in the FDs (Federal Districts) and the leaders of the FDs.

One of the most important elements of military reform was to transfer to the territorial principle of command and control over the military and other services of the Russian Federation. At present, Russia is trying its best for establishing a unified system of technical assistance and logistics for the armed forces and all other forces and military formations and institutions of the Russian Federation that are responsible for the state's military security. It has become one of the important tasks of military construction.

Another important area of concern for Russia is the future developments of the armed forces. It is very important for Russia to access the external threats correctly. Andrei Kokoshin points out that there is a changing nuclear balance in the world and it is not possible to maintain the former number of nuclear weapons. Hence, Russia should take steps to reduce the number of warheads on strategic platforms, and on operational –tactical platforms by the end of 2007. There are no direct threats right now but Chechnya and Central Asia might pose threats in ten years. Almost surely we should take steps to increase the strength of the armed forces by 2010.

The Federal programmes, 'On Operation Readiness of the Territory of the Russian Federation for Propose of Defence until 2025', is also a unique document (about Russian military reforms) as it brought together military planning within the Federal Districts and programmes of socio-economic development in its regions. The new administrative structure of the state is directly linked with the military reform, which is to be implemented on the basis of universally integrated effectiveness-cost-feasibility. It is also linked to the reform of established strategic commands, Operation Task Force (OTF) and joint logistics, which are essential for new cost effective approaches to defence and security. As the function of the OTF depends on the harmonization of the demarcation zones between the military and other force structure, hence proper steps ara taken to maintain it and to cut short the disunity of power structure. For improving the quality of its tactical and operational planning, the Command and Control (C&C) system was improved. The RF military doctrine defines the functions in the following way:

"The command and control of the Military Districts (MDs) provides command for the inter service groups of forces of general purposes, as well as planning and organizing joint activities with other military units, formations and institutions responsible for

military security within the boundaries of their responsibilities and a unified system of military administrative demarcation of the territory of the Russian Federation".[13]

Steps were also taken for the optimization of the infrastructure of the armed forces, logistic support service in accordance with the country's economic capabilities. At the heart of Russia's military reform, efforts were made to introduce a joint and combined doctrine for territorial defence. This reform aimed at the preparation for a local conflict. The Deputy head of the Committee in Defence and Security of Russian Federation Council, Vladimir Kulakov stressed on it, as it is essential to meet the military requirement of Russia. At present, there is also a need for single technological policy for weaponry as there are 26 different types of anti-aircraft weapon and 20 types of communication control system.

One of the biggest weakness in Russian military setup is lack of well-equipped infantry divisions. In accordance with military guidelines of RF, there should be a minimum of ten fully equipped infantry divisions in a state of combat readiness to ensure the defence and security of the country and its allies and to obviate a threat to national interests. For ensuring it there should be proper arrangement for their training, financing and regular supply of equipments. An economic assessment of the required financial expenditure for proper maintenance of armed forces revealed that Russia could not afford to have more than 800,000 servicemen. According to Security Council data 2001, there were around 2.5million servicemen in all power structures. There were proposals to reduce it to a reasonable size. Even before that on 9th November 2000, the Russian Security Council was unanimous in its vote to reduce its man power by 600,00.The Secretary of the Russian Security Council Sergei Ivanov told reporters that the 3million strong army was a 'crushing burden' for the Russian economy.[14] In late 2001, President Putin confirmed the decision made by President Yeltsin. However, the dates for transition to the professional armed forces that had been voiced were different.

In April 2003, the Putin's Government endorsed a long-term reform plan that clearly demanded compromise from the generals. The structure of this reform can be divided into five parts.

Conscription – There was a proposal to reduce the length of compulsory military service from two years to one year. The first six months would be spent at a training centre. During the second six months the conscripts would be attached to regular unit. At the end of six months conscripts would get the opportunity to sign a contract.

A Bifurcated Army- Assuming the April 2003 plan is actually implemented, Russia will have two different armies. A front line military force capable of being deployed at a short notice and reserve force useful in the event of national emergency.

A foreign legion - A decision was taken to integrate CIS volunteers with regular Russian troops. Individuals who volunteered to serve, as contract soldiers will be given accelerated citizenship.

Women in combat- Russian army decided to open up positions for women to serve 'in combat roles.'

NCOs (Non-Commissioned Officers)- At one level, Russian government felt the need of the kind of NCOs that exist in the West. The purpose is that with a well-trained NCOs Corps, the army can solve both internal and external threats better.

The most important reform Putin introduced was the subordination of General staff to political elites. After the terrorists attack on the twin towers in New York City, Putin successfully used the technique to push the military in the direction he wanted. He informed Moscow's Generals and Admirals that it was a right line to support US's move to fight terrorism on a global scale.[15] Meanwhile, Putin and secretary of the Russian Security Council Ivanov seized on a surprise attack by Chechen rebels in Ingushetia to carryout a purge of top officials in the military and security agencies including General Kavashnin. Putin government also made drastic changes in the relationship between General staff and the ministry of defence to strengthen the military setup of Russia.[16] Most of the Russian analysts argue that military reform has failed in Russia and is unable to ensure the security of Russia. They point out to four explanations for the failure of the military reforms in Russia:

- A lack of consensus among military and political elites regarding the substance of reforms.
- Fear among political elites of military intervention in internal political power struggle.
- A shortage of financial resources.
- The ongoing conflict in Chechnya.

Besides the above explanations, other explanations for failed reform efforts are:

The militaristic origin and development of the Russian state and its structure and ideational legacies contributed to the structural privilege and operational autonomy offered to military leaders and institutions. The dominant position of both was reinforced by the coercion and autocratic rule. Overtime these features combined to produce a culture of defence and sacrifice to military needs and priorities. The weak response of political officials and the public to the repeated failure of military reform. The causes underlying Russia's military reform failure suggest that actors out side Russia can do little over the short term to alter incentives for actors inside the military establishment to support reforms.[17]

The need of the time is to encourage both foreign governments and members of the private sector to support long-term measures to create pressure for reforms. Proper training should be imparted to Russian journalists and analysts of civil-military relations to monitor and report on developments in military affairs, and the relationship between the military, government, and a society as a whole. Russia also needed well-resourced independent research organizations for the study of defence and security issues. Adequate emphasis should be given to funding for human rights education, which can create right awareness and public activism in favour of policy changes. At the Government level, foreign militaries should give Russian junior officers training and educational opportunities abroad, which can help them lateron to handle complicated situations more efficiently. Interactions with academic institutions outside Russia are essential as these can provide better exposures to theoretical and strategic experts and access them to alternative military histories and social science research. And the most important need is the change of the attitudes of the people of Russia as military innovations could be brought about through pressures from civil society.[18]

7.1. Russia's external security: In the military sphere, Russian leaders particularly Putin tried seriously to strengthen external security. After the terrorist attack of September 11, 2001, he decided to side with the United States and join anti terrorist coalition to fight against global terrorism. In the meantime, Russia's relation with the EU (European Union) improved. As old defence worries are becoming less relevant, new security concerns work to bring Russia and US together. Besides terrorism, proliferation of weapons of mass destruction and missiles are common concerns for both of them. Russian leaders are also trying their best to turn this antiterrorist alliance into a permanent security relationship binding Russia to the West. The need of the time is to chalk out a proper strategy to Russia's stage-by-stage integration within the West's security structure. Such strategy would involve several important directions.[19]

There is a need for strategic accommodation from both sides, involving the problem of missile defence, offensive arms reductions and post parity, post-deterrence strategic posture. There should be cooperation instead of confrontation in dealing with the sensitive issue of missile defence.

Russia –NATO relations should be revived on the basis of Founding Act. The 2002 Rome declaration should be the basis for Russia's membership in a new led security arrangement stretching from the Atlantic to the Pacific.

Russia and the EU should take the opportunities given by the 'Baltic chance' and turn Kalingrad into a laboratory for Euro-Russian cooperation not a wall against NATO. Further, Russia should be ready for security cooperation with the EU in peace keeping on the basis of Petersburg tasks.

There should be Euro –Russian industrial cooperation with emphasis on aircraft industry that can make room for Russia in the arms market and reduce the power of Iranian, Iraqi and Chinese lobbies in the Russian establishment. To tackle the complicated problems in the South and East, special emphasis should be given for stability building in the south and balancing to the east. At present, Russian leaders should orient the nation's policy towards realities rather than relics. Russia should play a European with the EU, a Eurasian with China and a fellow post-soviet with CIS states but with a proper strategy and caution as it is the only way out.[20.] After military reforms, at present the RF is adhering to two basic principles for ensuring its military security.

7.1. Principles of strategic Deterrence: In the security concept of Russia, protection of sovereignty and territorial integrity gets prime importance for which defensive measures have taken both at regional and global level. For fulfilling this objective strategic deterrence plays a key role in the security framework of Russia. The basic components of strategic deterrence are nuclear deterrence and General Purpose Force (GPF) deterrence. Strategic deterrence is used in peacetime and the period of threats before and after the outbreak of war, before the use of nuclear weapons. Deterrence on the global level is ensured by the threats of a massive use of strategic conventional or nuclear weapons systems that would cause heavy damage to the opponent with the costs that would be too great to outweigh any military gains. On the regional level, it is ensured by the threats of the use of conventional weapons, if necessary nuclear weapons, primarily non-strategic in any regional wars started against Russia or its allies. Strategic deterrence mechanism is based on deterrence actions by the RF Armed forces. Hence, with the reduction of RF armed forces, nuclear deterrence may be considered as an alternative to ensure the security of Russia.[21.] But it should be used if and when situation warrants.

7.1. Principles of Non-Military Action: The present Russia considers non-military action be it political, diplomatic and any other means adhering to principles of international law in the prevention of war and armed conflicts. As use of nuclear weapons, particularly Ballistic missiles and Weapons of Mass Destruction (WMD) have negative effects on the environment, hence non-military action is a good alternative to ensure military security in a peaceful manner. For this purpose, at present Russia gives priority to summit diplomacy, political and other means like reduction of conventional forces and strategic arms through various measures of arms control. In START-II agreement signed in 1993 and ratified in 2000, Russia's share of destroying nuclear arsenal and nuclear strike capability was much more than that of the USA and its allies. Further, Russia's support to chemical weapons convention, extension of Non-Proliferation Treaty (NPT) in 1995, and Comprehensive Test Ban Treaty (CTBT) in 1996 and earlier Conventional Forces in Europe (CFE) treaty singed in May 1992 with USA to reduce its ability to deploy troops and tanks on its borders, and to destroy military equipments are positive moves in this direction. But at present, the use of violence, lack of compromising attitude and above all unilateral power action by passing UN Security Council, force Russia to change its stand and resort to strategic deterrence. At present, security through non-military action could be possible if the leaders of USA and the West change their hawkish attitude and co-operate with Russia, other major powers and international organizations adhering to principles of international law, which seems to be a distant dream.

The need of the time is to maintain a striking balance between the two principles and apply the principles judiciously considering various factors like the situation, military requirements and the attitude of the opponents. However a study of the above factors needs scientific-methodological support, which Russia really lacks.

7.1. Scientific-Methodological Support for Unresolved Problems in the Military Security: At present even after reforms Russia's military security is not free from problems. It is not sufficient to neutralize threats to its security in different spheres including threats backed by military force. As security is closely related to state's material, financial, human and moral resources and Russia is not sufficient in those resources, hence, the security problems of Russia is getting multiplied. The most important problem is the absence of a generally accepted methodology for military-political forecasting and evaluation of military security of the Russia. Monitoring and evaluation of threats to military security of the RF are important task for RF Security Council, but it ought to address the task involving protection of the national interests from outside and inner military threats. The main task before Russia is the proper estimation of those threats. Their underestimation leads to pacifism and overestimation, to excess militarism, both of which may have negative effect on military security. In the former Soviet Union, military security and protection of natural interests were assured by the country's economic might, international prestige and military potential that was sufficient to neutralize both internal and external threats. But the present day Russia is unable to bear the same burden and in present international situations, it is impossible to seek to achieve absolute protection of state interests in all spheres. Hence, there is a need of proper strategy and a monitor mechanism to handle threats both internal and external effectively.[22]

Another important problem is how to define the essence and content of military conflicts likely to be connected against Russia. Lack of knowledge on these parts will impede in chalking out a proper strategy for the organization of an armed defence of the state, forms and methods of employment and training of the armed forces. Right approach with appropriate military policies can be formulated for strengthening military security if the military setup knows about the kind of war for which they are preparing for. In this connection, the necessity of developing a theory and practice that will help to plan organizational development of the military organization as a unified system is a next important theoretical and applied problem in the development of military organization, which is due to contradiction between the objective unity of the military organization and actually independent development of its components.[23] The development of state's military organization requires a proper methodology and set of methodological techniques that will consider factors like the economy of the state, science, culture, education and morale of the people in evaluating the military organization's ability to ensure military security. In the practical sphere, emphasis should be given to target planning of organizational development of the military organization of the state and its implementation. The most important problem of RF is state military security funding. The defence expenditure of Russia goes on changing from time to time, so also the ratio of defence expenditure for inner and outer security, Currently Russia spends 60% of its defence expenditure for outer security and 40% for inner security. A scientific methodology is required which will be helpful for assessment of financial resources for the military organization of the state and their distribution between its elements.[24] The new method of economic support of 21st century wars being constructed today should be based on the maintenance of the critical military might and readiness for a multi variant economic mobilization which will finally form a new paradigm.[25] Today, Russia struggles hard for strengthening its military security, as it is essential to regain its power and prestige in international politics. But its efforts are not directed properly as there is no unanimous opinion among leaders and strategic experts about the ways and means to strengthen its security structure. In fact, Russia's military security problems are fundamental and often philosophical which needs a holistic approach and ideological and methodological framework for investigation into trends in military security and organization development of the military organization of the state for its solution.

7.2. Political Security

Due to unique geopolitical situation of Russia, changes in global politics particularly after 9/11, and internal politics of Russia, political scientists and strategic experts have tended to focus on the changing paradigm of political security in Russia. Political security of Russia is no more defined as the 'reasonable freedom of action that enables Russia to pursue and achieve the objectives that it deems essential to defend even the potential and /or actual presence of primarily external threat to it in world politics'.[26] The main argument is that internal security of Russia and internal threats perception overshadow even its external security. Earlier notion of changing the external environment to increase political security with the internal status quo taken for granted is no more relevant as internal mechanism plays an important role in shaping and restructuring political security. In Russia, inefficient governmental mechanism, corrupt bureaucratic apparatus, nexus of criminals and mafias with government officials, abuse of power by local self-government, dominance of oligarchs in public life, and problem of terrorism are causes for political instability and internal security problem of Russia. During Yeltsin period, Russia's eighty-nine constituent republics and regions enjoyed as much autonomy as they can swallow and they were allowed even to go beyond central control. Devolution did not make Russia more democratic. Instead there was a tendency towards regional authoritarianism. Regional governors developed an unholy alliance with local financial elites and controlled regional industries, the press, courts, mass media and law enforcement agencies in their territories. One third of legislation passed by regional legislature was in conflict with federal law. Regional Governors did not try to increase government revenues. Rather they took various moves to reduce the flow of tax revenues to the federal budget. Regional leaders explored to find ways for retaining part of the revenue that could have been remitted to the centre. Powerful republics and regions negotiated for special tax breaks with federal centre. Tatarstan enjoyed the right to retain all the tax and export revenues collected on its territory as it had signed a bilateral treaty with the federal center.[27.] While stronger regions manipulated bilateral treaties in their favour, the weaker had to find other ways to avoid remitting taxes to the federal center. As per provision, federal budget only accepted money, so regicnal leaders made use of barter, money surrogate and tax offsets to withhold funds from the center and to help local enterprises to grow their business. They also encouraged corruption, nepotism, favouritism, and crimes from which regional local officials benefited.[28.] After Putin assuming power, he tried to redraw the federal map by establishing 'a single legal economic space'. By this he ensured that the regions were all subject to the same body of laws, abolishing the inequitable tax advantages enjoyed by some of them and removing protection and trade barriers other regions had tried to create between themselves and their neighbours. Putin also curtailed the powers of Governors by creating a new level of bureaucracy between the Governors and federal center. Under presidential decree, on 13 May 2000, the eighty-nine regions were administratively divided into seven 'Federal Districts' (FDs). These new units were to be headed each by a 'plenipotentiary representative' or 'envoy' appointed personally by the president. Many of the powers including security and law enforcement enjoyed by regional Governors during Yeltsin period were transferred to these presidential representatives. In the appointment, he preferred his loyal men who had backgrounds in army and security services. Thus the *Siloviki* or the *Chekisty* (siloviki, i.e. military or security; the Chekisty a near synonym used because many of Putin's appointees have roots in the KGB) play an important role and wield very considerable influence. Putin not only tightened his grip over the regional elites but also over the federal government through its numerous federal branches. In this way Putin wanted to increase government revenues to finance policy objectives such as the fight against crime and terrorism and to enlarge the influence of the central apparatus on constituent entities.[29] Another objective of the installation of plenipotentiary was to prevent and neutralize separatist movements. An important reform measure taken by Putin was to check the dominance of plutocrats, which was a barrier for Russia's transition to democracy. During Yeltsin time, the oligarchs dominated Russian public life through massive fraud and misappropriation particularly in the oil sector. The entire regions of Russia were being impoverished by the oligarch's theft. The loyalty of official was secured through bribes, kickbacks and charitable contributions. Some times pay offs were more direct. In Moscow, $50.000 was used to stall a criminal investigation. Oligarchs even controlled political parties and political movements.[30] But Putin's centralization of power helps in checking it to a larger extent. 'Siloviki' or the 'Chekisty' for top posts in Russia replaces oligarchs. Criminal proceedings started against corrupt oligarchs.

A major reform of Putin's government was to fight against terrorism. Putin was more serious about it after Beslan tragedy (the tragedy of the school siege in Beslan) in August 2004 and tightened the security and ordered to attack terrorists wherever they are found. In fact, Putin's efforts to reform the federal system are a positive step for Russian economy, political stability and corrupt free society. But it is doubtful that simply increasing central authority over the regions would result in improvement of the relations between the center and regional power. After the replacement of oligarchs, Siloviki do the same thing. In fact, they are the major obstacles to the development of a rule of law. Putin deliberately helps them when he thinks this to be politically both desirable and feasible. Putin does not in fact behave impartially.[31] The threat to attack terrorists and shoot them immediately has also created security problem for states bordering Chechnya. For example, Georgia foreign affairs experts are worried that Russia will violate Georgian sovereignty in the name of fighting terrorism.[32] The most vital point is that centralization of power demands guarantees for democratic development, in order to prevent totalitarianism. In this respect it is important to realize that since the introduction of the constitution of 1993, the powers of legislatures to check the executive (president and government) have been restricted. Hence, there is a need for democratization of various institutions of Russia for a strong and stable political setup.

7.2. External security: Internal and external dimensions of security are inseparable. But more attention is paid to external security when one deals with political security in world politics. In political security 'external-revisionism and internal-statuesque' doctrine has a strong influence.[33] In the rapidly changing world Russia has under gone multi-layer changes.

Firstly, there are general changes of global character. Russia is also affected by the process of globalization and trying to catch up with 21st century. Secondly, there are specific changes caused by post socialist transition taking place in central and East European countries including Russia. Thirdly, due to many negative results attained in reforms in Russia, there is a need for changing the model of transition. But each of the layer of changes is intertwined in such a manner that it is difficult to untie and focus on one layer without associating the other. Hence, creator of changes is facing challenges that are very difficult to solve.[34] However, Putin's programmes, policies and practical measures have created hopes that changes in the RF will materialize in the future. At the beginning of his first term, he brought positive changes in the foreign policy concept of 2000 to meet the needs of the country. As he was very critical about Yeltsin and Kozyrov's foreign policy concept of 1993 where importance was given to ' unilateral alignment with the West' 'paternalistic partnership' 'voluntary dependence' and subjugation to the West, so he deviated from that course and retained important components of Primakov's political orientation to overcome the problems that had loomed large over him and also for a strong and stable Russia. The concept openly criticizes US dominance in global politics and the role of US in fixing up global agenda. The security concept clearly states that 'this is a growing trend towards the establishment of a unipolar structure of the world with the economic and power domination of the USA'. It points out that western institutions and forums are playing important role in solving principal questions of international security bypassing the role of U.N Security Council. Russia advocates the preservation and strengthening of UN organization, OSCE (Organisation for Security and Cooperation in Europe) and other acceptable global and regional international organization. This is of course related to Russia's desire to strengthen its position in international politics. In the UNSC (United Nations Security Council) the RF possesses the right to veto and thus is able to block undesirable resolutions. This concept denounces the 'strategy of unilateral actions' applied by the USA and NATO as this practice 'destabilizes the international situation, provokes tension and the arms race and deepens international controversies, ethnic and religious cleavages'. This concept also warns USA not to go for the development of a national missile defence system, as it would force Russia to adopt 'adequate measures'.[35] The concept indicates that major threats to global peace and security came from 'the growth of separation, ethnic-national and religious extremism' and in particular, from the growth of international terrorism, transnational organized crime, as well as illegal trafficking in narcotic drugs and arms. In the concept, it is also clearly mentioned,

"*Russia will make its full contribution to theattainment of a lasting and just settlement for the situation in the Balkans, based on the coordinated decisions of the international community. It is of paramount importance to preserve the territorial integrity of the federal republic of Yogoslavia, and to oppose the partition of this state, a development fraught with the threat of the emergence of Pan Balkan conflict with unpredictable consequences*".

The part of the concept that deals with the settlement of global problems clearly reflects Russia's three positions in foreign policy:

Firstly, Russia's foreign policy 'must be based on maintaining a reasonable balance between its objectives and possibilities for attaining them'.

Secondly, 'concentration of political-diplomatic, military, economic, financial and other means on resolving foreign policy tasks must be commensurate with their real importance for Russia's national interests, while the scope of participation in international affairs must be adequate to the actual contribution to strengthening the country's positions'.

Thirdly, 'the diversity and complexity of international problems, and the existence of crisis situations require a timely evaluation of the priority of each of them in the foreign policy activity of the Russian Federation'.[36] These positions refer to both global and regional problems. Though the materialization of this concept produces positive results, yet it is criticized for its ambitious objective and modest funds available for their attainment in the present distribution of world power.

7.2. Early phase of Putin's Foreign Policy Initiatives

After Putin assumes power in March 2000, he focused on CIS countries and China for balancing the power equation with US and checking the dominance of US in global politics. So far as Russia's relations with CIS countries were concerned, he continued the same foreign policy initiatives as his predecessor Yeltsin did in the last phase of his foreign policy that had achieved maximum possible integration of the CIS countries on the basis of voluntary cooperation and mutual benefit. In the practice of politics, Russia's approach on good neighborhood and on regional conflict resolution got mixed up. On some cases, the RF deliberately encouraged regional conflicts for example in Abkhazia, followed by an offer of conflict resolution, thus making Georgia dependent on Russia for ensuring its security. This dependency of CIS states in the field of security aimed at increasing the influence of Russian Federation, thus ensuring healthy neighbourliness. Russia's relations with China improved dramatically after Beijing Declaration of July 2000, signed by the President of Russia and China. Both countries opposed all attempts of USA at revising the basic norms of international law, use of force, interference in the internal affairs of sovereign states. They also condemned US attempts to revise ABM (Anti Ballistic Missiles) treaty. Even Putin and Jiang Zemin sounded serious warning to Washington that the 'states calling for revision of the ABM treaty will bear all responsibility for undermining international stability and for consequences that might follow'. Moscow and Beijing criticized NATO's hegemonic moves, not only in Europe but also in Central Asia. Both strongly condemned NATO for arbitrary use of force in the Balkans. The Russian and Chinese President also supported a peaceful political settlement of Kosovo and Metohija. In fact, Russian President Putin's Asia tour was considered as an attempt to strengthen the Moscow-Beijing-Pyongyang axis both politically and militarily. It was a positive step for creating a multi polar world by consolidating the stability in the region of North Eastern Asia. Besides, Russia's relations with China, Putin also traveled constantly to Austria, Canada, Cuba, France, Germany, India, Italy, Japan, North Korea, Poland, Serbia, Slovenia, South Korea, Sweden, Turkey, the United Kingdom and Vietnam- and every where he worked at upgrading Russia's ties. In this phase, Putin also gave attention to Russia's nearest neighbours. He toured extensively to Uzbekistan, Ukraine and Belarus and extended relations with all parts of the former Soviet Union. He put importance on economic ties but at the same time he also stressed on security ties with Central Asian countries to stall the threat from Islamic extremism.[38]

Russian foreign policy from 2000 has been mainly European oriented. Putin has recognized Europe as his natural partner. His government has developed healthy bilateral relations with West European countries particularly with Germany and Britain. British Prime Minister Tony Blair was Putin's first international partner. From an East and West point of view, Russian approach has been characterized by balancing European and Asian forces[39].

7.2. Post September 2001-The Policy Shift

International politics was completely changed after the terrorist attack of 11 September 2001 and the subsequent war waged by the US against terrorism. Putin was the first foreign head of state to express sympathy and condemn the attacks in a telegram to Bush and he wrote, 'without doubt such inhuman acts should not stand without punishment'. Russia supported the US offered co-operation, secret information and air corridors for NATO aircraft and agreed to the establishment of US military bases in Central Asia. Russia also developed partnership with the West for fighting against terrorism. Unlike previous years, after 9/11, Kremlin declared a long-term course of constructive dialogue and co-operation with the West, including the US. It was materialized during

Putin's visit to US in October 2001. Putin's government accepted Washington's decision to abrogate ABM treaty. Putin also accepted American military intervention in Georgia though he expressed his reservations about this later on.

The most astonishing change in the approach to global security was that of Russia NATO relations which focused on the mechanism of Russia's effective participation in NATO activities. In 2001, co-operation with Russia was offered by NATO within the formula '19+1' which means that 19 NATO countries would decide whether to accept it or not. But in May 2002, NATO-Russia Council (NRC) was created at the Reykjavik summit. In the Rome declaration of 28 May 2002, co-decision making rights in nine issue areas like military crisis management, counter terrorism, non-proliferation of weapons of mass destruction and theatre missile defence were given.[40] The council was a symbol of US-Russia rapprochement, but it did not play any substantial role in further developments. Russia was also supported by US administration to join WTO (World Trade Organisation) and became a full member of G8 in June 2002. In spite of the improved relations between Russia and USA, and the consultation that continued on Afghanistan in the Russian – US working group, no direct co-operation developed between the two powers relating to various issues of Central Asia. In fact, Russia-US security co-operation in Central Asia was important, but it could not materialize due to mutual suspicion. But it reinforced the geopolitical dependence of the Central Asia and Trans- Caucasian republics on Russia. It also silenced western critics of Russia's handling of Chechnya. The Chechen rebels, some of whom were linked to AlQueda, also suffered a setback in their public relation and image.

The most important achievement was the verbal agreement between two leaders at their November 2001 summit on reducing their 6,000 strong nuclear arsenals to 1700-2250 each. Though Putin's pro-western approach has helped in enhancing his standing in the West and won some significant benefits for Russia. Yet it has left him politically exposed, and there are also various issues where US expects more from Russia. In the words of Colin Powell, former US Secretary of State, "'We don't agree on everything, of course we had hope for more Russian support for our Iraq policy, and still hope Russia will change its attitude towards the Iranian nuclear programme. We also differ over aspects of Russian policy in Chechnya. But the relationship as a whole is no longer locked in a knee-jerk antagonism. We now have necessary level of trust to resolve the most difficult issues between us".[41]

7.2. Russia's Foreign Policy in 2004

At the end of 2004, there was difference of opinions among the Russian commentators about the success and failure of its foreign policy. But it is clear that Russia's international behavior in this period was continuation of previously existing tendencies. Of course Russia attempted to consolidate its influence in some parts of the world particularly in the 'near abroad' what most analysts referred to as the 'former Soviet space'. Relationship between Russia and US marked a difference between them over US policy toward Iran and Iraq and its interference in Georgia, Central Asia and Ukraine.

In the Iranian case, US and Europeans are against Teheran's pursuit of nuclear capability, but Yeltsin and Putin remain committed to the completion of the Bushehr nuclear reactor as it provides financial boost to Russian business and Ministry of Atomic Energy and at the same time it has become a symbol of Russia's independent foreign policy line. As Russia does not like to go against the decision of IAEA (International Atomic Energy Agency), so it has stated again and again that it would continue to work on Bushehr, but that Iran needed to comply with IAEA agreements. Russian foreign minister Sergei Lavrov continued negotiations on spent fuel from the Bushehr reactor, but emphasized that Iran must comply with all the demands of IAEA. In Washington the Bush Administration warned that Iran might be referred to UN Security Council for possible sanction over its decision. Russia however emphasized that dialogue with Iran under the IAEA framework was the best way forward.[42.]

Russian present Foreign Minister Sergei Ivanov told Russian television, "on the whole, I think that this problem must be resolved primarily within the political and diplomatic framework, and on the current stage within the IAEA framework".

The Iraqi situation remains as a bone of contention between two powers. Politically Russia opposed US's unilateralism. Economically, Russia hoped to protect LU Koil's interests in Iraqi oil production and financial gains from UN Administered Oil-for-Food Programme. Both sides publicly claimed interests in stabilizing the situation during the handover to Iraqi authorities, but Russia's interest lies in 'managed instability' that is a situation in which US would not free to focus its attention on other areas and at the same time, continuation of war in Iraq would deter Islamic forces to pose a threat to the rest of the Middle East. Sergei Lavrov has said that his government is in favor of UN's central role in Iraq.[43] In this year, Russia was very much critical of NATO expansion and NATO involvement in post-Soviet space. Putin expressed his dissatisfaction over NATO's refusal to alter conventional forces in Europe Treaty and alliance's inadequate recognition to Russia's role generally for which he declined an invitation to attend the 2004 NATO summit in Istanbul. In the words of observer Aleksander Golts:

'When you get right down to it, all Putin really needs is membership in an international club for the elect. A club where he can shake hands with George W. Bush and Tony Blair and be treated as an equal, as he is this week at G-8 summit. Putin regarded the role he would have played at the NATO summit- a second stringer mixed in with the Bulgarians and Slovenians – as beneath him. And that is why he turned down NATO's inviatation'.[44]

Unlike the year 2003, it was a hard task for Russia to maintain a striking balance with US. But it successfully used Germany and France to try to block Iraq war and US unilateralism. Russia's views of NATO in the year 2004 remained negative because of the inclusion of Baltic states and ties between NATO and other post summit countries. Russia is also careful of the talk in USA about forcefully fostering regime change in Syria and Iran-two of Moscow's friends in the Middle East.

In 2004,Russia supported the new Georgian President's move to reintegrate the several secessionist provinces. Putin also intervened in Ossetiya, Abkhaziya and Ukraine to reestablish Russian hegemony in the territory of erstwhile Soviet Union. In

Central Asia, there is keen competition between US and Russia. Russia has reopened its base in Kant and Kyrgyzstan and opened new base in Tajikistan to counter the dominance of United States in this region. Putin has reinvigorated his ties with Uzbek President Islam Karimov and signed a treaty of strategic partnership with him in the meeting of the Shanghai co-operation organization (SCO). But at the last part of 2004, Russia's intervention in the Ukrainian election exposes Russian intentions as well as its spectacular failure. It is time to watch and see how Moscow will handle its Ukrainian policy.[45]

From the above analysis, it is evident that Russia has made progress in adjusting to international realities. Putin's efforts of working with US by steering a middle course between the extremes of Gorbachev and Kozyrov's westernism on the one hand, and Primakov's great power -balancing on the other without jettisoning Russian interests reflect his pragmatism and vision. He has also tried to broaden the concept of Russian security which takes nothing for granted, internal and external, by replacing value loaded concept of security and emphasizing on the internal foundations of political security policy in which the focus of attention and level of activity are the key dimensions, nothing is taken for granted and over emphasized, be it internal and external securities, and policies are formulated according to the need of the time and requirements considering the national interest of Russia.

7.3. Economic Security

The biggest problem for Russia is its economic security. It struggles hard to cope with realities and to strengthen its economic position both internally and externally since its inception. Russia works genuinely hard to become a major economic power in the world and to catch up with 21st century through internal and external reforms in its economy. Though fundamentals have changed, yet Russian economic recovery is not up to expectation. But recently, Russia is moving too fast and gaining economic stability, which promises an important role for Russia in the world in coming days.

Since the financial crisis of 1998, the Russian economy has grown at an average annual rate of more than 5%. But there has been a slow down to about 4% in 2002. Recently Russia's economic performance is extremely good as everything is moving in a right direction and there are enough reasons to believe that rapid growth in Russian economy is likely to be sustained. Unlike earlier period, ruble devaluation stimulated Russian production; oil price raises further boosted revenues; political uncertainly was reduced. The negative trend in Russian economy is gradually eroding; the business environment is improving through Russian business confidence and right institutional change. In 2000, net exports of goods and services were equivalent to 21.1% of GDP and the growth of consumer demand also increased rapidly. At the same time domestic investment grew strongly and the large cut in tax break for re-investment of profits, effective in 2002 affected companies investment more than the reality. At the margin and over the period as a whole, the business community of Russia increased domestic investment more than it increased capital flight.[46]

Russia's recent growth, public spending restraint, budget surplus and paying- off of debt, in addition to rising foreign confidence largely fulfills the precondition for sustained growth. The only exception is the level of monetization. Russia remains at a low level of monetization; at the end of September 2002 ruble broad money supply (M2) was about 18% GDP, and after the addition of foreign exchange deposits the ratio was still 24%. The reason for this is that Russian banks continue to do rather little financial intermediation.[47] Two types of growth constraints worth mentioning here: Russia's present dependence on natural resources exports; poor and not readily changed economic institutions.

Today, everything in Russia depends on oil. Whenever oil production has declined, the GDP has declined. Whenever oil production has gone up, the GDP has risen. Hence, it largely matters both to near term policy particularly the implementation of federal budget and to longer-term prospects. For the sustained economic growth, it is necessary that oil price should remain high and there should not be quick fluctuation. Another important requirement is institutional reforms. Though Russian business environment is improving, but it is not up to mark so far as international standard is concerned. Important structural weaknesses are: a weak banking system; an illiquid and nontransparent stock market; state intervention helping some firms and hampering others; unclear property right; grossly distorted energy prices. Institutional reforms could be possible through a reform minded leadership pushing through market friendly legislation and implementation in practice.

The important areas of institutional reforms in Russia are banking and financial sector, taxation, land ownership, competition policy, state administration, the judicial system, the labour market, energy prices and corporate governance.[48] For a clear understanding of institutional reforms during Putin's period, some key areas where reform measures are successfully implemented and going to be implemented are worth mentioning here.

Putin's government has also brought changes on Russian markets. Russian business chains are rapidly assimilating the practice of the western operators who want to become leading market participants. Russian chains are trying to imitate transnational operators in their structural and institutional relations in order to meet new competitive situation.[49] In the mineral recourse sector Putin is determined that the Russian government should have a decisive voice in decisions about energy and natural resources. Though he is not in favour of total state control, yet he favours guided market with the possibility for multiple forms of ownership.[50]

During Putin's era, reform in taxation appears to have been a top priority of the Kremlin. He has appointed the champion of the free market economy Frederich Hayek as his economic advisor and brought changes in taxing system. The income tax was pared to 13 percent and the corporate tax to 24 percent; the sales tax was eliminated; and there was a sharp cut in the unified social tax, a move calculated to save private entrepreneurs an estimated $10 billion a year. These cuts have been supplemented by a tight control on government spending after Putin's reelection.

Steps have been taken to reduce federal bureaucratic work force by 20 percent.[51] Recently steps have been taken to strengthen the judiciary, to reduce regulatory obstacles and to improve the quality of administration. Efforts have been put to streamline administration and to take steps against corrupt administrators. In present Russia, constant renegotiations over property rights continue. Legislation in 2001 clearly clarified property rights in non–farmland, facilitating the development of market in real estate. In 2002, a new land code allowed trading in agricultural land. But the potential illegitimacy of the initial distribution of property rights has not been sorted out. Putin is determined to correct it. Some of his trusted aides have indicated that the Khodorkovsky/ Yakos affair is not end of the road. There is going to be continued attack on the oligarchs.[52] It is clear that the Putin's government is undoing the privatization and enacting its own vision of re-privatization. He is also following an extremely cautious path, as he knows re- privatization may result in public anger and even the dismissal of his government. In fact, Putin and his men have developed a new corporatist ideology within both the Kremlin and the Duma. They tolerate large private enterprises, but on the condition of their subservience to the state's political and economic agenda.[53] The fruits of these policies have not only affected industrial sector but also agricultural and service sectors. In the service sector, it has provided opportunities to people to get more jobs particularly in technical filed. In 2002, 32 percent of working young people up to age twenty, including 40 percent of women, were employed in the informal sector. The level of in formal employment of young people in August 2002 rose to 39.4 percent in comparison to 26.3 percent in February. Of course in this sector inefficient employment is perpetuated and low quality of human capital is preserved. At present, government is taking measures to streamline the informal sector overcoming the negative phenomenon associated with development of this sector and creating more jobs in the formal sector. In the agricultural sector, Russia has achieved spectacular result. This sector had been systematically destroyed by six decades, but today, Russia has moved from being the world's largest importer of grains to a net exporter.

From the above analysis, it is clear that there has been a progress in all these areas under Putin's government. But still there are some problems, which may stymie strong performance of Russia. The drilling of exploratory wells inRussia fell by 20% in between January to October 2004, which affected Russia's growth rate for September 2004.

Demography is another major concern. Lower birth rate and life expectancy affect Russian economy particularly labour market as they are related to human capital. Making better use of the labour force is the key problem today and it will make the situation worse as the potential work force will decline after 2006. During the period of market reforms, less importance was given to labour as a factor in economic development. The labour market adjusted to the altered conditions through under utilization of the labour force, a sharp reduction in wages and deterioration in the economic and legal status of employees, forced unemployment wages below the minimum subsistence level. Lack of legal protection for employees and reduction in labour force participation had also negative effects on the quality of human capital.[54] In this situation, informal employment helps people by offering an alternative to unemployment. It not only makes the work force more mobile but also limits the decline in the living standards. But this informal sector is also not free from problems. The irregular nature of informal employment, lack of legal protection, and widespread infractions (tax evasion, working without a license etc.) negatively affect the level of motivation of the workers who are working in this sector.[55]

The most important problem in today's Russia is the gap between rich and poor. It is widening day by day; *Silovakis* are replacing old oligarchs. There are currently thirty-six billionaires in Russia, Thirty-three of them in Moscow alone. Most of the rich people prospered from privatization in the 1990s. Most of their wealth derives from raw materials excluding few those have made their fortunes in manufacturing. But the same problem still continues as *Silovakis* are in important positions of companies, either as the Chief Executive Officers (CEOs), chairman of the board, or members of the board. Their approach is, ' it is our time to share in the loot'. Unless Putin overhauls the administrative setup and controls them, it may hinder the process of development. Really, it is a tough task ahead for Putin. It is also time to watch how he is able to pursue his reform measures and overcome the problems that are looming large over Russia.

7.3. Economic Security: External Dimension

External dimension of economic security plays an important role in Russian economy as Russia's integration into Liberal International Economic Order (LIEO) strengthens its economic stability by improving its BOP (Balance of Payment); developing trade relations with West and other countries including CIS; becoming member in international organizations; making the economy open for FIIs (Foreign Institutional Investors) and MNCs (Multinational Corporations) to invest money in Russian market. Russia was struggling hard to overcome its economic problems up to the end of Yeltsin period due to lack of sufficient investment, faulty tax system and massive tax evasion coupled with poor balance of payment and trade relations with its neighbouring and European and Asian countries. But due to Putin's sincere efforts, the economic situation both internal and external has improved, the negative trends in Russian economy are getting neutralized, and above all it is gaining economic stability.

In November 2000, Putin said that Russia's genuine efforts were to create a favourable condition for integration into global economy.[56] This could not only speed up the economic growth of Russia, but also increase Russia's attractiveness to foreign investors. Putin also expressed his keenness to liberalize the economy by joining WTO. Russia's membership of WTO helped Russia in many ways:

Greater access to international markets.
Greater domestic competition and increase inefficiency.
An increase in Foreign Direct Investment (FDI).
Legal recourse to settle trade disputes.

Another conspicuous step in this direction was Russia's full membership in G8 at the Birmingham Summit 1998 where it was accepted as a new member of a new G8. At the G8 summit in Okinawa in July 2000, Russia discussed problems of international trade and information and communication technology with other members. In fact Russia's importance on liberalization, privatization and globalisation help foreign institutional investors to invest money in Russian market. As mentioned earlier, an increase in foreign direct investment has been recorded in Russia. But still the level of FDI in Russia is low in comparison to other transition economies. In Russia, most of the FDI is confined to mainly energy and recourses. And the share of FDI is much higher in Moscow than other parts of Russia. Even FDI continues to flow into Russia despite the Yakos affair; capital outflow has increases in response to the same trends.[57]

The macro economic environment of Russia in the year 2003 indicated that investment spending was high. Macro fundamentals were strong. The budget was in surplus,[58] the current account balance was in surplus and foreign reserves were very high.[59] External debt of the government was about $110 billion that was a manageable limit. Even capital flight increased after the arrest of Khodorkskiy, it was around the $15 billion to $18 billion marks. The Current macro economic environment is even better than 2003 to 2005, which clearly indicates that Russia's economy is moving in a positive direction.

7.3. Economic Relations

Recently, Russia has developed healthy relations with EU (European Union) and other Asian countries. It has rightly emphasized on bi-lateral trade relations and multilateral agreements to strengthen its economy. Putin in his 'Russia at the turn of the millennium' speech released on 31st December 1999 stressed on the need for deeper integration into global economy, he set Russia's direction down the westernizing. Further, he emphasized on strengthening of economic relations leading to a 'Russia-European Union Free Trade Zone'. At the EU-Russia summit in may 2001, the decision was taken to establish a Common European Economic Area (CEEA)[*] by 2003. The creation at the Brussels Summit in October-2001 of a high level group for developing closer economic relations with Russia was a positive step in this direction.

Since the beginning of 21st century the policy of the Russian government and private sector was to expand its export capabilities in every possible direction in Europe, the US, and the Asia–Pacific region. To materialize it, the idea of Russia-EU joint energy policy has been under consideration since the EU-Russia summit in Paris in 2000. When leaders Putin and Prodi addressed the possibility of a joint response to the oil crisis, Russia was ready for external capital investment into oil and gas sector. At the end of September 2001, during Putin's visit to Germany, he gave his consent to export oil to Europe if the oil supplies from the Middle East were cut off. The year 2000-2004 was focused on attracting foreign, particularly European investments into energy industry. On 26 June 2003 the memorandum on cooperation for the construction of the North European natural gas pipeline project was signed between U.K. and Russia, which will be extremely useful for sending Russian natural gas to Britain, as well as into the markets of continental Europe. In this respect, British and Russian energy companies are working together on the Russian market and engaging in joint ventures in the markets of other countries. The joint projects are discussed not only for Europe, but also for Asian countries to meet their shortage of energy resources.[60] It was pointed out at the Russia-UK energy conference held in London in June 2003 that energy deals have an impact on business philosophy and international politics. In this context, Viktor Vekselberg, chairman of the TNK management, a Russian company said, that "TNK–BP joint project open new horizon for cooperation. It will strengthen Russian link with the industrial world. It facilitates Russia's transformation from a regional exporter to global energy supplier". These plans were confirmed at the Russia-EU energy summit that took place in London on March 2004.

Russia's bilateral relations with United States are at the lowest ebb since the Soviet collapse. But after 9/11, both the countries are seriously thinking for constructive engagement in various fields particularly in trade and commerce. At present, US is encouraging American firms to cultivate relations with experts and managers in defence heavy regions that might otherwise seek partners in West Asian states.[61]

Russian president Vladimir Putin put much importance on Asia Pacific region. In the Asia Pacific Economic Cooperation (APEC) organization summit in Brunei, he said, "Russia's transport arteries and space lunch facilities held great potential for cooperation with the Asia-Pacific region". Russia's participation in the process of economic collaboration in the Asia and Pacific Ocean is natural and inevitable due to its unique geo-political setup. Russia has extended co-operation in power engineering, environmental issues and the exploitation of the sea shelf to the development of transport communications and the implementation of specific economic and investment projects. Russia is a supplier of raw materials and modern technologies in the region. The Russian-Vietnamese Vietsovpetro joint company is constantly building up oil extraction in Vietnam. A large oil refinery was constructed there in collaboration with Russian technology. Russian oil industry together with Caltex Pacific Indonesia Company implemented a pilot project, which helped to increase the oil yield at Sumatra's oilfields. These technologies were recommended further for use in all the oilfields of the 'land of thousand lands'. Another milestone in this direction was that in February 2000, the Indonesian Garuda-1 artificial satellite was put into orbit with the aid of a Russian booster rocket. At present, Indonesian business circles have taken interests in the use of the Russian technology in non-traditional energy sources, in medicine, information technology and other industries. In many Asian countries Russia is known as a reliable economic partner. Russia's initiative proclaimed at the UN Millennium Summit regarding the joint development of innovative reactor technology and naturally safe nuclear cycle is appreciable to the APEC states as it can be used to overcome their problems of recycling of nuclear waste and thus strengthening their economic potential by using cheap electricity.[62]

7.3. Economic Relations with CIS Countries

Putin in his speech to Russian Parliament in April 2002 emphasized on the economic aspects of foreign policy. In this speech he gave utmost importance on the economic relations with CIS states. He said:

"CIS was crucial to Russia in securing competitive advantages on the world market. The Commonwealth of Independent States (CIS) is a genuine factor in stability across an extensive part of the world's territory, an influential group of states with a wide range of objectives and interests. Work with the countries of the CIS is Russia's main foreign policy priority. This

priority is linked, among other things, to the securing of competitive advantages on world markets. The CIS countries have many opportunities to carryout large-scale, joint infrastructure, transport and energy projects. I am sure that there implementation will increase the solidarity of our integration, and will provide new opportunities for the Russian economy, and for others besides".

Though in his speech, he did not mention Central Asian States by name, but he clearly indicated these states in his reference to CIS energy and transport projects. It was a fact that it did not seem to offer any economic benefit in the short term but in long-term perspective Central Asia was regarded as of economic interest to Russia. When he came to power, he came up with a new proposal in October 2000 to lunch a new organization, the Eurasian Economic Community (EEC), to replace the CIS Custom Union, but it could not materialize. After the September 2001, Russia put importance on the energy assets of four Central Asian States. Previously oil and gas resources were confined to Caspian region but it has extended to non-Caspian states like Uzbekistan, Tajikistan and Kyrgyzstan and also to include hydro energy.[63] In January 2002, Putin came forward with a proposal for Eurasian Alliance of Natural Gas Producers consisting of Russia, Kazakhstan, Turkmenistan and Uzbekistan. On 1st March 2002, the leaders of these states intended to cooperate with each other in energy policy and measures to defend the interests of Natural Gas Producers. Further, the four countries intended to coordinate their import-export and investment policies and to promote a common ' energy security strategies'. A gas alliance would open up Russian natural gas pipeline network to Central Asian producers, which are eager to extend it to European market.[64] Russia wanted to push for alliance, which would help Russia to increases energy exports to western customers with the help of Central Asian counties. But either for political or economic reasons most of the projects for gas pipelines were not completed. For Russia to succeed in creating a gas alliance with Central Asian states, it had to complete the projects and made them operational. After September 11, Russia is genuinely trying for economics co-operation with Central Asian states particularly in energy sector.

From the above analysis, it is clear that Russia's well being largely depends on the energy sector as it provides stable incomes and helps in strengthening its economy.[65] It is a matter of astonishment that during the years of its economic growth, Russia has not introduced a single new manufactured product on the world market. Science intensive goods are almost non-existent in the structure of Russian exports. It is high time for Russia to stress on science intensive goods that can be exported to other countries. In fact, it is necessary for a balanced relation of 'import substitute and export promotion' with other countries.

Another aspect of Russia's involvement in the global economy is its human capital. Russia has produced well-qualified scientists, economists and technocrats but their expertise is not utilized properly in Russia as a result of which they are forced to migrate to America and European countries. It is right time to provide jobs to those experts and utilize their potentialities for the growth of Russian economy. Russia's economic programmes seem to be lopsided as those programmes do not look into the future and do not look for solutions to difficult economic problems. The main task before the political leaders and policy makers is to sort out them immediately for strengthening its economics security.

7.4. Human Security

At present human security plays an important role in the concept of security of New Russia. Russian security is no more confined to the development of state mechanism; it is concerned with all-round development of the citizens of Russia. In present day Russia, organized crimes and terrorism are two major threats to the stability of Russia and weaken the human security idea in New Russia. The rate of organized crimes is increasing day by day as the problem of homeless and neglected children in Russia has not been solved properly as yet. The homeless and neglected children have spent their maximum time on the streets. Most of them are members of informal groups and most of which have leaders. In maximum cases, leader of the group has criminal tendencies, which help the youngsters to involve in various types of crimes. A survey has revealed that more than 42 percent are still engaged in stealing. Females are also engaged in crimes and prostitution. In terms of their way of life, youngsters try to imitate adults. As a result 77.2 percent smoke, 64.2 percent drink alcohol,

27percent use narcotics, 29.7 percent are sexually active. The behaviors of females are also same as the behavior of males. Among them, 62.3 percent smoke, 54.4 percent drink and 17.3 percent use narcotics and 36.8 percent sexual active. Most of them suffer from various diseases and face heath problems due to excess smoking, drinking, and sexually activities. The root causes of the problems are their broken family, excess use of alcohol and narcotics by their family members particularly their parents, and faulty socialization. The need of the time is that government, social organizations and educational institutions should take concerted efforts to remove the root causes of the problems by creating a healthy atmosphere for homeless and neglected children of Russia.

Terrorism is a major threat to Russia. Besides terrorism, ethno-separatism and ethnic violence have taken their ugly heads in Russia. In August and September 2004, there were series of attacks on major cities of Russia by terrorists. On 24 August, two Russian planes exploded in flight. One crashed near Tula and the other near Rostov. In this plane crash 89 passengers died. On 30 August, 10 people were killed and more than 50 wounded in the Moscow city by a suicide bomber. On 1 September a group of 32 terrorists took hostage School Number One in the North Ossetian town of Beslan, holding prisoner over one thousand children, parents and teachers who had come to celebrate the first day of Term. This hostage crisis ended in a firefight where 326 died including 159 children and some 540 wounded. Putin took it seriously, the president declared that 'our country is under attack' and considered the terrorist attack on a part of co-ordinated assault by international terrorism.[66] After the Beslan incident, Putin tightened the security set up of Russia. He stresses on an integrated security system to combat terrorism. He recognized the need for a 'fundamental revision of all policies in the North Caucasus'. Putin openly admitted that terrorism had got strengths from desperate living standards; he proposed the creation of Special Federal Commission (SFC) in the North Caucasus for redressing the socio economic situation. Putin has been fighting against terrorism since coming to power. He said publicly that Chechen rebels have link with terrorist outfits led by powerful leaders of various Islamic groups. But after September 11, he successfully convinced United States about this and persuaded to fight jointly against International terrorism. Russia also got the support of CIS, EU, NATO, China and other countries to curb terrorism, which is a menace to global peace and stability.

A primacy of focus was on the former Soviet Union, with the development of anti-terrorist structures in the CIS. The Shanghai Co-operation Organization (SCO) brought together Russia, China, Kazakhstan, Uzbekistan, Kyrgyzstan and Tajikistan to fight against terrorism for which efforts were made to create an International Convention on Combating Terrorism.[67] In April 2003, members of CIS countries created the Collective Security Treaty Organization (CSTO). In December 2003, Putin stated that efforts were made to create rapid action forces and air defence structures to combat terrorism.[68] Moscow also got support from most CIS states in tackling Chechen war and cutting off external sources of support. Putin also used counter terrorism to align Russia within the Euro-Atlantic community. After 9/11, US-Russian relations progressed quickly. Counter terrorism is also a part of Russia-NATO relations. In May 2002 the NATO Russia Council (NRC) was created to work together as 'equal partners in areas of common interest'. Russia also became an active member in the Security Council's Counter Terrorism Committee (CTC). The CTC was created to combat international terrorism in accordance with rules of international convention and protocols.

Russia's efforts to check international terrorism and terrorism inside Russia are widely acclaimed. But still it is not adequate to root out it completely. People of Russia sacrificed their freedom in exchange for security during Putin's first term. But series of terrorist attacks in 2004 revealed the weakness of Russia's security structure and posed a threat not only to peace and stability of Russia but also to global peace and security. How long will the people of Russia restrict their freedom in the wake up new attacks? No doubt, America and West are supporting the Russian move to curb terrorism where their interests coincide, for example during the war in Afghanistan. But largely they differ on various issues with Russia, particularly the violation of human rights in Chechnya; anti-terrorist campaign to include new targets such as Iraq and Iran where Russia has political and economic interests.[69] Hence, it is right time for Russia to take a cautious and judicious path to align with USA and West in their anti-terrorist campaign without sacrificing the national interests of Russia.

Ethnic violence is also a threat to the security of Russia. Of course ethnic violence was a common feature in former Soviet Union. Though it has been reduced after the disintegration of Soviet Union, yet ethnic conflicts in CIS countries has come to cost more than 180 thousand people. More than 80 thousand people died in Chechen war. Putin's government is trying seriously to solve the ethnic conflicts, but it has not been solved yet.

Another important threat to human security in Russia is the physical health of the nation. In Russia, cardiovascular diseases, cancer, AIDS, alcoholism, drug addiction and the reduction in birth rate and life expectancy were very common up to the end of 2000. More than half a million people were infected with AIDS. Most of the diseased people were unable to pay for medical treatment they needed. A survey in the year 2000 revealed that the majority of Russians were unable to get balanced diet. Even at present an average Russian eats food worse than the people of developing nations.

One of the most important problems in the life of Russian citizens is the family crisis. More than half of the marriages were unsuccessful and divorce rate was unusually high. More than 650 thousand children in Russia were officially registered as orphans.[70.] The situations in Russia have been improved dramatically during Putin's period. He is sincerely trying to solve the problems of New Russia. But his efforts in this direction are not sufficient to change the social scenario by removing the problems. He will have to work hard to remove social maladies. It could be possible only through wholehearted efforts by government, various organizations, NGOs and above all by creating consciousness among people without which no *dues-ex-machina* (God) can alter the fates of Russians.

Another important threat to the values of human security is environmental security. There are many links between environment and security, some of them of historical dimension. Threats to environmental security are threats to human security values. In Russia, outdated military equipments and facilities piled up owing to the disarmament process, which was a cause for environmental pollution. Large deposits of chemical weapons accumulated in the country for many decades were destroyed in the last decade. There are proposals also for further destruction following international agreement and appropriate commitments, despite shortages in economic resources and technical capacities. The environmental risk is attributed to submarines stored with radioactive fuel. In the Russia arctic zone alone about 70 nuclear submarines have been anchored, 53 of them stored with fuel. The transportation of fuel to the existing Russian treatment facilities would cost huge amount of money, and seems to be a difficult task. Hence, there should be efforts by Russia to eliminate environmental risks from military installations and facilities, both those in service and outdated ones, considering the limited Russian economic and technical capacity, deficiencies in institutional arrangements to meet the target in the foreseeable future in accordance with Arctic Military Environmental Co-operation (AMEC) agreement between USA, Norway, and Russia.[71] During Soviet regime the leaders and policy makers had not cared for ecology while planning industrial growth. As a result in present Russia more than 26 percent of drinking water has failed to meet the sanitary and chemical standards. Various types of pollutions including air and land have increased to a sufficiently high level in and around major urban and industrial conglomerates that adversely affect the health security of Russia.[72] At present steps are being taken by Putin's government to make substantial improvement in environmental issues which have been neglected for a long time.

From the beginning of the Chechnya issue Russians were criticized severely by the US and the West for violation of human rights and rejection of political settlement of this problem through OSCE mediation. Though the situation has been changed after 9/11, yet the question of human rights is still in the air. The conciliatory approach taken by Russian delegation in OSCE summit on various issues despite criticism of its Chechnya campaign clearly revealed that Russia had been trying to strengthen OSCE. Of course one of the important reasons is the fight of OSCE for protection of the rights of Russian minorities abroad. As mentioned earlier Russia has been trying to protect the rights and interests of Russian minorities in Baltic States, which is reflected in Putin's Foreign policy concept:

" to protect the rights and interest of Russian citizens compatriots abroad on the basis of international law and operative bilateral agreements. The Russia Federation will seek to obtain adequate guarantees for the rights and freedoms of compatriots in states where they permanently reside and to maintain and develop comprehensive ties with them and their organizations".[73]

Putin's 'Federative Reforms on Democratization in Russia' also helps to protect the civil rights of the people of Russia. The Russian constitution in its articles such as 19, 30, and 55 and recent court ruling indicate that power to regulate and limit civil rights is the exclusive prerogative of federal authorities. At present federal authorities are in a better position constitutionally to constrain regional actions limiting civil rights.

In the ethnic Russian dominated North Caucasus region of Krasnodar *Kray*, governor Aleksandr Tkachev made a policy of deporting 'illegal' immigrants from the *Kray*. Chechens, Azeris and Meskhetian Turks could become the victims of this policy. But the federal prosecutor in the region challenged the policy as a violation of the constitution and the federal law and ultimately stalled it.[74] At present human rights organizations are playing an active role in Russia. They are not only fighting for the protection of rights of the people, but also pressurizing the government to give justice equally to all the citizens of Russia including minorities. Women movement has also gained momentum in Russia, which is a healthy sign of freedom, and democratization in Russia. In fact, Russia is moving in right direction so far as human rights issue is concerned except its military action in the break away republic of Chechnya which is still in controversy.

7.4. Transnational Threats to Human Security: Russia's Role

At present, many emerging problems cannot be addressed through unilateral initiative by the super power alone. For about 30 years, international system was becoming inter dependent and threats to well being becoming transnational in scope, and needs multilateral solutions to the existing problems.[75] The issues like international terrorism; proliferation of weapons of mass destruction of many kinds (nuclear, chemical and biological); organized crime and the large scale trade in drugs; diseases and plagues; large scale population movements: refugees; genocide that drive some of these population movements need multilateral efforts for solutions. In present day world Russia really matters as it has more power than we might ordinarily think. It has the ability, through acts of omission and commission to cause unacceptable damage to the wealth, health and security of USA and its allies. If Russia does not upgrade the security of its stockpiles of nuclear, chemical and biological weapons and know how, it will increase the probability of the proliferation of WMD (Weapons of Mass Destruction) to non-state actors that belong to transnational terrorist outfits. If Russia does not improve its public health system, it will increase the probability of spreading deadly viruses and bacteria globally. If the government of Russia does not check environmental pollution with its borders, the threat of transnational environmental disaster will definitely increase. If steps are not taken by Russia to check its slow population growth or even population decline, it will adversely affect other societies. If Russia does not come forward to check organized crimes within its border, the global trade in drugs, human beings and nuclear technology will threaten humanity. Hence, it is clear that Russian governments passivity in all these areas poses threat to transnational human security.[76.] Russia acts of commission could also cause irreparable damage to USA, its allies and rest of the world. For example, supply of nuclear reactor to Iran could jeopardize US interests internationally. Similarly if leaders of Moscow are inclined to help US can do as they have been assisting in curbing international terrorism and the military efforts in Afghanistan. They could also play a constructive role in the stabilization of Iraq. They can also help USA and rest of the world, of course excluding Middle East by exporting energy resources. Their acts of commission either for better or worse, largely depend on the interests of Russia and bargaining power of US and other nations through their diplomatic channels.

At present, Russia has taken some positive steps to check international terrorism. As discussed, Russia stresses on international convention for the suppression of acts of nuclear terrorism. It also emphasizes the need to prevent terrorists from acquiring WMD, their means of delivery and related materials. Russia supports efforts to prevent the deployment of weapons in outer space while preserving it for peaceful purposes. Russia's genuine efforts for economic growth and democratic progress of the Central Asian states are definitely a positive move in this direction. The Russian side also advocates a time frame for the formation of a new democratic Iraq in compliance with UN Security Council resolution 1546. Russia also supports the objective of a just and lasting settlement of Arab-Israel conflict. Russia reiterates its support for the reconstruction process in Afghanistan. But at the same time expresses its concern over the increase in the cultivation, production and trafficking of narcotic drugs in Afghanistan and decides to take effective steps to counter act drug and terrorist threats.[77]

No doubt, Russia is trying to minimize the human security threats to it and rest of the world. Russian government is making policies and programmes to over come the problems that are threatening the well being of Russians. It also collaborates with other global powers to solve the transnational threats by making special efforts from its side and encouraging others for multilateral initiatives for the solutions of emerging transnational human security problems. But in the eyes of the rest of the world, its achievement in this direction is just average. Russia will have to work hard without ifs and buts and make an excellent performance for the projection of a better image internationally, but it should not be at the cost of its national interests.

Notes and References

1. A.F. Klimnenko, "Osobennosti novoy Voyennoy doktriny", *Voyennaya Mysl*, 5, (2000).
   Also Marcel de Haas, *Russian security and Air power 1992-2002* (London: Frank Cass, 2004).
2. C.J. Dick, "The Military Doctrine of Russian Federation", *Journal of Slavik Military Studies*, Vol.7, no.3 September 1994, pp. 503-504.
3. NATO's use of military force without the consent of the Security Council of the UN. It is justified
   according to NATO's strategic concept for the maintenance of security and stability in Euro-Atlantic area.
   See *The Alliance Strategic Concept* (Brussels: NATO office of information and press, 1999), p.14.

4. *The Alliance's Strategic Concept (*Brussels: NATO Office of Information and Press, 1999), p.14.
5. National Security Concept (January2000): Russian: 'Kontseptsiya natsionalnoy bezopasnosti',*Nezavisimoye Voyennoye Obozreniye*, 1(14 January2000), p.1.http://www.scrf.gov.ru/Documents/Decree/2000/24-1.html. English: www.fas.org/nuke/guide/russia/doctrine/gazeta 012400.htm
6. *Ibid.*, p.1.
7. Foreign Policy Concept(June 2000):Russian: 'Kontseptsiya Vneshey Politiki Rossiyskoy Federatsii', *Nezavisimoye Voyennoye Obozreniye*, 25 (14 July2000), p.4.http://www.scrf.gov.ru/Document/Decree/2000/07-10.html English: http://www.fas.org/nuke/guide/russi/doctrine/econcept.htm 012400.htm
8. *Ibid.*, p.4.
9. S.A. Bogdanov, "The Economic Components of Russia's Military Security", *Military Thought*, Vol.14, no.1 (2005), pp.12-13.
10. *Ibid.*, p.16.
11. *Interfox News Agency*, in Russian 1440 gmt, 9 November 2000, See also *Summary of World Broad Cast* (SWB) Su/3995/SI/1, 11 November 2000.
12. Irina Isakova, *Russian Governance in the Twenty first Century* (London: Frank Cass, 2005), pp. 232-273.
13. Russian Military Doctrine, (April 2000):
    Russian: 'Voyennaya doktrina Rossiyskoy Federatsii', *Nezavisimoye Voyennoye Obozreniye*, 15 (28 April 2000).www.Scrf.gov.ru/document /decree/2000/706-1.html.
    English: www.freerepublic.com/forum/a394aa0466bfe.htm.
    See also Irina Isakova, *Russian Governance in the Twenty first century*, (London: Frank Cass, 2005), pp. 235-236.
14. *ITAR-TASS News Agency*, Moscow, in English 1750 gmt, 9 November 2000.See also *Summary of World Broad Cast* (SWB) Su/3995/ SI/1, 11 November 2000.
15. Russia's Putin says Armed forces should focus on opposing terrorism. *ITAR-TASS* 26 November 2002 in *WNC Military Affairs*, 27 November 2002. See also "Vladimir Putin and Military Reform in Russia", *European Security*, Vol.14, no.1 (March2002), pp.137-155.
16. "The Elite's Feeling the Heat", *Moscow Times*, 10 April 2003 in Johnson's List, 10 April 2003.

17. Alexander M. Golts and Tonya L. Putnam, "State Militarism and its Legacies", *International Security*, Vol. 29, no. 2 (Fall 2004), pp.156-157.
18. Barry R. Posen, *Sources of Military Doctrine: France, Britain, and Germany between the world wars* (Ithaca, NY: Cornell University Press, 1986), pp. 225-226. See also Jeffery A. Isaacson, Christopher Layna, and John Arquilla, *Predicting Military Innovations* , RAND Documented Briefing (Santa Monica, Calif: Rand 1999), http:// www.rand.org/publications/DB/DB242/
19. Dmitri Trenin, "From Pragmatism to Strategic Choices: Is Russia's Security Policy Finally Becoming Realistic", in Andrew C. Kuchnins, ed., *Russia after the fall* (Washington DC :Carnegie Endowment For International Peace, 2002), pp. 191-196.
20. Ibid., pp.197-203.
21. A.L. Khryapin, "Conceptual Principles of Strategic Deterrence", *Military Thought*, Vol.14, no. 205, pp.30-35.
22. V.I. Ostankov, "Scientific –Methodological Support of Military Security of the Russian Federation", *Military Thought*, Vol.14, no.1,2005, p.56.
23. *Ibid.*, p.58.
24. *Ibid.*
25. A.I. Pozharov and V.V. Grebenik, "Theory of War Economics: Need for a New Paradigm", *Military Thought,* Vol.14, no.1, 2005, pp.165-171.
26. This definition is given by Takashi Inoguchi, "Political Security: Toward a Broader Conceptualisation", *International Studies* (New Delhi), Vol.14, no.2, 2003, p.106.As it has been applied in a Russian context, hence the word Russia appears in the definition.
27. *Russian Regional Report*, 12th February 1998, Published by East West Institute, Moscow.
28. Philip Hanson etal., "Federal Government Responses to Regional Economic Change in Russia", in Philip Hanson, and Michael Bradshaw, eds., *Regional Economic Change in Russia* (Cheltenham: Edward Elgar, 2000). See also Elizabeth Teague, "Putin reforms the federal system" in Cameron Ross, ed., *Regional Politics in Russia* (Manchester: Manchester University Press, 2002), pp.208-209.
29. Marcel de Haas , *Russian Security and Air Power* (London: Frank Cass, 2004), pp.78-79. See also N.A. Smith, *Putin's Regime: Administer Democracy,* E108 (Camberley: Conflict Studies Research Center, 2000).

30. Lee S.Woolskey, "Putin's Plutocrat Problem", *Foreign Affair*, Vol.79, no.2 (March/April), 2000, pp.26-27.
31. Peter Reddaway etal., "Russia in the year 2003", *Post-Soviet Affairs*, Vol. 20, no.1, 2004, pp.1-6.
32. Timothy J.Colton etal., "Russia in the year 2004", *Post-Soviet Affairs*, Vol.21, No.1 (January-March), 2005, p. 24.
33. Takashi Inoguchi, "Political Security: Towards a Broader Conception", *International Studies* (New Delhi), Vol. 40, no. 2, 2003, p.109.
34. Sava Zivanov, *Review of International Affairs*, Vol.LI, no.1096, (August) 2000, p.13.
35. *Ibid.,* p.17.
36. Robert Legvold, "Russia's Unforced Foreign Policy", *Foreign Affair*, Vol. 80. no. 5, (September/October), 2001.
39. Ludmilla Seleneva, "Post-Soviet Russian Foreign Policy: Between Doctrine and pragmatism", *European Security* (A Frank Cass Journal), Vol.11,no.4, 2002.
40. "The New Alliance", *The Times*, 15 May 2002.
41. Colin L. Powell, "A Strategy of Partnerships", *Foreign Affairs,* Vol. 83, no.1(January/February), 2004, p. 31.
42. *The Hindu* (Chennai), January 11, 2006.
43. Colton etal., " Russia in the year 2004", *Post Soviet Affairs,* Vol.21,no.1(January-March), 2005, pp. 20-21.
44. *St. Petersburg Times*, June 11, 2004. See also Tomothy J.Colton etal., p. 21.
45. Andrei P. Tsyganov, "Vladimir Putin's Vision of Russia as a Normal Great Power", *Post Soviet Affairs*, Vol.21, no. 2 (April-June), 2005, pp.147-149.
46. Phillip Hanson, "The Russian Economic Recovery: Do Four Years Growth tell Us that the Fundamentals have changed?", *Europe-Asia Studies*, Vol.55, no. 3,2003, pp. 366-367.
47. *REMIR*, 11 November, 2002, p.3, see also Phillip Hanson, "The Russian Economic Recovery: Do Four Years Growth tell Us that the Fundamentals have changed?", p. 369.
48. Phllip Hanson, "The Russian Economic Recovery: Do Four Years Growth tell Us that the Fundamentals have changed?", pp.374-375.
49. V. Radaev, " Competitive Changes in Russian Market", *Russian Social Science Review*, vol.46,no.4 (July-August), 2005, pp.31-58.

50. Harley Balzor, "The Putin Thesis and Russian Energy Policy", *Post-Soviet Affairs,* Vol.21, no. 3, 2005, p. 211.
51. Leon Aron, "Is Russian Going Backward?", *Commentry,* Vol.118, no.3 (October), 2004, pp. 51-52.
52. Timothy J., Colton etal., "Russia In The Year 2004", pp. 6-11.
53. Leon Aron, "Is Russian Going Backward?", p.51.
54. S.Gorisov, "The Scale and Structure of Informal Employment in the Russian Economy", *Russian Social Science Review*, Vol. 26, no. 3 (May-June), 2005, p.6.
55. *Ibid.,* p.6.
56. *Summary Of World Broad Cast*, Su/399/B/13, 16 November 2000.
57. Timothy J. Colton etal., "Russia in the year 2004", *Post Soviet Affairs*, Vol. 21, no.1, 2005, pp.10-11.
58. The primary surplus of the federal government is about 3.8 percent of GDP. The nominal balance is about 2.1 percent.
59. About $48 billion at the end of 2002. It could be $67 billion by the end of 2003 or about 15 percent of GDP. See Peter Reddaway etal., "Russia in the year 2003", pp. 24-25.
60. Irina Isakova, *Russian Governance on the Twenty first century*, pp. 283-284.
61. Sam Nunn and Adam N. Stulberg, "The Many Faces of Modern Russia", *Foreign Affairs,* Vol.79, no. 2 (March-April), 2000, pp. 61-62.
62. *Nezavismaya Gazeta*, 14 November 2000. See also *Summary of World Broad Cast* ,Su/3999B/3, 16 November 2000
63. Lena Jonson, *Vladimir Putin and Central Asia(* London: LB Tauris, 2004), pp. 100-101.
64. *Ibid.,* pp.102-103.
65. Leonid Grigoriev, "Russia's Place in Global Economy", *Russia in Global Affairs,* Vol.3, no.2(April-June), 2005, pp.128-141.
66. Putin's address of 4 September 2004 , on the presidential website: www.kremlin.ru.
67. Li LIFAN and Ding SHIWU, "Geo political interest of Russia, the US and China in Central Asia", *Central Asia and the Caucasus,* Vol.3, no. 27, 2004, pp.151-154.
68. *IPD, Moscow,*11 December 2003, www.mid.ru.
69. Gail W. Lapidus, "Putin's war on Terrorism: lessons from Chechnya", *Post Soviet Affairs*, Vol.18, no.1(January-March), 2002, pp. 41-48.
70. Zafar Imam, *Yeltsyn years in Russia 1990-1999*, (Delhi: Samskriti,2002), pp.115-165.

71. Ruff Nathan etal., *Reports on Applying Military and Security Assets to Environmental Problems*, in Environmental change and security project, no. 3, spring 1997, (Washington DC: the Woodrrow Wilson Center) 1997.
72. Zafar Imam and N.V. Romanovsky, *Yeltsyn Years in Russia 1990-1999*, (New Delhi: Samskriti, 2002).
73. *The Foreign Policy Concept of the Russian Federation* approved by President Vladimir Putin on June 28, 2000.
74. *Nezavisimaya gazeta*, April 25, 2002, p.5.
75. Robert keohane and Joseph Nye, eds., *Transnational Relations and World Politics* (Cambridge, MA: Havard University Press),1971.See also Reddaway etal., "Russia In the Year 2003", p. 39.
76. Reddaway etal., "Russia In the Year 2003", p. 41.
77. Joint Declaration between the Russian Federation and the Republic of India, New Delhi, 3 December 2004. Published in *Peace and Conflict*, Vol.8, no.1, 2005, pp. 42-44.

Conclusions

Russian concept of security has traversed a long way from peaceful co-existence to mutual security, from the days of October revolution led by Lenin to *Post-perestroika* set into motion by Putin. The first Soviet leader Vladimir Illyich Lenin was a pragmatist and gave importance to national considerations over international priorities during the early years of communist rule, when he sought to consolidate the base of communism in Soviet Union. But as far his international agenda was concerned he was not a pacifist as his main objective was to overthrow capitalism and to establish supremacy of communism practised in Soviet Union over capitalism. He also supported the struggle of colonised people for independence, against imperialism and worked towards global peace and security. Besides this external dimension of security, he also stressed on internal security in all its dimensions. With his sincere efforts, Soviet Union gained political and economic stability and developed military capability. But after Lenin when Stalin came to power, he gave priority to offence rather than defence as his views on security was based on the assumption that Soviet Union was surrounded with enemies who were desperately trying to destroy it. He was against détente as he thought it would work to the advantage of the forces opposed to Soviet Union. As such, he was in favour of adopting policies that would deter enemies of Soviet Union from contemplating sudden attack against it. No doubt his military theory was influenced by the Clausewitzian themes – that war was an act of violence. During the last part of his tenure, he challenged the hegemonistic tendency and imperialistic designs of USA and during the Second World War, Soviet Union extended its influence over its bordering nations and even militarily occupied

Eastern Europe. The East European countries acted like Satellite States and helped Soviet Union in its agenda of expansion of communism on one hand and strengthening its economy through mutual trade relations on the other. However, Soviet Union's over-emphasis on military might and faith in armed forces for preserving Soviet security interests underwent significant changes during the time of Khrushchev, who tried his best to meet the exigencies of time. He was the first Soviet leader who intertwined proposals for peace and military strategy for ensuring Soviet security. His defence strategy in the 1950s was aimed at averting the possibility of any nuclear war and the settlement of crisis by peaceful means. But at the same time, he laid emphasis on the development of nuclear technology, especially on the designing of high quality nuclear weapons. Thus, Khrushchev's offensive détente was the strategic ideology for ensuring the security of the Soviet Union. Of course, the objective conditions of Soviet Union forced Khrushchev to take this peculiar approach to security, which laid emphasis on peace, yet at the same time prepared unabashedly for war. With the emergence of Brezhnev again, the Soviet approach to security changed again and strengthening of Soviet forces was given top priority. In late 60s, Breznev undertook serious efforts for the accumulation of military force and modernization of technology to improve the quality of the Soviet forces. During this time, while formulating security policies, he gave top priority to the expansion of communism and at the same time sought to check the belligerent activities and the supremacy of United States over other nations. But during 70s, he changed his stand and accorded importance on détente when he realized that the world was on the brink of a nuclear war and that the entire world would perish if the nuclear war were to break out. Thus, he broadened the concept of security and tried to ensure the security of Soviet Union through the security of the entire world. His keen efforts to develop friendly relations with USA, Europe and Asian countries clearly reflected his inner desire for global peace and security. Besides military security, he also tried hard to strengthen political and economic security of Soviet Union by establishing good political and economic relations with CMEA and other countries of the world. Thus, during the later part of his rule, the tree of détente planted by Khrushchev came to blossom. Though he stressed on détente as it was the cardinal principle of his security policy, this was not to be at the cost of his ideological conviction. After Brezhnev, there were no spectacular changes in the Soviet concept of security during the time of Andropov and Chernenko. Andropov was convinced that peace could be achieved and security could be ensured not by arms build up, but by reducing existing armaments to lower levels.

In the mid 80s when Gorbachev came to power, there was economic stagnancy coupled with political instability and international turmoil. Gorbachev introduced the policy of "acceleration" (*Uskorenie*) to boost the efficiency of the ailing Soviet economy and allowed people to enhance their abilities appropriately – just after his assumption of power. But he announced *perestroika* (restructuring) officially in the 27th CPSU Congress, 1986 and continued it upto December 1991, i.e., the end of his tenure. During this *perestroika* phase, he came out with a package of security proposals. The proposal for *perestroika* did not come as manna from the heaven; it was his own brain-child, prepared after a careful and realistic assessment of the politico-economic situation of Soviet Union. A statesman and a visionary, his approach to security was humanistic. For him security was a holistic concept. His concept of security was integrated with the security of all members of the international community, where the opponents of Soviet Union became partners in its security endeavour and together they aimed at achieving universal security. In his words, "it is a way of mutually advantageous and reciprocal compromise, on the basis of which the supreme common interest prevents any conflict where there should be no striving for security for oneself at the expense of the other". This concept of Soviet security during *perestroika* known as 'comprehensive universal security' or common security which was enshrined in the 27th CPSU Congress. It was broader in connotation as it encompassed military, political, economical humanitarian aspects of security and tried to ensure the security of the Soviet Union through the security of the entire world. Though the external dimension of security was emphasized in such a universalistic security paradigm, the internal military, political, economic and humanitarian spheres were not underplayed but they were made to adopt a direction that would lead to universal security.

In the military sphere, there was a growing need of new institutions and ideas because the military-industrial complexes, old style ideologues and autarkic interests seemed outdated by then. Drastic changes were brought about in the Soviet armed forces and personnel. In fact, Gorbachev went in for drastic cut in resources aimed at slimming down the corpulent military bureaucracy. At the institutional level, changes were brought about in the Politburo, Defence Council and Central Committee Secretariat. The old military doctrine was rejected; the role of KGB was also drastically reduced and it was accorded responsibilities of lesser importance.

New military strategy and doctrine of reasonable sufficiency was given prominence for ensuring the security of the Soviet Union on the one hand and the security of the world on the other. The external dimension of military security during *perestroika* concerned 'the renunciation by the nuclear powers of war against each other or against any third country with either nuclear or conventional weapons'. When the world was on the brink of nuclear war, Soviet Union under the leadership of Gorbachev took consistent efforts to ease out the tension from the globe. Soviet concept of security also aimed at the "prevention of arms race in space, cessation of all nuclear weapons tests and total destruction of chemical weapons and renunciation of the development of other means of mass annihilation".

Soviet security model during *perestroika* was known as the doctrine of 'reasonable sufficiency' to guarantee security not by the highest possible but by lowest possible level of strategic parity with the western block. The disbanding of military alliance and the renunciation of the policy of parity along the upward spiral clearly reflected the New Thinker's desire for ushering in a noble world of cooperation and friendship instead of hatred and enmity. Thus the Soviet decision to spend money in civilian sectors, cutting down of the defence budget was the manifestation of the slogan 'Disarmament for development'.

In the political sphere, Gorbachev introduced changes in the Soviet state's approach to security at both internal and external levels. At the internal level, he introduced his policy of *Glasnost* (openness) which aimed at democratization of Soviet polity and freedom to the people through open debates and discussions.

During this time, Soviet Union witnessed a fundamental political and constitutional revolution that sought to lead his country towards an open system. Gorbachev thought it was needed for strengthening the internal environment and political structure of Soviet Union. His introduction of the factor of openness into internal political structure had had tremendous impact on the domestic decision-making apparatus and resulted in the gradual withering away of the ideological stiffness that led the block-politics going. This was something fundamentally different happening to the Soviet political system known for its 'rigid command structure' and its inscrutable ways that had led many to call it 'a mystery wrapped in an enigma inside a riddle'.

Thus the external dimension of Soviet security, ensuing from such openness, aimed at removing all the factors that led to antagonistic relationship between the two power blocs. It laid stress on the 'right of each people to choose the ways and forms of its development independently'. It also prepared the grounds for the 'just political settlement of international crises' and regional conflicts. Gorbachev realized that regional conflicts would weaken the security structure of the world and for a better and prosperous world these problems had to be solved amicably. His bold steps in this direction helped him in solving some of these problems. Soviet decision for creating an all embracing system of international security resulted in the 'elaboration of a set of measures aimed at building confidence between States and the creation of effective guarantees against attack from without and for inviolability of their frontiers'. This idea materialized in the Stockholm Conference, which created barriers against the use of force or constant preparation for war, whether on land, sea or air. Soviet Union also took steps for prevention of international terrorism, which was a threat to international security by destabilizing various parts of the world.

The economic security of Soviet Union under *perestroika* had two main extrapolations. In the domestic front, it tried to bring in reforms to boost the stagnant Soviet economy through structural changes and integrate Soviet economy into the new global economic order. Gorbachev revised the traditional Soviet approach to the world economy and sought to integrate Soviet economy with the economies of the rest of the world through mutual friendship, economic co-operation and trade relationship and the issue of ideological divide was pushed to the background. During this *perestroika* phase, Soviet Union improved the quality of Soviet manufactured goods and increased its exports. It expanded its trade with the West. The co-operation in the form of joint ventures was a major step taken by Soviet leader Gorbachev to strengthen the economic security of Soviet Union internally. As far as accession to international economic organizations was concerned, Soviet Union tried to become a member of GATT/WTO, World Bank and IMF. This had had good effects on the crisis-ridden Soviet economy and thus Gorbachev sought to transform it by preparing it to adjust to the new rules of the game in the world market.

In 1988, Soviet Union established official relations with EC. This was followed by the signing of the first long-term agreement on trade, economic and commercial cooperation in the year 1989. The 1989 agreement, which came into force on 1 April 1990, served as a legal foundation for the USSR-EC relations. As the situation in Europe and Soviet Union started changing during the *perestroika* period, Soviet Union was forced to take steps to integrate itself into the new European space; otherwise it would lead to isolation and threaten the stability and security of Soviet Union on the Continent. The relations between Soviet Union and EC also cleared the way for bilateral trade and cooperation between individual CMEA countries and EC.

Under Gorbachev's leadership, Soviet Union also tried its best to improve the efficiency of the CMEA, obviously, to get maximum economic benefits out of it. It initiated measures to strengthen the CMEA by intensifying the cooperation in the field of science and technology, the establishment of joint ventures, direct links between CMEA enterprises, joint exploitation of energy sources and convertibility of the transferable of the ruble. In the international front, several proposals were introduced and Gorbachev genuinely tried to implement those proposals for ensuring peace and security of the entire world. The most important proposal relating to international economic security was the "exclusion of all forms of discrimination, renunciation of the policy of economic blockades and sanctions, if this is not directly envisaged in the recommendations of world community". It condemned the policy of economic blockades and sanctions and demanded the abolition of those practices pursued by imperialist powers, which aimed at the economic isolation of certain State or group of States. It endorsed the UN move that States could only use collective measures for the purpose of maintaining international peace and security and only by the decision of the UN Security Council.

Another important proposal of this economic security was the "call for joint quest for ways of settlement of the problem of debts". In this context, Soviet Union supported the move taken by NAM, UN and the Latin American countries to solve this debt problem in a proper way adhering to the principle of justice and equality. Soviet leader Gorbachev favoured the NAM appeal for an urgent action to ease the burden of the debt. Soviet Union also took concrete steps in this direction. The third world countries and those who were in debt trap were to benefit from that measure.

During this phase, Soviet Union also supported the move of the Third World countries for the establishment of NIEO which aimed at creating cooperation among all States irrespective of their social economic systems, correction of existing inequalities, elimination of gap between developed and developing countries and ensuring economic and social development and peace and justice for coming generation. During this phase, Soviet Union expressed its keen desire to cooperate UN and other organizations in order to remove discriminatory restrictions and other artificially created obstacles for international economic relations.

Soviet Union also emphasized on North-South dialogue, which it considered essential, for strengthening international economic system. As Soviet Union considered the solution of international economic problems was closely connected with the termination of confrontation and arms race. So, it stressed on the "elaboration of principles for utilizing part of the funds released as a result of a reduction of military budgets for the good of the world community, of developing nations in the first place". Gorbachev tried seriously in this direction and even succeeded in changing the attitude of USA to cooperate in reducing armaments.

Another important proposal, which was emphasized by Soviet Union at the UN, was the one that sought to project a reasonable alternative to an arms race in outer space – a stage by stage programme for international cooperation in the exploration of outer space for peaceful purposes.

Humanitarian security during *perestroika* stressed on the inter-State relations and contacts among the people of various nations for the solution of the global problems as it believed in the principles of mutual trust and understanding of common problems and joint efforts for the solution of those problems. It concerned with Soviet human rights policy as a domestic issue and the issue of foreign policy. In the domestic sphere, democratization and glasnost (openness) were introduced which provided adequate freedom to the people by encouraging people of the Soviet Union to participate in open debates and discussions. It also tried to ensure a decent living to the people by improving Soviet economy as it was essential for them. During *perestroika* direct personal contacts in the cultural field both on individual and collective basis and contacts between cultural institutions and associations were encouraged. Soviet Union also took adequate steps for the abolition of genocide, apartheid and racial discrimination against the people. New laws were enacted for guaranteeing freedom of expression and freedom from religious persecution.

Soviet Union also tried to ensure socio-economic rights such as right to work and right to housing for its citizens. The provision of the international covenant on economic, social and cultural rights were formalized not only in the constitution of Soviet Union, but also in the fundamentals of labour legislation.

Soviet Union took genuine steps for re-orienting families, marriage and the promotion of contacts between people. It stressed on the exchanges of ideas in the sphere of art, science, education and medicine.

It is a fact that the concept of security evolved during *perestroika* was an alternative to power paradigms for it put least importance on power and considered security not as a derivative of power. However, even if the ideas of 'New Thinking' were idealistic in nature, the Soviet doctrine of 'reasonable sufficiency' took note of the fact that the issue of power could not be divorced from the concept of security. Thus, it was a complex combination of realism and idealism.

Soviet concept of security during *perestroika* had both theoretical and operational flaws for which it could not ensure the security of the Soviet Union from the conventional point of view. The fact that the policy of openness led to disintegration of the mighty Soviet Union has led many to conclude that the Gorbachev's approach to security had many loopholes in it. Firstly, his concept of security over-emphasized international security or universal security at the cost of security of the nation-state. It tried to ensure the security of the Soviet Union through the security of the entire world, which was not possible as nations could not change their attitudes at the cost of their national interests.

Secondly, the Soviet concept of security during *perestroika* was not enduring as it was a subjective concept and depended on the perceptions of the individuals, leaders in power, which were unpredictable. As international actors change, so do their approaches to security.

Thirdly, it could not hold good as objective factors were not under absolute human control.

Fourthly, there were inherent inconsistencies among the different levels of security, as was enunciated by Gorbachev's New Thinking. Particularly, the internal security of Soviet Union was not assessed properly. The peculiar problems facing the Soviet state at the internal level were not taken into consideration. The adoption of a liberal domestic policy at the internal sphere, which was a product of Soviet leader Gorbachev's international outlook made Soviet Union pay a heavy price as it led to disintegration of Soviet Union. In the military sphere, the internal and external changes in Soviet Union during *perestroika* had some negative effects, which made the Soviet security weak and not viable. It encouraged dissatisfaction among military personnel by its policy of appeasement of the civilians through military reforms. It also weakened the security set up as Soviet Union's broader reform agenda was having paradoxical consequences for it. The very strategy of *glasnost* and *perestroika* removed the rationale for a large standing military which stimulated internal political developments as secessionist movements and ethnic strife in a number of republics in Soviet Union. The doctrine of reasonable sufficiency, unilateral cut, attitudes of compromise were interpreted as weakness of the Soviet Union by the West and contributed also to the rise of his opponents inside his country which contributed to the shattering of the internal fabric of security. As military security was under-emphasized in relation to political and economic security, the concept of security did not evolve properly.

At the operational level, it did not succeed in changing the belligerent attitude even after Soviet leader took peace initiatives. Soviet Union's efforts to reduce military weapons and expectations of USA's cooperation in this direction had not produced expected result; on the other hand many analysts believed that USA penetrated into the internal politics of Soviet Union and hastened the fall of the Soviet empire.

In the political sphere, the internal reforms through '*Glasnost*' or openness provided enough liberty to the people to raise voice against the Soviet leader. The internal liberalization also encouraged the secessionist movements inside Soviet Union. The changes in Eastern Europe and unification of Germany had also influenced other nations, so also the republics of Soviet Union when they realized that Gorbachev would not resort to 'Stalinist' measures to suppress them. So this internal and external liberalization which led to social, environmental change together with Gorbachev's liberal attitude of non-interference and encouragement to the people to 'choose the ways and forms of its development independently' accelerated the process of disintegration. In fact, Gorbachev was not solely responsible for disintegration of Soviet Union but he committed a mistake without visualizing the 'destructive potential' of the *perestroika,* which belied his expectations by weakening the security set up instead of strengthening it. Another important factor, which accelerated the process of disintegration, was the attitudinal changes of the people of Soviet Union. As the Soviet Socialist System matured at the time of Gorbachev and citizens came to know about the pitfalls of the system, so the citizens of 80s and 90s were very much critical of the system than their predecessors. When freedom was given to them, ethnic, nationalist and regional problems, which were suppressed for a long time, surfaced in violent forms and those forces encouraged the secessionist trend in Soviet Union.

In the international front, the political changes aimed at a peaceful world. But when Soviet Union was out of power race, the balance of power tilted in favour of USA and made USA more powerful. Thus, it helped in a 'world to be ordered than a new world order'. In the economic sphere, Soviet concept of economic security did not succeed in overcoming its economic crisis. There were innumerable problems obstructed for an effective participation of Soviet Union in global economy. Though Western technology provided relief, yet it was constrained by foreign currency reserve as the COCOM regulations restricted technology transfer. In such a situation, it was too difficult on the part of the Soviet Union to involve seriously in the international economic system. Even western countries did not come forward to help *perestroika* by extending subsidized credits or allowing Soviet products to be sold in their market. Several other factors like the shortage of skilled and experienced executives to run things in a new way; the rigid bureaucratization; the imbalance between demand and supply; the difficult system of export licensing; the problem relating to internal convertibility of the rouble; the constraints of getting financial help from international institutions obstructed to engage actively in world economy. Further, the mismanagement of Soviet economy and misutilization of foreign borrowing coupled with the ineffectiveness of CMEA partners pushed Soviet Union into economic crisis.

In the international front, the economic security did not yield an expected result as USA and other western powers responded half-heartedly being guided by their interests rather than purely humanitarian concern. Even they were not keen to take some benevolent measures like helping the poor nations and spending a sizeable amount of money for solution of global problems.

Complete disarmament was also not possible as it required attitudinal changes of international actors, which was too difficult. Even Soviet Union did not play that much effective role as it was hard pressed with its own problems. Its poor economy, collapse of CMEA and resistance from Gorbachev's opponents brought obstacle in realizing his dream of a New World. Further easy way of accepting the payment of debts and assistance to third world countries during the early *perestroika* period aggravated the economic situation. Soviet leader Gorbachev even took some measures at the cost of Soviet economy only to exhibit his noble desire for a peaceful world, which of course, later on put him into real problem. Although it is too difficult to establish any direct linkage between economic security during *perestroika* and the end of Soviet system, yet, there is a perceptible link between economic changes at the internal level in Soviet Union and openness (*Glasnost*) and a positive international environment, which worked together to lead to the fall of Soviet Union.

In the humanitarian sphere, changes in Soviet culture, art, literature and the emphasis on human rights through *Glasnost* had some negative effects as Soviet society was toiling under the repressive policies of the communist dispensation for a long time. When people enjoyed liberty, they started revolting against the state mechanism and tried to secede from Soviet Union. Further, good relations with the West, compromising attitudes of Soviet Union, relying heavily on Western science and technology provided enough space to USA and other Western powers to penetrate into the internal security of the Soviet Union, which ultimately helped in the process of disintegration.

From the above analysis, it is clear that even if it was ideally designed, the Soviet concept of security during *perestroika* was unable to resolve the security problems of Soviet Union. Soviet concept of security during *perestroika* could have been more viable and sound had it looked into following questions.

1. There could have been efforts aimed at striking a balance among the three levels of security, i.e. individual, national and global security. Individual security should have been guaranteed not at the cost of national security and national security not at the cost of global security. An intelligent compromise between national security and international security or universal security was the need of the hour. The

domestic security arrangements could have been evolved in such a way that it would not have created any operational complications during this phase.

2. While formulating Soviet security policies, psychology of the individuals, nation state, peculiarities of that nation, world public opinion should have been taken into consideration. As perceptions vary so do the concepts of security, that is why some individuals feel secure with minimum security arrangements and some feel insecure with relatively better security arrangements. It is same also in case of nation states. Another important factor, which was not given due weightage by the 'New Thinkers', was the peculiarities of Soviet Union, which constituted its social structure, geography, culture and attitudes of the people.

   At the time of formulating security policies, these factors should have been considered and security arrangements should have been done in such a way that they should have catered to the needs of the people of Soviet Union without leading to security breakdown. It could have been possible if security policies were formulated after studying the situation in a proper context.

3. Soviet concept of security during *perestroika* could have been really universal in scope if it would not have been stable and could have adapted itself to the changing needs of the people.

4. A compact security system without any systemic problem could have been possible, if two sets of security set up would have been evolved. One could be 'Common Security' i.e. security for all nations. The other could be 'particular security', i.e. security arrangements taking the peculiarities of the domestic environment of the erstwhile Soviet Union.

5. As the concept of security is multidimensional and new dimensions can be added at anytime, the concept of security during this phase should have been flexible enough to accommodate the changes.

6. In fact, there was need of rational contextual study while formulating Soviet security policy, which could have been given a new direction to Soviet security.

Whatever might be the effects of Soviet security during *perestroika*, still it has contributed positively to the world and it has still some relevance after the disintegration of Soviet Union, particularly in the post-Soviet era, as it brought changes in military, political, economic and humanitarian spheres. It led to a new era by ending the cold war in a more peaceful way. At the same time, it liberated Soviet Union from the conceptual and ideological baggage that had heavily influenced in the past. Though Soviet Union is no more, the military reforms have had an enduring impact in post-Soviet phase. The ideas like renunciation of war, the danger of inadvertent nuclear war, prevention of arms race, interdependence in the sphere of security contributed positively in the making of a peaceful world free from nuclear holocaust. During this phase, confidence building mechanism between super powers, efforts for settling international conflicts, preventing terrorism, improving an atmosphere of peace and security ushered a new era. In the post-Soviet world, the Soviet concept of 'Comprehensive Universal Security' has been re-conceptualized and reformulated in a better way and strategic experts are trying to apply this for solving the problems of the world including the problems of South Asia.

In the economic sphere, though Soviet efforts for ensuring security did not succeed too much, yet it integrated Soviet economy wi h the global economic order and strengthened the relations between East and West, which moved towards stabilization and rapprochement. It also helped Soviet Union in various ways like exporting high quality of manufactured goods, improving trade with European community and the West by enjoying Most Favoured Nation (MFN) status, encouraging private investment in Soviet economy and also favouring the presence of MNCs in Soviet Union. It also encouraged cooperatives, individual enterprises and developed the idea of cost accounting culture. Though Soviet Union is no more, still this process of liberal economy is continuing in CIS countries including Russia. In fact, it can also be interpreted as a failure of socialism to pose as an alternative to capitalism for which it has been striving. It also exhibited the inner weakness of socialist system, which cannot be corrected and systemic change is inevitable. Soviet concept of international economic security tried sincerely for strengthening international economic system through various measures as discussed and also restructuring of it towards the establishment of the New International Economic Order (NIEO) based on sovereign equality, justice, equity mutual interest and benefit.

In the humanitarian sphere, though this concept of security has negative effects, yet it is more positive nature as it makes the system open and stresses on the human rights policies by giving complete liberty to the people, which is essential for the growth of the society. Its emphasis on democratization, cooperation among people and organizations in various spheres of activities like art, science, culture also exhibited the desire of Soviet leader Gorbachev and the 'New Thinkers' for a better mutual dependent 'one world' which in fact the need of the present world.

Though Soviet Union is no more, the broader framework during last two years of *perestroika* is still continuing in CIS, which came into existence after the declaration of Minsk and Alma Ata in December 1991. The CIS does not have a security structure as such and the efforts for an Unified Armed Forces (UAF) do not materialize due to internal differences among the states of CIS. CIS members such as Azerbaizan, Moldova and Ukraine discarded the unified command structure, Belarus adopted a 'middle position' and other CIS states including Central Asian Republics are also reluctant to remain within the structure as they fear the hegemony of Russia. Thus CIS states are no more a force to be reckoned with. The CIS including Russia are following Gorbachev and Andrei Kozyrov's approach of cooperation with the West in military, political, economic and other spheres of activities. Though Yeltsin, the President of Russia, mentioned that 'Russia has a right to act tough when it is really necessary' yet it cannot stop NATO's expansion and bend to the pressure of the West. In fact, the disintegration of Soviet Union has made the West more powerful and the West has known the weakness of Russia. So, it does not consider new Russia as a major power. The cooperation with the West can also be interpreted as inevitable for Russia to overcome its economic and social problems. Another factor is that Russia is a fractured nuclear power and it has much difference with other CIS members. Another important factor, which hinders the relationship between Russia and rest of the CIS states, is Russia's interference in the internal affairs of other states for protecting the rights of the Russian minority. The Russia's indirect backing to those minorities encourages secessionist trend, thus impedes in framing a security set up for the CIS.

In fact, initially, CIS members were misdirected; but gradually they are in a better position and moving towards integration. But they may take time to evolve the security structure provided they sort out their differences. The efforts in the sphere of disarmament, reduction of military budget and emphasis on 'conversion process', i.e. converting military expenditure to civilian products also reflect the significance of Gorbachev's security approach in CIS. In Russia, the Yeltsin government has pledged to continue with strategic arms reduction process began during Reagan Gorbachev period. Russia has also taken concrete steps in the direction by signing START II Treaty and CFE Treaty.

In the political sphere, CIS members are gradually gaining political stability. In the recent elections liberal political forces have won the election in the states of CIS which reflect people's support for democracy, liberty and open system, which has been started during *perestroika* period. But some states of CIS, particularly in Central Asia troublemakers and rabble-rousers have dominated and they are abetting terrorism, which is threatening to the security of those states. Serious steps should be needed to check it. The members of CIS should iron out their internal contradictions for strengthening political security, which is the need of the time.

At present, there is a need of confidence building mechanism for the stability of the CIS and to solve the problems of the world. Here, one can argue in favour of Soviet security during *perestroika,* as it was the cardinal idea in Gorbachev's concept of 'Comprehensive Universal Security'. In the economic sphere, CIS members have failed to integrate economically as they have differences. Central Asian states are supporting the move, but other CIS members are opposing it. At present, successor states of Soviet Union, particularly the Central Asian states, are in deep economic crisis and they are in need of economic stability, which may not be possible in near future for which they continue dependence on Russia. But, Russia is unable to help them as it is also in economic crisis. Russia is seriously trying to overcome its economic crisis and help other CIS members by its new economic policy and getting financial support from other countries and institutions like G7, IMF and World Bank. The only prescription for the treatment of the CIS including Russian economy is the reduction of the burden of the state through various measures. As far as the economic policy of the states of CIS are concerned, they are following the same liberal economic policy of the *perestroika* period and trying to integrate fully with Liberal International Economic Order. Now CIS members are trying seriously to improve trade relationship among themselves and with the West, which can reduce and redress their economic hardship. Russia– the true successor of erstwhile Soviet Union is taking measures like reducing state spending; providing a non-deficit budget; going for new borrowings; moving towards the paying off the debts; completing the privatization of the remaining state enterprises; pursuing tough monetary policies; de-regulating economic activity in sweeping fashion to strengthen its economic security etc. In fact, all the members of CIS including Russia are supporting the move of the Third World countries for the establishment of NIEO.

In the humanitarian sphere, the CIS members are determined to take steps to further human rights both at the national and international level. In this direction, Russia is trying its best to uphold personal rights and freedoms inside Russia and other parts of the world. Russia's efforts for ensuring minority rights are significant for the cause of peace and stability. Further, Russia is also trying to safeguard the economic and cultural interests of every nationality in the territory of the Russian Federation in accordance with national identity. Thus the humanitarian face of Soviet security during *perestroika* is reflected in Russia as it is trying for improving its relationship with other nations including the West and a transformation of the international political system towards humanization of international politics.

In the conclusion, one should admit the elements of continuity in post-Soviet phase. But in the present time, CIS can be a viable alternative to the USA if they iron out their differences and make efforts for a security structure with rational contextual study of the situation under the dynamic leadership of Russia and adhere to a common policy in the days to come. But it seems to be a distant dream as the security of New Russia is not stable and moving slowly from the state of Uncertainty to certainty.

In fact, it is a difficult task to sketch a map of threats to Russian security, as security of a nation is no more confined to neo-realistic view. At present, the concept of security is multi dimensional as it covers wide range of issues from the security of a nation to the security and well being of all the people everywhere. In Russian context, it is more complicated as New Russia is in the transitional phase and in the midst of security threats. In the military, political, economic and humanitarian spheres, it is facing different types of threats and new threats are surfacing as global politics is changing too fast. Here attempts have been made to enlist the threats to Russian security and steps taken and going to be taken by Russia to neutralize the negative trends in all the dimensions of Russian Security. At present Russia is in process of defining a democratic and nationalist concept of security unlike Soviet regime's global and hegemonic one.

In the military sphere, reforms have been introduced to improve the military capability of Russia to defend its national interests and to meet the threats emanating from different quarters. Emphasis has been given to reform the administrative system within the framework of military reform to make the military setup more effective and to strengthen the military system to meet the need of time. For making the military security more effective, it not only introduced modern methods and techniques for renovation of its military buildup but also reduced the number of nuclear weapons and manpower from army to save the Russian economy from huge military expenditure. But strategic experts of Russia and the West think that military reforms in Russia have not brought desired results due to lack of consensus among military and political elites, shortage of financial resources, the conflict in Chechnya, the weak response from political officials and the public to the repeated failure of military reform, inadequate outside support to create pressure for reforms.

In the external dimension, Russia is also taking sincere steps to reduce the tension of the globe and to curb international terrorism for which it has supported the move of US and the rest of world, and also taking initiatives to integrate within West's security structure. Though it has tried genuinely for ensuring military security, yet its efforts are not adequate and at present Russia's military security is not free from problems. It needs a holistic approach, ideological and methodological framework for its solutions.

In the political sphere Russia introduced federative reforms with emphasis on harmonization of regional constitutions and legislation with federal law and the RF constitution in the name of the "reintegration of Russia's legal space". This reform not only reorganized and reduced the administrative regimes of Russia, and curtailed the powers of governors but also helped in checking corruption, nepotism, favoritism, and thus ensuring political stability to a larger extent.

So far as the external dimension of political security of Russia is concerned, it tries to develop healthy relations with China and CIS countries for balancing the power equation with US. At the same time it also took initiatives to strengthen its relations with Central Asia, South East Asia and other Asian countries to generate capital from outside in order to resuscitate its economy that have fallen off the charts since 1991. Russia under the leadership of Putin also reflected its pragmatism and vision by choosing a middle course between the extremes of Gorbachev and Kozyrov's westernism and Primakov's great power balance to work with USA. He has broadened the political security of Russia by replacing the value-loaded concept of security to the requirements considering the national interests of Russia. At present Russia has improved its political relations with USA and West excluding Iraqi and Iranian case where USA and West are against Russia's move.

In the economic sphere Russia is working hard to cope with the pulse of realities. It has two extrapolations, internal and external.

In the internal dimension, it has brought institutional reforms in key areas to revamp its economy. Putin has brought changes in taxing system and reduce regulatory obstacles to improve the quality of administration as well. He has streamlined the administration to certain extent by checking the privatization that started in 1990 and still continues, and massive corruption by oligarchs. At present unlike earlier period, the negative trends in Russian economy are gradually eroding, the business environment is improving and consumerism is spreading through Russian business confidence. But there are problems like decline of work force, post unemployment, reduction in labour force participation and wide spreading infractions etc. The gap between rich and poor has not been reduced and illegitimacy of initial distribution of property rights have not been sorted out which affect the Russian economy. Now it is a right time to implement policies to overcome these problems otherwise Russian economy may lag behind and cannot catch up with the fast growing economy of developed nations.

In the external dimension, Russia is trying to integrate into global economy through constructive efforts like healthy bilateral and multilateral trade relations with powerful Asian and European countries, opening up its economy for MNCs and FIIs by loosening trade and tariff system, emphasizing on 'import substitute export promotion'. Russia's membership of WTO, G8 and financial institutions has accelerated the process of stabilization of its economy. Russia's wholehearted efforts to improve its ties with Asian and European countries and decision for establishment of Common European Economic Area are positive steps in this direction. At present Russia is also exploring possibilities for joint ventures with Asian and European companies in oil and gas sector to expand its export capabilities.

After 9/11, Russia has improved its relations with USA and seriously thought for constructive engagement in trade and commerce. But unless and until Russia cleans up its economic acts at home, it is a grueling task to improve its relations with immediate neighbours, USA and the West. In Russia's security framework, human security has not been underscored. Putin's unflagging zeal and indomitable spirit to ensure the safety and well being of all the people including Russians 'everywhere-in their homes, in their streets in their communities and in their environment' prove his keenness and interest in human security and love for humanity.

Appendix

27th CPSU Congress Political Report on Comprehensive Universal Security

We are living in a world of realities and are building our international policy in keeping with this specific features of the present phase of international development. Creative analysis of this phase and vision of prospects have laid us to a conclusions that is highly significant. Now, as never before, it is important to find ways for closer and more productive cooperation with governments, parties, and mass organisations and movements that genuinely concerned about the destines of peace on earth, with all peoples in order to **build an all- embracing system of international security**.

We see the fundamental principles of the system in the following

1. In the Military Sphere

- renunciation by the nuclear powers of war- both nuclear and conventional-against each other or against third countries;
- prevention of arms race in outer space, cessation of all nuclear weapons tests and the total destruction of such weapons, a ban on and the destruction of chemical weapons, and renunciation of the development of other means of mass annihilation;
- a strictly controlled lowering of a the levels of military capabilities of countries to limits of reasonable adequacy;

- disbandment of military alliances, and as a stage towards this- renunciation of their enlargement and of the formation of new ones;
- balanced and proportionate reduction of military budgets.

2. In the Political Sphere

- strict respect in international practice for the right of each people to choose the ways and forms of its development;
- a just political settlement of international crises and regional conflicts;
- elaboration of a set of measures aimed at building confidence between states and the creation of effective guarantees against attack from without and of the inviolability of their frontiers;
- elaboration of effective methods of preventing international terrorism, including those ensuring the safety of international land, air, and sea communications.

3. In the Economic Sphere

- exclusion of all forms of discrimination from international practice; renunciation of the policy of economic blockades and sanctions if this is not directly envisaged in the recommendations of the world community;
- joint quest for ways for a just settlement of the problem of debts;
- establishment of a new world economic order guaranteeing equal economic security to all countries;
- elaboration of principles for utilizing part of the funds released as a result of reduction of military budgets for the good of the world community, of developing nations in the first place;
- the pooling of efforts in exploring and making peaceful use of outer space and in resolving global problems on which the destinies of civilization depend.

4. In the Humanitarian Sphere

- cooperation in the dissemination of the ideas of peace, disarmament, and international security; greater flow of general objective information and broader contact between peoples for the purpose of learning about one another; reinforcement of the spirit of mutual understanding and concord in relations between them;

- extirpation of genocide, apartheid, advocacy of fascism and every other form of racial, national or religious exclusiveness, and also of discrimination against people on this basis;
- extension-while respecting the laws of each country- of international cooperation in the implementation of the political, social, and personal rights of people;
- decision in a humane and positive spirit of questions related to the reuniting of families, marriage, and the promotion of contacts between people and between organisations;
- strengthening of and quests for new forms of cooperation in culture, art, science, education, and medicine.

These Principles stem logically from the provisions of the Programme of the CPSU. They are entirely in keeping with our concrete foreign policy initiatives. Guided by them it would be possible to make peaceful coexistence the highest universal principles of relations between states. In our view, these Principles could become the point of departure and a bilateral and multilateral-among leaders of countries of the world community.

Source: ***27th CPSU Congress, Documents and Resolutions*, (New Delhi: Allied Publishers, 1986), pp. 96-99.**

Mikhail Gorbachev's Message to International Conference on the Relationship between Disarmament and Development

I send you my heartfelt greeting and express the hope that the international conference will find new possibilities in the approach to solving this cardinal problem of our time.

The obstacles on the road to the conference created by the opponents of disarmament have confirmed once again the interdependence of disarmament and development and the urgency of the task.

It is time for all to realise that by leaving, willingly or not, the peoples of some regions and even of while continents in the position of exploited and destitute ones, mankind risks causing an explosion that would be no less lethal than a thermonuclear clash.

The conference is opening at a time favourable for the study of the problem – at the juncture of the ripe requirement and already existing possibilities. Only recently, prior to Reykjavik and the "double global zero" variant, it seemed to be very remote. But today, the roads to disarmament and development are coming closer not only in wishes but also in real politics.

I have in mind the possible agreement on the total elimination of two classes of nuclear missiles which could be signed even tomorrow if the United States and the RFG removed the obstacle that is known to all.

I have in mind the possibility of substantially reducing the strategic offensive arms of the two biggest nuclear powers in conditions of strengthening the ABM Treaty.

A certain optimism is being instilled by the progress at the talks in Geneva and within the framework of the conference on disarmament where representatives of 40 countries have closely approached the conclusion of a convention on banning chemical weapons and destroying their stockpiles.

The principle of development through disarmament is organically built into the concept, of creating an all-embracing system of international peace and security which was proposed to the world community by the group of socialist countries. And the fact that this concept is getting the moral and political support of many states, I also refer to the category of favourable conditions of the conference's work.

Last but not least, there is the obvious acute concern of the world community and influential political circles over the economic situation in the zone of developing countries. Many people now see the connection between their unprecedented debt, generated by non-equivalent exchange, this new form of colonialist plunder, and the growth of the military budgets of imperialist States The horrific unfairness of the fact that the former are paying for a big part of the latter's military expenditures is obvious as well.

We and our friends propose sure ways and means of putting an end to this situation. I hope that the conference will take into consideration the document of countries of the socialist community "On Overcoming Underdevelopment and Establishing a New International Economic Order", which was adopted in Berlin.

There is no end to work for the world community in this direction. I am convinced that the conference will be able to make an appreciable and competent contribution to the internationalisation of efforts to turn disarmament into a factor of development.

The participants in the conference can count on our vigorous participation and support. The Soviet Union has already demonstrated in practice that it stands for the intensification of the work of international forums tackling problems of the arms race, including the Geneva conference on disarmament.

We will further do everything possible to strengthen the authority of the United Nations Organization and its role in assisting development through disarmament. We believe that the United Nations Security Council should address itself to this directly as well.

It would be useful to discuss problems of disarmament and development in terms of fundamentals at a special meeting of the top leaders of the United Nations Security Council's member-states.

The implementation of the basic principle "disarmament for development" can and must rally mankind and help the formation of its global outlook.

We stand for more openness in respect of military activity and military expenditures and persistently propose to conduct a comparison of the military doctrines of NATO and the Warsaw Treaty. This would make it possible to approach a realistic comparison of military budgets as well with the aim of putting a stop to their swelling and limiting them to the level of reasonable sufficiency.

It is necessary to stop and reverse the process of militarisation. The drawing up by each State of its own national plan of conversion would be an important step along this road strengthening international trust and testifying to the resolve to scale down military production.

In order to transfer to the needy countries the means that would be made available in the course of disarmament, it would be desirable to create within the framework of the United Nationals Organization an international fund "Disarmament for Development" that would be open to all States. The USSR is prepared to take part in such a fund.

Mankind wants to be confident that it has a future. Your decisions will help strengthen the faith that there will be a future.

Source: *TASS*, August 26, 1987.

Political Report of the 28th Congress of the CPSU, On Security.

The Security of the Country

As long as the danger of armed conflict exists, the country needs a reliable defence. The party deems it necessary:

- to carry out military reform on the basis of a new defence doctrine, the principle of reasonable sufficiency, and the priority of quantitative parameters in the development of the armed forces;
- to retain the fundamental questions of the country's defence and security, as well as the development, training and employment of the Armed Forces under the exclusive jurisdiction of the Union of Soviet Socialist Republics;
- to enhance social security (including life and health insurance for servicemen) and to improve the living conditions of servicemen and their families;

- to use the army strictly for its intended purpose and in full accordance with legislation;
- to exercise effective political leadership in the sphere of defence and control by the supreme bodies of power over the military department which must operate with the utmost openness, taking into account the level of trust achieves between states;
- to strengthen the ideological influence of the CPSU on personnel through Party branches and Communists in the Armed Forces;
- to carry through their state conversion programme and to use the potential released for civilian production, providing social protection for the employees.

Remaining a vital institution, in present conditions, defending the constitutional system and maintaining public order, the internal affairs and state security organs should act strictly within the law and be controlled by the representative authorities. It is necessary to raise the standard of professional training and material security of those employed in the law-enforcement organs.

Towards a Renewed Union of Sovereign Republics

For a Voluntary Union of Peoples. The CPSU maintains that the development of centrifugal tendencies can be prevented only on the basis of the democratisation of relations among nations and national-state formations of the Union of Soviet Socialist Republics, and the successful economic development of all regions and of the integral nationwide market system. The Party proceeds from the recognition of the right of nations to self-determination, including secession, but does not confuse the right to withdrawal from the USSR with the expediency of such a withdrawal. It considers that, bearing in mind the interests of the peoples themselves and the tendency of world processes towards integration, it is important to preserve the integrity of the renewed Union as a dynamic multinational state. The CPSU advocates the friendship and international unity of all nations and ethnic groups in the country.

The Party will pursue the policy of strengthening the sovereignty of the Union Republics. It proposes the political and legal multiplicity of relations among the republics themselves and with the Union as a whole and their diverse economic relations on the basis of the economic independence of enterprises.

The CPSU is in favour of raising the constitutional status and expanding the rights of the autonomous republics, regions, and areas.

The Party deems it necessary to provide favourable conditions for the development of all nations and ethnic groups:

- to strengthen legal guarantees for cultural and ethnic communities with no administrative or territorial status, as well as their right to table draft laws in the state organs of the USSR and republican authorities and to have a quota representation in them;
- to take urgent economic, legal and ecological measures to preserve the environment and to reproduce conditions ensuring the normal development of ethnic minorities;
- to confirm the right of peoples deported in the past from their historical homeland or traditional places of residence to return to them, and also citizens' right to return to their historical homeland from abroad.

Human Rights and the Rights of Nations

The CPSU is:

- in favour of expanding the rights of nations while recognising the priority and unfailing and unconditional guarantees to the rights of every human being;
- against the existence of any legal norms or laws allowing inequality of citizens on the basis of their nationality, and in favour of a complete freedom of choice in individual national self-determination;
- in favour of respect for the cultural traditions and interests of all the ethnic groups of the population in adopting the republican legal norms and laws.

Towards the Peaceful Development of Mankind

The Party believes that soviet foreign policy should proceed from the ideas of peace, cooperation, interaction, progress and humanism and promote in every way both domestic reform and international stability.

Foreign Policy Guidelines. In order to strengthen universal security, the Party advocates:

- a vigorous continuation of the successfully launched policy of demilitarisation of international relations, armament and armed force reductions to the limits of reasonable defence sufficiency, the complete exclusion of the use or threat of force from international practice, the further lessening and then utter elimination of military confrontation;
- the building of a global and regional security structures on the basis of the balanced interests of all parties to preclude conflicts and international instability;
- putting the relations between states on a legal footing guaranteeing the freedom of social and political choice, sovereignty, independence, and the development of cooperation and partnership with all countries of the world;
- the further normalisation of Soviet-American relations and their channeling into constructive partnership; creative participation in the all-European process and putting an end to the historical split in Europe; the development of new forms of political and economic cooperation with the East European countries; the consolidation in all areas of positive trends in relations with the People's Republic of China; active policies in the Asia-Pacific Region, with the aim of turning in the political settlement of regional conflicts; interaction with the non-aligned movement and cooperation with the developing states.

Towards Qualitatively New International Cooperation

The Party deems it of vital importance to pool the efforts of all members of the international community in solving problems common to all mankind.
It is in favour of:

- vigorous joint initiatives to improve the environment and prevent an ecological disaster;

- our country's participation in the efforts of the international community to overcome hunger, poverty, mass epidemics, serious diseases, drug addiction, international terrorism and critical imbalances in the development of different parts of the world;
- intensive expansion of world economic contacts, the elimination of impediments to scientific, technological and economic exchanges and the development of contacts in the humanitarian field;
- interaction and cooperation with all international organisations on a regional and global scale, acting on the principle of historical responsibility for the future of mankind.

The CPSU is in favour of overcoming the historical split in the workers' movement and developing cooperation between Communist, Socialist, Social-Democratic and National Democratic parties, as well as all organisations and movements advocating peace, democracy, and social progress.

The Renewal of the Party

Being the core of the command system of administration for many years, the Party itself has undergone serious deformations. The over-centralisation and suppression of critical thought have had a pernicious effect on inner-Party relations. The ideological and moral degradation of some party leaders has caused enormous damage.

The Congress points out that the CPSU, as the ruling party, is politically and morally responsible for the situation in this country. It has been frank about the mistakes made by the country's party and government leaders and has denounced Stalinist crimes and gross violations of human rights. The congress, however, resolutely opposes wholesale accusations leveled against honest Communists of both the past and selflessly served the people, working and fighting courageously for the freedom and independence of their homeland. Progressive forces have always been active in the CPSU and it was they who initiated and spearheaded the restructuring of society.

The CPSU firmly renounces political and ideological monopoly and supersession for the bodies of state and economic management. Dynamic changes call for a speedy transformation of the CPSU into a genuine political party which reflects and defends the vital interests of the working class, the peasants and the intelligentsia and acts within the framework of a civil society.

Sources: *28th Congress of the CPSU, Documents and Materials*, (Moscow: Novosti Press, 1990), pp. 87-91.

Bibliography

1. Primary Sources

Andropov, Y.V., *Speeches, Articles, Interviews- A Selection* (New Delhi: Allied Publishers, 1984).

Arms Control and Disarmament Agency: World Wide Military Expenditures and Arms Transfers (Washington D.C.: US Government Printing Office, 1980).

Brezhnev, L. I., "Reports of the CPSU Central Committee and the Immediate Tasks of the Party in Home and Foreign Policy", *Socialism Theory and Practice*, No. 3, (March 1976).

"*Brighter Prospects for US-Soviet Trade?*", Current Digest of Soviet Press, Vol. 37, No. 50, (January 8,1986), pp. 1-5.

Chernenko, V., *Selected Speeches and Articles* (New Delhi: Allied Publishers, 1984).

Congress of Peoples Deputies of the USSR, Moscow, Kremlin, May 25-June 9, 1989, Documents and Materials (Moscow: Novosti Press, 1989),

Documents of the meeting of the Political Consultative Committee of the Warsaw Treaty Member States, Berlin, May 28-29, 1987 (Moscow: Novosti Press, 1987).

Facts on File, (New York: Facts on File Inc.).

Foreign Policy Concept (June 2000):

Foreign Policy Reports 1945-1952 (New York: Foreign Policy Association).

For Building New Relations in the Asia-Pacific Region, Speech by Mikhail Gorbachev, at Krasnoyarsk, September 16, 1988 (New Delhi: Allied Publishers, 1988).

Geneva, *The Soviet-USA Summit, November 1985, Documents and Materials* (Moscow: Novosti Press, 1985).

Geneva, Reykjavik, Washington, Moscow (Moscow: Novosti Press, 1988).

Gorbachev's, Speeches and Writings (Oxford: Pergamon, 1986).

Gorbachev: Bringing Out the Potential of Socialism More Fully (Moscow: Novosti Press, 1988).

Gorbachev: At the Crucial Stage of Perestroika (Moscow: Novosti Press, 1989).

Gorbachev: New Political Thinking (Moscow: Novosti Press, 1989).

Gromyko, A., *On the International Situation and the Foreign Policy of the Soviet Union* (Moscow: Novosti Press, 1983).

Interfox News Agency, in Russian 1440 gmt, 9 November 2000.

ITAR-TASS News Agency, Moscow, in English 1750 gmt, 9 November 2000.

ITAR-TASS 26 November 2002 in *WNC Military Affairs*, 27 November 2002.

Ivashchenko, A., "Foreign Trade in the Perestroika Era", *The Current Digest of the Soviet Press*, Vol. XL, No. 34, (September 21, 1998), pp. 7-9.

Lenin, V. I., *Collected Works*, Vols. 22 & 30, (Moscow: Progress Publishers, 1964).

Mikhail Gorbachev's Answers to Questions Put by L'Unita (Moscow: Novosti Press, 1987).

Mikhail Gorbachev Interviewed by Der Spiegel (Moscow: Novosti Press, 1988).

Mikhail Gorbachev, "For a 'Common European Home', For a New Way of Thinking", Speech by the General Secretary of the CPSU CC at the Czechoslovak-Soviet Friendship Meeting, Prague, 10 April 1987, *Documents and Materials* (Moscow: Novosti Press, 1987).

Mikhail Gorbachev, "Address at the 43rd Session of the UN General Assembly", New York, 7 December 1988, *Soviet Review Documents* (New Delhi: New Age Printing Press, 1988).

Mikhail Gorbachev, "Address at the Meeting to mark the 40th Anniversary of the German Democratic Republic", Berlin, 6 October 1989, *Documents and Materials* (Moscow: Novosti Press, 1989).

Mikhail Gorbachev, *The Speech in Murmansk, October 1, 1987* (Moscow: Novosti Press, 1988).

Mikhail Gorbachev, *Peace has no alternative, Speeches, Articles, Interviews* (New Delhi: Patriot Publishers, 1986).

Mikhail Gorbachev talks to the Delegation from the House of Representatives of the US Congress (Moscow: Novosti Press, 1987).

Mikhail Gorbachev's address to the Congress of Deputies on May 30, 1989 (Moscow: Novosti Press, 1989).

Mikhail Gorbachev's Visit to Cuba, Address to the National Assembly of the Republic of Cuba, April 2-5, 1989, *Soviet Review Documents* (New Delhi: New Age Printing Press, 1989).

National Security Concept (January 2000):

"Pavlov Sets Hard Line on Economic Reform," *The Current Digest of Soviet Press,* Vol. XLIII, No. 6, (March 13, 1991), pp. 1-5.

Putin's address of 4 September 2004 , on the presidential website: www.kremlin.ru.

Prime Minister Nikolai Ryzhkov's Speech before Congress of People's Deputies, June 8, 1989 (Moscow: Novosti Press, 1989).

Russian: 'Kontseptsiya Vneshey Politiki Rossiyskoy Federatsii', *Nezavisimoye Voyennoye Obozreniye*, 25 (14 July 2000).http://www.scrf.gov.ru/Document/Decree/2000/07-10.html

English: http://www.fas.org/nuke/guide/russi/doctrine/econcept.htm 012400.htm

Russian: 'Kontseptsiya natsionalnoy bezopasnosti', *Nezavisimoye Voyennoye Obozreniye*, 1(14 January 2000). http://www.scrf.gov.ru/Documents/Decree/2000/24-1.html.

English: www.fas.org/nuke/guide/russia/doctrine/gazeta 012400.htm

Russian Regional Report, 12th February 1998, Published by East West Institute, Moscow

Russian Military Doctrine, (April 2000):

Russian: 'Voyennaya doktrina Rossiyskoy Federatsii', *Nezavisimoye Voyennoye Obozreniye*, 15 (28 April 2000).www. Scrf.gov.ru/document /decree/2000/706-1.html.English:www.freerepublic.com/forum/a394aa0466bfe.htm.

Soviet Military Power (Washington D.C.: US Department of Defence, 1983).

St. Petersburg Times, June 11,2004.

Summary Of World Broad Cast, Su/399/B/13, 16 November 2000.

Summary of World Broad Cast (SWB) Su/3995/SI/1, 11 November 2000.

Summary of World Broad Cast (SWB) Su/3995/ SI/1, 11 November 2000.

Summary of World Broad Cast ,Su/3999B/3, 16 November 2000.

The Result and Lessons of Reykjavik Summit Meeting in the Iceland Capital, Oct.-12, 1986 (Moscow: Novosti Press, 1986).

The Alliance Strategic Concept (Brussels: NATO Office of Information and Press,1999).

"The Elite's Feeling the Heat", *Moscow Times*, 10 April 2003 in Johnson's List, 10 April2003

US Defence Department, *Soviet Military Power*, (Washington, D.C.: US Government Printing Office).

USSR-US Summit, Washington, December 7-10, 1987, *Documents and Materials* (Moscow: Novosti Press, 1987).

USSR-US Summit, Moscow, May 29-June 2, 1988, *Documents and Materials* (Moscow: Novosti Press, 1988).

Visit of Mikhail Gorbachev to France, July 4-6, 1989, *Documents and Materials* (Moscow: Novosti Press, 1989).

Visit of Mikhail Gorbachev to China, May 15-18, 1989, *Documents and Materials* (Moscow: Novosti Press, 1989).

Visit of Mikhail Gorbachev to Great Britain, April 5-7, 1989, *Documents and Materials* (Moscow: Novosti Press, 1989).

Yaremenko, Y., "Key to Perestroika: Market Plus Plan", *The Current Digest of Soviet Press,* Vol. XL. No. 40, (November 2, 1988), pp. 17, 18 and 31.

1st Session of the USSR Supreme Soviet, *Mikhail Gorbachev's Address, Moscow, Kremlin* (Moscow: Novosti Press, 1989).

19th All Union Conference of the CPSU, Report by Mikhail Gorbachev, *Documents and Materials* (Moscow: Novosti Press, 1988).

28th Congress of the CPSU, *Documents and Materials* (Moscow: Novosti Press, 1990).

XXVII CPSU Congress, Political Report of the CPSU Central Committee of the Communist Party of the Soviet Union, Delivered by Mikhail Gorbachev, General Secretary of the CPSU Central Committee, *Soviet Review Documents*, Vol. XXIII, No. 10, (New Delhi: New Age Printing Press, 1986).

XXVII CPSU Congress, *Documents and Resolutions* (New Delhi: Allied Publishers, 1986).

2. Secondary Sources

2. (i). Books

Abram, B., *Planning and Performance in Socialist Economics* (London: Unwin Hyman, 1989).

Aganbegyan, A., *The Challenge: Economics of Perestroika* (London: Hutchinson, 1988).

Alford, J., (ed.), *The Soviet Union Security Policy and Constraints* (New York: St. Martin's, 1985).

Allison, Roy., Bluth, Christoph.,(ed.),*Security Dilemmas in Russia and Eurasia*(London:Royal Institute of International Affairs,1998).

Alvin, Z., and Stein, R., *Soviet Foreign Policy since World War II: Imperial and Global* (New York: Harper Collins, 1992).

Aron, R., "The Quest for a Philosophy of Foreign Affairs", in Stanley Hoffman (ed.), *Contemporary Theory in International Relations* (New Delhi: Printence-Hall, 1964).

Asirvatham, E., *Political Theory* (New Delhi: S. Chand & Co, 1988).

Barnet, Richard J., and Falk, A., (eds.), *Security in Disarmament* (Princeton: Princeton University Press, 1965).

Barringer, Richard E., *War: Patterns of Conflicts* (Cambridge: The MIT Press, 1972).

Baylis, J., Booth, K., Garret, J., and Williams, P., *Contemporary Strategy* (London: Croom Helm, 1975).

Bennett, Paul R., *The Soviet Union and Arms Control* (New York: Praeger, 1989).

Breslauer, G., (ed.), *Soviet Strategy in the Middle East* (Winchester, MA: Unwin Hyman, 1990).

Brezhnev, L. I., *Following Lenin's Course* (Moscow: Progress Publishers, 1975)

Brezhnev, L. I., *Pages From His Life* (New Delhi: Allied Publishers, 1979).

Bugajski,Janusz., *Cold peace:Russia's new imperialism* (Westport:Praeger, 2004).

Bull, H., *The Control of the Arms Race* (New York: Frederick A. Praeger, 1961).

Bull, H., *The Control of the Arms Race: Disarmament and Arms Control in Missile Age* (London: Weidenfeld & Nicholson, 1961).

Bull, H., *Arms Control* (London: Macmillan, 1987).

Bush, K., *From Command Economy to the Market Economy* (Aldershot: Dartmouth Publishing, 1991).

Buzan, B., *People, States and Fear* (Great Britain: Wheatsheaf Books, 1983).

Buzan, B., (ed.), *The International Politics of the Deterrence* (London: Frances Pinter, 1987).

Buzan, B., Wæver, O., and Wilde, Jaap De., *Security: A New Framework for Analysis* (Boulder: Lynne Reinner, 1998).

Carnesale, A., and Haas, Richard N., *Superpower Arms Control* (Cambridge: Ballinger, 1987).

Carr, E. H., *The Bolshevik Revolution 1917 to 1923*, Vol. 3, (London: Penguin, 1977).

Chopra, V. D., (ed.), *Mikhail Gorbachev's New Thinking in Asia-Pacific* (New Delhi: Continental Publishing House, 1988).

Chopra, V. D., Gidadhubli, R.G., Mishra, G., (eds.) *Soviet Economic Reforms in the USSR* (New Delhi: Patriot Publishers, 1989).

Cimbala, Stephen J., and Dunn, Keith A., *Conflict Terminations and Military Strategy* (Boulder: Westview Press, 1987).

Clausewitz, Carl, V., *On War* (London: Routledge, 1962)

Clemens, Walter C, Jr., *Can Russia Change? The USSR Confronts Global Interdependence* (London: Unwin Hyman, 1990).

Cohen, Ariel.,(ed.), *Eurasia in Balance* (Aldershot:Ashgate, 2005).

Couch, M., *Revolution and Evolution: Gorbachev and Soviet Politics* (New Delhi: Prientice-Hall 1990).

Davis, M., (ed.), *Security Issues in the Post-Cold War World* (Cheltanham: Edward Elgar, 1996).

Davis, R. W., *Soviet History in the Yeltsin Era* (New York: St Martin's Press, 1997).

Deger, S., and Sen, S., *Military Expenditure: The Political Economy of International Security* (New York: Oxford University Press, 1990).

Desai, P., *Perestroika in Perspective* (London: I. B. Tauris & Co, 1989).

Deutscher, I., *The Prophet Arm* (Oxford: Oxford University Press, 1976).

Dinerstein, Herbert S., *War and the Soviet Union* (New York: Praeger, 1959).

Donaldson, R. etal., *The Foreign Policy of Russia,Changing systems, Eunduring Interests* (London:M.E.Sharpe,1998).

Dunlop,John B.,*The Rise of Russia and the Fall of the Soviet Empire* (Princeton: Princeton University Press, 1994).

Dyke, Vernon Van., *International Politics* (Bombay: Vakils Feffer and Simons, 1969).

Dyker, David A., *The Future of the Soviet Economy Planning System* (London: Croom Helm, 1985).

Earle, Edward M., *Makers of Modern Strategy: Military Thought from Machiavelli to Hitler* (New York: Atheneum, 1966).

Edwards, David E., *Arms Control in International Politics* (New York: Rinhart and Winston Inc, 1969).

Enzor, G., *The European Community and the Developing Countries* (London: Cambridge University Press, 1993).

Feffer, J., *Beyond Détente: New Options on East-West Relations* (London: I.B. Tauris and Co, 1990).

Flynn, G., *The Internal Fabric of Western Security* (Allenheld: Osmun & Co, 1981).

Francois, H., (ed.), *The Strategic Implications of Change in Soviet Union* (London: Macmillan, 1990).

Friedlander, M., (ed.) *Foreign Trade in Eastern Europe and Soviet Union* (Boulder: Westview Press, 1990).

Garthoff, R., *Soviet Military Policy: A Historical Analysis* (London: Faber and Faber, 1966).

Gati, C., *The Bloc that Failed* (Bloomington: Indian University Press, 1990).

Ghali, B. B., *An Agenda for Peace* (New York: United Nations, 1992).

Gilberg, S.,(ed.), *Security Implications of Nationalism in Eastern Europe* (Boulder: Westview Press, 1986).

Gilpin, R., *War and Change in World Politics* (Cambridge: Cambridge University Press, 1981).

Gnevushev, N., *Disarmament for Development* (New Delhi: Allied Publishers, 1987).

Goodman, Malvin A., *Gorbachev's Retreat to the Third World* (New York: Preager, 1991).

Gorbachev, M. S., *Perestroika: New Thinking for Our Country and the World* (London: Fontana/Collins, 1987).

Gorbachev, M. S., *On Major Directions of the USSR's Domestic and Foreign Policy* (Moscow: Novosti Press, 1989).

Gormley, Denis, M., *Double Zero and Soviet Military Strategy* (Shrewsbury: Triservice, 1990).

Gotfried, K., and Blair, Bruce G., (eds.), *Crisis Stability and Nuclear War* (New York: Oxford University Press, 1988).

Graham, B., *Security Analysis: Principles and Techniques* (New York: McGraw Hill, 1962).

Gray, Collin, S., *The Geo Politics of Super Power* (Kentuky: University Press of Kentuky, 1988).

Grazini, G., *Gorbachev's Economic Strategy in the Third World* (New York: Praeger, 1990)

Green, William C., and Karasik, T., (eds.), *Gorbachev and His Generals: The Reform of the Soviet Military Doctrine* (Boulder: Westview Press, 1990).

Grudzinski, Premyslaw Ham.,Peter Vam., *Integrating Russia in Europe:mission impossible?* (Esbjerg:South Jutland University Press,1997).

Gupta, A., *Ideology and Soviet Foreign Policy: Lenin to Gorbachev* (New Delhi: A. V. Genus Publishing House, 1993).

Hall, R., *Soviet Military Art in a Time of Change: Command and Control of the Future Battlefield* (London: Brassey's, 1991).

Ham Peter, V., *Western Doctrines on East-West Trade* (London: Macmillan, 1992).

Hanson, Philip and Bradshaw, Michael eds., *Regional Economic Change in Russia* (Cheltenham: Edward Elgar, 2000).

Harle, V., and Livonen, J., (eds.), *Gorbachev and Europe* (London: Printer, 1990).

Hasegawa, T., and Pravda, A., (eds.), *Perestroika: Soviet Domestic and Foreign Policy* (London: Sage Publications, 1990).

Hanson, Philip and Bradshaw, Michael eds., *Regional Economic Change in Russia* (Cheltenham: Edward Elgar, 2000).

Hassalla, A., *The Balance of Power 1751-1789* (New York: Macmillan, 1914).

Hedenskog, jakob.,Konnander,Vilhelm., Nygren, Bertil.,Oldberg,Ingmar.,(eds.), *Russia as great power: dimensions of security under Putin* (London:Routledge, 2005)

Heisburg, F., *The Strategic Implications of Change in the Soviet Union* (London: Macmillan, 1990).

Herz, John H., *Political Realism and Political Idealism* (Chicago: University of Chicago Press, 1951).

Hewatt, Edward A., and Winston, Victor H., (eds.), *Milestones in Glasnost and Perestroika* (Washington DC: The Brookings Institute, 1991).

Hill, Ronald J., and Dellenbrant, Jan A., (eds.), *Gorbachev and Perestroika: Towards a New Socialism* (England: Edward Elgar, 1989).

Hillsman, R., and Good, Robert C., (eds.), *Foreign policy in the Sixties: The Issues and the Instruments* (Baltimore: John Hopkins Press, 1965).

Hoffman, S., *State of War: Essay on Theory and Practice of International Politics* (London: Pall Mall, 1965).

Holden, G., *Soviet Military Reform* (London: Pluto Press, 1991).

Hudson, George E., (ed.), *Soviet National Security Policy under Perestroika* (Boston: Unwin Hyman, 1990).

Imam, Z., (ed.), *Restructuring Soviet Society: An Appraisal of the New Programme of the Communist of the Soviet Union* (New Delhi: Panchsheel, 1987).

Imam, Z., *Soviet Foreign Policy 1917-1990* (New Delhi: Sterling Publishers, 1991).

Imam, Z., *New Russia: Disintegration and Crisis- A Contemporary Chronicle 1988-1994* (New Delhi: ABC Publishing House, 1995).

Imam, Zafar., *Yeltsyn years in Russia 1990-1999*, (Delhi: Samskriti, 2002).

Isakova,Irina., *Russian Governance in the Twenty first Century* (London: Frank Cass, 2005).

Jacobsen, Carl G., *The Soviet Defence Enigma: Existing Costs and Burden* (Oxford: Oxford University Press, 1987).

Jacobsen, Carl G., (ed.), *Soviet Foreign Policy: New Dynamics, New Themes* (London: Macmillan, 1989).

Jane, Davis, M., (ed.), *Security Issues in the Post Cold War World* (Cheltham: Edward Elgar, 1996).

Jervis, R., and Bialer, S., *Soviet American Relations after the Cold War* (London: Duke University Press, 1991).

Johnson, Lena., *Valdimir Putin and Central Asia* (London:I.B.Tauris, 2004).

Kaldor, M., *The Disintegrating West* (New York: Hill and Wang, 1978).

Kakonen, J., (ed.), *Perspectives on Environmental Conflict and International Politics* (London: Printer, 1991).

Kanet, Roger E.,(ed.), *New security environment* (Aldershot:Ashgate, 2005).

Kanet,Roger E., Kozhemiakin,A.V., *The Foreign Policy of the Russian Federation*(London:Macmillan,1997).

Katz, Mark N., (ed.), *The USSR and the Marxist Revolutions in the Third World* (Cambridge: Cambridge University Press, 1990).

Kennan, George F., *The Realist of American Foreign Policy* (New Jersey: Princeton Hall, 1954).

Kennan, George F., *The Nuclear Dillusion: Soviet American Relations in the Atomic Age* (New York: Panthem, 1982).

Kennedy, P., *The Rise and Fall of Great Powers: Economic Change and Military Conflict from 1500 to 2000* (London: Unwin Hyman, 1988).

Keohane, Robert and Nye, Joseph eds., *Transnational Relations and World Politics* (Cambridge,MA:Havard University Press,1971).

Khrushev, N. S., *For Victory in Peaceful Competition with Capitalism* (London: Hutchinson and Co, 1960).

Knorr, K., and Verba, S., *The International System* (Princeton: Princeton University Press, 1961).

Kovalenko, I., and Touzmohammadov, R., (eds.), *Disarmament for Development* (New Delhi: Allied Publishers, 1989).

Kuchnins, Andrew C., ed., *Russia after the fall* (Washington DC :Carnegie Endowment For International Peace, 2002).

Kumar, S., (ed.), *Gorbachev's Reforms and International Change* (New Delhi: Lancer Books, 1993).

Kugler,Richard L Kozintseva., Marina V.,*Enlarging NATO: the Russia factor* (Santa Monica:Rand Corporation,1996).

Lavigne, M., *The Soviet Union and Eastern Europe in the Global Economy* (Cambridge: Cambridge University Press, 1992).

Leites, N., *A Study of Bolshevism* (New York: Free Press, 1953).

Lenin, V. I., *War and Peace* (Peking: Foreign Language Press, 1960).

Lenin, V. I., *On the Foreign Policy of Soviet States* (Moscow: Progress Publishers, 1968).

Light, M., *The Soviet Theory of International Relations* (Great Britain: Wheatsheaf Books, 1958).

Lynn, Sean M., Miller, Jones Steven E., and Evera, Stephen V., (eds.), *Soviet Military Policy: An International Security Reader* (Cambridge, Mass.: The MIT Press, 1989).

Macridis, Roy C., (ed.), *Foreign Policy in World Politics* (New York: Prentice-Hall, 1992).

Malcolm, N., (ed.), *Russia and Europe: An End to Confrontation* (London: Pinter, 1994).

Mandel, E., *Beyond Perestroika* (London: Verso, 1989)

Mastny, V., *Helsinki Human Rights and European Security: Analysis and Documentation* (Durham, NC: Duke University Press, 1986).

McAinsh, Garrett L., *World Encyclopedia of Peace*, Vol.1, (Oxford: Pergamon Press, 1986).

McCauley, M., *Gorbachev and Perestroika* (London: Macmillan, 1990).

MccGwire, M., *Military Objectives in Soviet Foreign Policy* (Washington DC: Brookings, 1987).

Mc Nair, B., *Glasnost, Perestroika and the Soviet Media* (London: Routledge, 1991).

McNamara, Robert S., *Out of the Cold* (New York: Simon & Schuster, 1989).

Mehrotra, S., *India and the Soviet Union: Trade and Technology Transfer* (New Delhi: Oxford University Press, 1991).

Miller, Robert F., *Gorbachev at the Helm* (London: Croom Helm, 1987).

Miller,Steven E., Trenin, Dmitri., *Russian military: Power and policy* (Cambridge:MIT Press, 2004).

Moiseyev, M., *The Soviet Military Doctrine: Orientation towards Defence* (Moscow: Novosti Press, 1989).

Morgenthau, Hans J., *Scientific vs. Power Politics* (Chicago: University of Chicago Press, 1946).

Muller, B., *Common Security and Non-Offensive Defence* (Boulder: Lynne Rienner, 1992).

Myers, M., *Ultimate Security: The Environmental Bases of Political Stability* (New York: W. W. Norton, 1993).

Neumann, Iver B., *Russia and the Idea of Europe* (London: Routledge, 1996).

Newton, Julie M., *Russia, France and the Idea of Europe*(New York: Plagrave Macmillan, 2003).

Niiscki, K., (ed.), *The Soviet Union in Transition* (Boulder: Westview Press, 1987).

Nikolsky, N., *The Philosophy of New Thinking and the Soviet Initiatives* (New Delhi: Allied Publishers, 1988).

Niou, Emersion M. S., Ordeshook, Peter C., and Rose, Gregory F., *The Balance of Power* (Cambridge: Cambridge University Press, 1989).

Nogee, Joseph A., and Donaldson, Robert H., *Soviet Foreign policy since World War II* (Oxford: Pergamon Press, 1988).

Obminsky, E., and Bugrov, A., *International Economic Security: A Major Factor of Peace* (New Delhi: Allied Publishers, 1988).

Patnaik, A., *Common wealth of Independent States: Problems and Prospects* (New Delhi: Konark Publishers, 1995).

Pekka, S., *Economic Thought and Economic Reform in Soviet Union* (New Ycrk: Cambridge University Press, 1991).

Peter, Z., *Soviet Foreign Relations: Process and Policy* (New Jersey: Prentice-Hall, 1990).

Pipes, R., *US-Soviet Relations in the Era of Détente* (Boulder: Westview Press, 1981).

Potter, Brian E., *World Encyclopedia of Peace*, Vol. II (Oxford: Pergamon Press, 1986).

Potter, Bruce D., *The USSR in Third World Conflict* (Cambridge: Cambridge University Press, 1984).

Richard, S., *Gorbachev and His Reforms 1985-1990* (London: Phillip Allan, 1990),

Richardson, J. L., *Germany Atlantic Alliance* (Cambridge, Mass.: Harvard University Press, 1966).

Rigby, T.H., *The Changing Soviet System: Mono-organizational Socialism from its Origins to Gorbachev's Restructuring* (England: Edward Elgar, 1990).

Roberts, G., *The Soviet Union in World Politics: Co-existence Revolution and Cold War 1945-1991* (London: Routledge, 1999).

Robinson, Neil., *Russia: A state of uncertainty* (London:Routledge, 2002).

Rosenau, James N., *International Politics and Foreign Policy* (New York: Free Press, 1961).

Rosenau, James N., *The Scientific Study of Foreign Policy* (London: Frances Pinter, 1979).

Rubinstein, Robert A., and Foster, Mary Le Corn. (eds.), *The Soviet Dynamics of Peace and Conflict* (Boulder: Westview Press, 1988).

Ryavec, Karl W., *United States – Soviet Relations* (London: Longman, 1989).

Saikal,Amin., Maley,Williams.,(eds.),*Russia in search of Its Future* (Cambridge:Cambridge University Press,1999).

Saikal, A., and Maley, W. (eds.), *Russia in Search of its Future* (Cambridge: Cambridge University Press, 1995).

Sakwa, R., *Russian Politics and society* (London:Routledge,1996).

Schwartz, M., *Soviet Perceptions of the United States* (Berkeley: University of California, 1978).

Sharma,R.R.,(ed.), *India and Emerging Asia*(New Delhi:Sage Publications, 2005).

Shearman, Peter.,(ed.), *Russia's Foreign Policy Since 1998*(Boulder:West View Press, 1995).

Sheehan, Michael J., *Arms Control: Theory and Practice* (Oxford: Basil Blackwell, 1988).

Shelling, T. C., and Halperin, M. H., *Strategy and Arms Control* (New York: Twentieth Century Fund, 1961).

Shmelyov, N., *Perestroika as seen by an Economist* (Moscow: Novosti Press, 1989).

Shultz, R., Godson, R., and Greenwood, T., (eds.), *Security Study for the 1990s* (Washington DC: Brassey's, 1993).

Singer, David J., *Deterrence Arms Control and Disarmament* (Ohio: Ohio State University Press, 1962).

Slyunkov, N., *Restructuring the Economy is the Paramount Political Task* (Moscow: Novosti Press, 1988).

Smith, Theresa C., and Singh, Indu B., *Security versus Survival: The Nuclear Arms Race* (Boulder: Lynne Rienner, 1985).

Snidal, D., "The Game Theory of International Politics", in Kenneth A. Oye (ed.), *Cooperation under Anarchy* (Princeton: Princeton University Press, 1986).

Snow, Donald M., *National Security: Enduring Problems of US Defence Policy* (New York: St. Martin's, 1987).

Snow, Donald M., *The Necessary Peace* (Lexington, USA: Lexington Books, 1987).

Sokolovskii, V. D., (ed.), *Voennaia Strategiia* (Moscow: Voenizdat, 1962).

Spanier, J., *Games Nations Play* (New Delhi: Macmillan, 1990).

Spiegel, Steven L., (ed.), *Conflict Management in the Middle East* (Boulder: Westview Press, 1992).

Sprout, H., and Sprout, M., *Foundations of International Politics* (Princeton: D. Van Nostrand Inc, 1962).

Spykman, Nicholas J., *America's Strategy in World Politics* (New York: Macmillan, 1942).

Starr, Richard, F., *Foreign Policies of the Soviet Union* (Stanford: Hoover Institution Press, 1991).

Subrahmanyam, K., *Security in Changing World* (New Delhi: B. R. Publishing, 1990).

Tedstrom, John E., (ed.), *Socialism, Perestroika and the Dilemmas of Soviet Economic Reform* (Boulder: Westview Press, 1990).

Thompson, K. W., and Morgenthau, Hans J., (eds.), *Principles and Problems of International Politics* (New York: Praegar, 1968).

Tucker, R. C., *The Soviet Political Mind* (New York: W. W. Norton, 1963).

Tucker, R. C., *Political Culture and Leadership in Soviet Russia: From Lenin to Gorbachev* (Sussex: Wheatsheaf Books, 1987).

Urban, G.R., *Can the Soviet System Survive Reform*? (London: Pinter, 1989).

Urban,Michael., *The rebirth of politics in Russia* (Cambridge: Cambridge University Press, 1997).

Vernon, Graham D., (ed.), *Soviet Perceptions of War and Peace* (Washington, DC: National Defence University, 1984).

Volkan, Vanik D., Montville, Joseph V., and Julien, D., (eds.), *The Psychodynamics of International Relationship,* Vol. 2, (Massachusetts: The MIT Press, 1991).

Vyas, A. and Vernikov A., *The Economics of Perestroika (*New Delhi: Ajanta Publications, 1991).

Walker, R., *Six Years that Shook the World* (Manchester: Manchester University Press, 1993).

Waltz, K., *Theory of International Politics* (Reading, MA: Addison-Wesley, 1978).

Webber,Mark., *The International Politics of Russia and the Successor States* (Manchester: Manchester University Press,1996).

Westing, Arthur H., (ed.), *Global Resources and International Conflict* (New York: Oxford University Press, 1986).

White, S., *Gorbachev and After* (Cambridge: Cambridge University Press, 1992).

Wolfe, Thomas W., *Soviet Power and Europe 1945-1970* (Baltimore: John Hopkins University Press, 1970).

Wolfe, Thomas W., *Soviet Strategy at the Cross Roads* (Cambridge, MA: Harvard University Press, 1964).

Wolfers, A., *Discord and Collaboration* (Baltimore: John Hopkins University Press, 1962).

Wright, M., *Power Politics* (London: Penguin, 1978).

Wright, Q., *On Predicting International Relations: The Years 2000*, Morgenthau Series in World Affairs, Monograph No.1, (Colorado: University of Denver, 1970).

Yahuda, M., *The International Politics of the Asia-Pacific 1945-1995* (London: Routledge, 1996).

Zagladin, V., *Peace the Only Option* (New Delhi: Allied Publishers, 1987).

Zdenek, M., *Can Gorbachev Change the Soviet Union? The International Dimensions of Political Reform* (Boulder: Westview Press, 1990).

Zloch, Christy I., *East-West Financial Relations* (New York: Cambridge University Press, 1991).

2. ii. Articles From Journals

Adelman, K. L., "The Road from Reykjavik", *World Affairs*, Vol.149. No.1 (Summer 1986), pp.11-14.

Adragna, Steven P., "A New Soviet Military? Doctrines and Strategy", *Orbis,* (Spring, 1989), pp. 165-179.

Aleksander, M., "Soviet Security Needs", *Link*, Vol. 33, No. 53, (11 August 1991), pp. 25-29.

Arbotov, A., "Reasonable Sufficiency", *International Affairs*, No. 10, (October 1988), pp. 78-87.

Arbotov, G., "The Cold War is Ending", *World Marxist Review*, Vol. 31. No. 8, (August 1988), pp. 43-47..

Aron,Leon., "Is Russian Going Backward?", *Commentry* ,Vol.118, No.3 (October),2004,pp.51-52.

Aspaturian, V.V., "Farewell to Soviet Foreign Policy", *Problems of Communism*, Vol. XL. No. 6, (November-December 1991), pp. 53-62.

Balzor, Harley., "The Putin Thesis and Russian Energy Policy", *Post-Soviet Affairs,* Vol.21, No.3,2005, p. 211

Bakshi, J., "Russia's Post-Pokhran Balancing Act", *Mainstream*, (August 1, 1998), pp. 32-33.

Behar, N., "East-West Cooperation and the Concept of Economic Security: A View Point from a Small Country", *The Korean Journal of International Studies (Seoul)*, Vol. XX. No. 4, (Winter 1989), pp. 289-303.

Bell, C., "Why an Expanded NATO Must Include Russia", *Strategic Studies*, Vol. 17. No. 4, (December 1994), pp. 27-41.

Benson, S., "Will Modern Technology Remilitarize Russia?", *Orbis*, Vol. 39. No. 3, (Summer 1995), pp. 403-415.

Bezymensky, L., and Falin V., "Who started the Cold War", *Reprints from the Soviet Press*, Vol. 47. No.11-12, (December 15-30, 1988), pp. 5-17.

Blank, S., "Soviet Perspectives on Asian Security", *Asian Survey*, Vol. 31. No. 7, (July 1991), pp. 646-661.

Bluth, C., "Russia and European Security", *The World Today*, Vol. 50. No. 4, (April 1994), pp. 73-76.

Bogdanov, S.A. "The Economic Components of Russia's Military Security", *Military Thought*, Vol.14,No.1 (2005), pp.12-13.

Booth, K., "Redefining East-West Security: Steps Towards Stable Peace in Europe, A Theory and Practice of Co-existence", *International Affairs*, Vol. 66. No. 1, (January 1990), pp. 17-46.

Borisov, N., "USSR's Scientific and Technological Cooperation with Capitalist Countries", *Foreign Trade*, No. 9, (1984), pp.12-17.

Boysen, S., "Gorbachev's Disarmament Proposals", *Aussen Politik*, Vol. 38. No.1, (1987), pp. 11-22.

Brusstar, James H., "Russian Vital Interests and Western Security", *Orbis*, Vol. 38. No. 4, (Fall 1994), pp. 607-620.

Brzezinski, Z., "Is the Cold War Over", *International Affairs*, (November 1989), pp. 32-37.

Brzezinski, Z., "Towards a Common European Home", *Problems of Communism*, Vol. XXXVIII. No. 6, (November – December 1989), pp. 1-10.

Brzezinski, Z., "Consequences of the End of the Cold War for International Security", *Adelphi Papers*, No. 265, (Winter 1991/92), pp. 3-17.

Burns, N., Hartman, A., Matlock, J., Ross, D., and Winston, V., "Three Years After the Collapse of the USSR: A Panel of Former and Current Policymakers", *Post-Soviet Affairs*, Vol. 11. No. 1, (January-March 1995), pp. 1-22.

Buszynski, Leszek., "Russia and the commonwealth of independent states in 2002:going separate ways" *Asian Survey* Vol.43,No.1 (January-February 2003),pp.15-24.

Buzan, B., "New Patterns of Global Security in the 21st Century", *International Affairs*, Vol. 67. No. 3, (July 1991), pp. 431-452.

Buzan, B., "Rethinking Security After the Cold War", *Cooperation and Conflict*, Vol. 32. No. 1, (1997), pp. 5-28.

Caldwell, L.T., "Soviet-American Relations: The Cold War Ends", *Current History*, Vol. 89. No. 549, (October 1990), pp. 305-308, 343-346.

Chandra, N.K., "Russia's Sinking Economy: External Dimensions", *Economic and Political Weekly*, Vol. 28. No. 20, (May 15, 1993), pp. 995-1003.

Chakravarty, S., "Foreign Policy- The Primakov Factor", *World Focus*, Vol. 18. No. 5, (May 1997), pp. 9-12.

Checinski, M., "Warsaw Pact/CMEA Military – Economic Trends", *Problems of Communism*, Vol. XXXVI. No. 2, (March-April 1987), pp.15-28.

Chervov, N., "Soviet-American Military Dialogue", *Problems of Peace and Socialism*, Vol. 17. No. 3, (March 1989), pp. 7-10.

Chubarian, A., "European Home", *Review of International Affairs*, Vol. XI. No. 984, (5 October 1989), pp. 6-8.

Cimbala, Stephen J., "US and Russian Strategic nuclear forces under cooperative security Moscow and after" *journal of Slavic Military Studies* Vol.18,No.2 (September 2005),pp.169-187.

Clark, Susan, L., and Graham, David, R., "The Russian Federation's Fight for Survival", *Orbis*, Vol. 39. No. 3, (Summer 1995), pp. 329-351.

Cook, Linda, J., "Brezhnev's Social Contract and Gorbachev's Reforms", *Soviet Studies*, Vol. 44. No. 1, (1992), pp. 37-56.

Colton etal., " Russia in the year 2004", *Post Soviet Affairs*, Vol.21,No.1 (January-March), 2005,pp. 20-21.

Csaba, L., "Russia Beyond Perestroika", *Communist Economics and Economic Transition*, Vol. 4. No. 3, (1992), pp. 333-359.

Davenport, Brian, A., "The Ogarkov Ouster: The Development of Soviet Military Doctrine and Civil/Military Relations in the 1980s", *The Journal of Strategic Studies*, Vol. 14. No. 2, (June 1991), pp. 129-147.

D'estaing, V., G., Nakosone, Y., and Kissinger, Henry A., "East-West Relations", *Foreign Affairs*, Vol. 68. No. 3, (Summer 1989), pp. 1-21.

Debroy, B., and Mago, L. D., "Issues in Indo-Soviet Trade", *Foreign Trade Review*, Vol. 26. No. 1&2, (April- September 1991), pp. 40-55.

Desch, Michael, C., "Why the Soviet Military Supported Gorbachev, But Why the Russian Military Might Only Support Yeltsin for a Price", *The Journal of Strategic Studies*, Vol. 16. No. 4, (December 1993), pp. 455-489.

Dhar, B., "Economic Reforms in the USSR: the Emerging Scenario", *RIS Digest*, Vol. 7. No. 2-4, (December 1990), pp. 40-49.

Dibb, P., "Is Soviet Military Strategy Changing?", *Adelphi Papers*, No. 235, (Spring 1989), pp. 35-47.

Dick, C.J., "The Military Doctrine of Russian Federation", *Journal of Slavik Military Studies*,Vol.7,No.3 September 1994, pp.503-504.

Dobrynin, Anatoly, F., "New Thinking in the Fight for Peace", *Political Affairs*, Vol. 66. No. 8, (August 1987), pp. 22-29.

Dracheva, N., and Diikov, S., "USSR Economic Ties with West European Countries: Tasks and Priorities", *Foreign Trade,* No. 7, (1991), pp. 10-13.

Dubey, M., "Halt Arms Race: Build Global Security Based on Cooperation, Equality and Justice", *New Perspectives,* Vol. 19. No. 6, (1989), pp. 6-7.

Dunay, P., "Euphoria and Realism in Post-Cold War European Security", *Journal of Peace Research*, Vol. 30. No. 3, (1993), pp. 347-35.

Dunlop, J., "Soviet Cultural Politics," *Problems of Communism*, Vol. 36. No. 6, (November-December 1987), pp. 34-56.

Dunn, L. A., "The Super Power Dialogue: Prospects and Limits", *Adelphi Papers*, No. 248, (February 1990), pp. 3-16.

Ermith, F., "Evolution of Soviet Doctrine", *Adelphi Papers*, No. 206, (Spring 1986), pp. 3-10.

Evangelista, M., "New Soviet Approach to Security", *World Policy Journal*, Vol. 3. No. 4, (Fall 86), pp. 561-600.

Feldbrugge, F., "Can the Soviet Economy be Reformed", *NATO Review,* Vol. 37, No. 3, (June 1989), pp. 15-20.

Ganyushkin, V., "Visit off to a Good Start: A New Trend towards Common European Home", *New Times*, No. 28, (11-17 July 1989), pp. 5-7.

Gidadhubli, R.G., "Russian Economy: Why No Resurgence?, *World Focus*, Vol. 18. No. 5, (May 1997), pp. 6-8.

Goetz, R., "Russian Security Policy Options and Their Price", *Aussen Politik*, Vol. 47. No. 3, (1996), pp. 255-262.

Goetz, R., "Structural Legacy and Systemic Transformation in the Former USSR: Experience With *Perestroika*", *Aussen Politik*, Vol. 45, No. 11, (1994), pp. 166-175.

Golan, G., "Gorbachev's Middle East Strategy", *Foreign Affairs*, Vol. 66. No. 1, (Fall 1987), pp. 41-57.

Goldberg, P., "Economic Reforms and Product Quality Improvement Efforts in the Soviet Union", *Soviet Studies*, Vol. 44. No. 1, (1992), pp. 113-122.

Goldman, Mardshall I., "Gorbachev and Economic Reforms", *Foreign Affairs*, Vol. 64, (1985), pp. 56-73.

Golts ,Alexander M., and Putnam, Tonya L., "State Militarism and its Legacies", *International Security*, Vol.29, No.2 (Fall 2004), pp.156-157.

Gonchar, K., "Military Spending in the USSR: A Reconsideration", *Journal of Peace Research*, Vol. 31. No. 2, (1994), pp. 219-228.

Gonsalves, E., "USSR Initiates a New World Order", *World Focus*, Vol. 9. No,10-12, (October- December,1988), pp. 32-40.

Goodwin, Robert, E., "Mood Matching and Arms Control", *International Studies Quarterly*, Vol. 12. No. 4, (December 1988), pp. 32-40.

Gordon, Michael, R., "Russian Military Turns to Regional Peacekeeping", *Strategic Digest,* Vol. 24. No. 2, (February 1994), pp. 221-223.

Gorbachev, M. S, "Soviet Proposals for Complete Disarmament", *Political Affairs*, Vol. 65. No. 2, (February 1986), pp. 33-39.

Gorisov, S., "The Scale and Structure of Informal Employment in the Russian Economy", *Russian Social Science Review*, Vol.26,No.3 (May-June), 2005, p. 6.

Gregory, Paul, R., "The Impact of Perestroika in the Soviet Planned Economy: Results of a Survey of Moscow Economic Officials", *Soviet Studies*, Vol. 43. No. 5, (1991), pp. 859-873.

Grigoriev, Leonid., "Russia's Place in Global Economy", *Russia in Global Affairs,*Vol.3,No.2 (April-June),2005,pp.128-141.

Gromyko, A., "Along A Leninist Course in Foreign Policy", *Problems of Peace and Socialism*, Vol. 13. No. 4, (April 1985), pp. 8-17.

Grueder Andreas, H., "The Russian Military and the Crisis of State", *Aussen Politik*, Vol. 45. No. 1, (1994), pp. 79-89.

Gupta, A., "Problems and Prospects of Defence Conversion in the USSR", *Strategic Analysis*, Vol. XIII, (November 1990), pp. 965-976.

Gupta, R., "Science and Technology and Soviet Security", *Strategic Analysis*, Vol. 13. No. 9, (December 1990), pp. 1069-1080.

Gupta, R., "CIS: Prospects and Paradoxes of Military Union", *Strategic Analysis,* Vol. 16. No. 4, (July 1993), pp. 493-511.

Gurov, A., "Economic Foundation of the Soviet Defence Capability, *Soviet Military Review*, No. 3, (March 1986), pp. 4-6.

Gusev, N., "Leninist Principles of Soviet Military Development", *Soviet Military Review*, No. 11, (November 1984), pp. 10-12.

Hall, J., "Glasnost and Soviet Culture", *Problems of Communism*, Vol. 38. No. 6, (November-December 1989), pp. 40-50.

Hansen, L., "A Case for Seduction? Evaluating the Post-Structuralist Conceptualisation of Security", *Cooperation and Conflict*, Vol. 32. No. 4, (December 1997), pp. 369-397.

Hanson, Phillip "The Russian Economic Recovery: Do Four Years Growth tell Us that the Fundamentals have changed?", *Europe-Asia Studies*, Vol.55, No.3, 2003,pp.366-367.

Harman, W., "Quest for Security Viewed as a Whole System Problem", *Transnational Perspectives*, Vol. 14. No. 3, (1988), pp. 12-19.

Herspring, Dale, R., "Soviet High Command Looks at Gorbachev," *Adelphi Papers*, No. 235, (Spring 1989), pp. 48-62.

Herspring,Dale R., "Vladimir Putin and military reform" *European Security* Vol.14,No.1 (March 2005), pp.137-155.

Herz, J.H., "Political Realism Revisited", *International Studies Quarterly*, Vol. 25. No. 2, (June 1981), pp. 182-97.

Holloway, D., "Gorbachev's New Thinking", *Foreign Affairs*, Vol. 68. No. 1, (1988/89), pp. 66-81.

Homer-Dixion, Thomas F., "Environmental Scarcities and Violent Conflicts: Evidence and Cases", *International Security,* Vol. 19. No. 2, (1994), pp. 5-40.

Homer-Dixion, Thomas F., "On the Threshold: Environmental Change and Acute Conflict", *International Security,* Vol. 16. No. 2, (1991), pp. 76-116.

Howard, M., "1989, A Farewell to Arms!", *International Affairs*, Vol. 65. No. 3, (Summer 1989), pp 407-14.

Hyland, W. G., "The Gorbachev Succession", *Foreign Affairs*, Vol. 63. No. 4, (Spring 1985), pp. 800-809.

Huntington, Samuel P., "The Clash of Civilizations?", *Foreign Affairs*, Vol. 72. No. 3, (Summer 1993), pp. 22-49.

Huntington, Samuel P., "If Not Civilizations, What?", *Foreign Affairs*, Vol. 72. No. 5, (November-December 1993), pp. 187-194.

Inoguchi, Takashi "Political Security: Toward a Broader Conceptualisation",

International Studies (New Delhi), Vol.14, No.2,2003,p.106.

Izynmov, A., and Kortunov, A., "The Soviet Union in the Changing World", *International Affairs*, (August 1988), pp. 46-56.

Jagan, C., "Soviet Concept of New Thinking Opens the Way to a Lasting Peace", *International Affairs*, (Moscow), No. 3, (March 1988), pp. 86-90.

Jung, Young S., "New Thinking of the Soviet Security Strategy and its Impact on the International Order in Asia", *Korean Journal of International Studies*, Vol. 21. No. 3, (Autumn 1990), pp. 353-366.

Kamath, P. M., "American Perception of the Gorbachev Reforms", *Strategic Analysis*, Vol. 15. No. 1, (April 1992), pp. 17-27.

Kamath, P M., "US Russia security relations in 1990s :from cooperation to condominium or cold war again?" *Strategic Analysis* Vol.17,No.5 (August 1994),pp.593-606.

Kambaluris, N., "Rapprochement and Prospects: Relations between EC and the COMECON", *Review of International Affairs* (Moscow), Vol. XI. No. 930, (5 January 1989), pp. 9-15.

Kapchenko, N., "Political Aspects of International Security", *International Affairs*, No. 9, (September 1986), pp. 84-92.

Kaushik, D., "Russia: Five Years of Radical Reforms?", *World Focus*, Vol. 18. No. (May 1997), pp. 3-5.

Kaufman, Stuart, J., "Organisational Politics and Change in Soviet Military Policy", *Strategic Digest*, Vol. 24. No. 8, (August 1994), pp. 1080-1098.

Khromov, I., "Conversion, Reforms and Security", *Problems of Economic Transition*, Vol. 36. No. 7, (November 1993), pp. 37-51.

Khryapin, A.L., "Conceptual Principles of Strategic Deterrence", *Military Thought*, Vol.14, No. 205, pp. 30-35.

Klaiber, Klaus P., "The NATO-Russian Relationship a Year After Paris", *NATO* Review, Vol. 46. No. 3, (Autumn 1998), pp. 16-18.

Klimnenko, A.F., "Osobennosti novoy Voyennoy doktriny", *Voyennaya Mysl*, 5, (2000).

Koizumi, N., "Gorbachev and Soviet Arms Control Policy", *Japan Review of International Affairs*, Vol.3. No.1,(Spring/Summer 1989), pp.187-202.

Kokoshin, A. A., "Arms Control: A View from Moscow", *Daedalus*, Vol. 120. No. 1, (Winter 1991), pp. 133-143.

Korneyev V. "A New Stage of Soviet Indian Economic Relations", *Foreign Trade* (Moscow), No. 2. (1989), pp. 20-24.

Kozyrev, A., "East and West From Confrontation to Cooperation and Co-development", *International Affairs,* (October 1989), pp. 3-13.

Kozyrev, A., "Russia and Human Rights", *Slavic Review*, Vol. 52. No. 2, (June 1992), pp. 287-293.

Kozyrev, A., "The New Russia and the Atlantic Alliance", *NATO Review*, Vol. 41. No. 1, (February 1993), pp. 3-6.

Kozyrev, A., "Russia and NATO: A Partnership for a United and Peaceful Europe", *NATO Review*, Vol. 42. No. 4, (August 1994), pp. 3-6.

Kuznetsov, A., "Economic Reforms in Russia: Enterprise Behaviour as an Impediment to Change", *Europe Asia Studies*, Vol. 46. No. 6, (1994), pp. 955-970.

Labahn, A., "Political and Economic Effects of *Perestroika* in the Soviet Union and its relations to Eastern Europe and the West", *Aussen Politik*, Vol. 39. No. 2, (1988), pp.107-124.

Lapidus, G. W., "Gorbachev and the Reform of the Soviet System", *Daedalus*, Vol. 116, No. 2, (Spring 1987), pp. 24-30.

Lapidus, Gail W., "Putin's war on Terrorism: lessons from Chechnya", *Post Soviet Affairs*, Vol.18, No.1(January-March),2002,pp. 41-48.

Larrabee, F. S., "Gorbachev and the Soviet Military", *Strategic Digest*, Vol. 18. No. 9, (September 1988), pp. 1141-1153.

Larrabee, F. S., and Lynch, A., "Gorbachev: The Road to Reykjavik", *Foreign Policy*, No. 65, (Winter 1986-87), pp. 3-28.

Lebahn, A., "Political and Economic Effects of Perestroika on the soviet Union and Its Relation s to Eastern Europe and the West", *Aussen Politik*, Vol. 39. No. 2, (1988), pp. 107-124.

Legvold,Robert., "Russia's Unforced Foreign Policy", *Foreign Affair,* Vol.80. No.5, (September/October), 2001.

Lemaıtre, P., "Eastern Reforms Process and Policy of the West", *Journal of Peace Research*, Vol. 26. No .4, (1989), pp. 337-340.

Lepingwell, John W. R., "Towards a Post-Soviet Army", *Orbis*, Vol. 36. No. 1, (Winter 1992), pp. 87-104.

Lipmann, W., "The Cold War", *Foreign Affairs*, Vol. 65. No. 4, (Spring 1987), pp. 869-884.

LIFAN Li and SHIWU, Ding "Geo political interest of Russia, the US and China in Central Asia", *Central Asia and the Caucasus,* Vol.3, No.27, 2004, pp.151-154.

Lobov, V., "Towards more Security", *New Times* (Moscow), No. 29, (17-24 July, 1989), pp. 8-10.

Mackintosh, M., "Russian Attitude to Defence and Disarmament", *International Affairs,* Vol. 61. No. 3, (Summer 1985), pp. 385-394.

Malasshenko, I., "Non-Military Aspects of Security", *International Affairs*, (Moscow), (January 1989), pp. 40-51.

Malcolm, N., "The Common European Home and Soviet European Policy", *International Affairs*, Vol. 65, No. 4, (Autumn 1989), pp. 659-676.

Malcolm, N., "The New Russian Foreign Policy", *The World Today*, Vol. 50. No. 2, (February 1994), pp. 28-32.

Malhotra, J., "Indo-Russian Relations", *World Focus*, Vol. 18. No. 5, (May 1997), pp. 13-15.

Malkevich, V., "East-West Economic Relations and their Prospects", *Foreign Trade*, No. 1, (1989), pp. 25-28.

Mandelbaum, M., "Ending the Cold War", *Foreign Affairs*, Vol. 68. No. 2, (Spring 1989), pp. 16-36.

Manning, R. A., "Moscow's Pacific Future: Gorbachev Rediscovers Asia", *World Policy Journal*, Vol. 5. No. 1, (Winter 1987-88), pp. 55-78.

Marantz, P., "Soviet New Thinking and East-West Relationship", *Current History*, Vol. 87. No. 531, (October 1988), pp. 309-12.

Marantz, P., "Russian Foreign Policy During Yeltsin's Second Term", *Communist and Post Communist Studies*, Vol. 30, No. 4, (1997), pp. 345-351.

Masow, T. D., "Non-Military Dimensions of Soviet Security Policy in Asia", *Bulletin of Peace Proposal*, Vol. 20. No. 4, (December 1989), pp. 405-420.

Mastny, V., "Europe in US-USSR Relations: A Topical Legacy", *Problems of Communism*, Vol. 37. No. 1, (January-February 1988), pp. 16-29.

McCarthy, P., "Seven Steps to Expand East-West Trade", *Bulletin of Atomic Scientists*, Vol. 44. No. 5, (June 1988), pp. 26-29.

MccGwire, M., "Soviet Military Objectives", *World Policy Journal*, Vol. 3. No. 4, (Fall 1986), pp. 667-696.

Mehrotra, O. N., "Gorbachev and Western Europe", *Strategic Analysis*, Vol. 9. No. 9, (December 1985), pp. 895-899.

Mehrotra, O. N., "Gorbachev's Proposal for a Secure World", *Strategic Analysis*, Vol. XI. No. 10, (January 1988), pp. 1039-48.

Menon, R. C., "New Thinking and North-East Asian Security", *Problems of Communism*, Vol. 38. No. 2-3, (March-June 1989), pp. 1-29.

Meyer, Stephen, M., "Soviet Strategic Programme and the US SDI," *Survival,* Vol. 27. No. 6, (November-December 1985), pp. 274-292.

Mishra, A., "Problems in Security: Quest for a New Theoretical Paradigm", *Journal of Peace Studies*, Vol. 4, No. 21, (March-April 1997), pp. 3-13.

Morozov, Viatcheslav., "Russia in the Baltic Sea Region:Desecurization or Deregionalization?" *Cooperation and Conflict* ,Vol.39.No.3, (September 2004), pp. 317-331.

Nikitin, V., "USSR-Austria: New Trends in Economic Cooperation", *Foreign Trade* (Moscow), No. 2, (1989), pp. 12-14.

Noren, James, H., "The Controversy Over Western Measures of Soviet Defense Expenditures", *Post-Soviet Affairs*, Vol. 11. No. 3, (January- March 1995), pp. 238-276.

Notzold, J., "East-West Trade at the Cross Roads", *Aussen Politik*, Vol. 37. No. 4, (1986), pp. 400-12.

Notzold, J., "Several European Economic Blocs? The Future Significance of the COMECON", *Aussen Politik*, Vol. 40, No. 3, (1989), pp. 277-92.

Nunn Sam and Stulberg, Adam N. "The Many Faces of Modern Russia", *Foreign Affairs,* Vol.79, No.2 (March-April), 2000, pp.61-62.

Odom, W. E., "Soviet Military Doctrine," *Foreign Affairs*, Vol. 67. No. 2, (Winter 1988/89), pp. 114-134.

Ostankov, V.I. "Scientific –Methodological Support of Military Security of the Russian Federation", *Military Thought*, Vol.14, No.1, 2005, p. 56.

Oudenaren, John V., "Deterrence, War Fighting and Soviet Military Doctrine", *Adelphi Papers*, No. 210, (Summer 1986), pp. 3-47.

Ozhegov, A., Rogovskii, E., and Iaramenko, I., "Conversion of the Defence Industry and Transformation of the Economy of the USSR", *Problems of Economics*, Vol. 34. No. 6, (October 1991), pp. 79-94.

Parrot, B., "Soviet National Security Under Gorbachev", *Problems of Communism*, Vol. 37. No. 6, (November-December 1988), pp. 1-36.

Perkovich, G., "Counting the Costs of the Arms Race", *Foreign Policy*, Vol. 85, (Winter 1991-92), pp. 83-105.

Pick, O., "Perestroika and the Warsaw Pact", *NATO Review*, Vol. 36. No. 5, (1988), pp. 28-33.

Piskvlov, M., "The ECE and East-West Trade and Economic Cooperation", *Foreign Trade* (Moscow), No. 3, (1989), pp. 26-28.

Powell, Colin L., "A Strategy of Partnerships", *Foreign Affairs,* Vol.83, No.1(January/February), 2004, p.31.

Pozharov A.I., and Pozharov V.V. "Theory of War Economics: Need for a New Paradigm", *Military Thought,* Vol.14, No.1, 2005, pp.165-171.

Primakov, Y., "USSR Policy in Regional Conflicts", *International Affairs*, No. 6. (January 1988), pp. 4-9.

Radaev, V. " Competitive Changes in Russian Market", *Russian Social Science Review*, Vol.46, No.4 (July- August), 2005, pp. 31-58.

Radu, M., "The Soviet Tragedy", *Orbis*, Vol. 39. No. 1, (Winter 1995), pp. 121-125.

Rajamohan, C., "Perestroika and International Security", *Social Scientist*, Vol. 17. No. 11-12, (November –December 1989), pp. 13-29.

Reddaway Peter etal., "Russia in the year 2003", *Post-Soviet Affairs*, Vol.20, No.1, 2004, pp.1-6.

Renaud Jean C., "East-West Economic Relations in the Conflict of *Perestroika*", *NATO Review*, Vol. 36. No. 4, (August 1988), pp. 17-19.

Robinson,Collin., "Russian ground forces today a structural status examination" *Journal of Slavic Military Studies,* Vol.18,No.2, (June 2005), pp.189-206.

Rosefietde, S., "Economic Foundations of Soviet National Security", *Orbis*, Vol. 30. No. 2, (Summer 1986), pp. 317-30.

Rosefielde, Steven., "Back to the future ? prospects for Russia's military industrial revival" *Orbis* Vol.46,No.3 (Summer 2002),pp.499-509.

Rubanov, V., "From the Cult of Secrecy to the Information Culture", *Soviet Review*, Vol. 30. No. 5, (September-October 1989), pp. 1-35.

Saksena, J., "Reykjavik, Euromissiles and West European Security", *Strategic Analysis*, (January 1987), pp. 1183-98.

Sachs, Jeffrey D., "Privatisation in Russia: Some Lessons from Eastern Europe", *American Economic Review*, Vol. 82. No. 2, (May 1992), pp. 43-48.

Schmemann, S., "For Russia's Army, A Humiliating Retreat: Dismantling of a Once-Mighty Force Poses Critical Problems for Moscow", *Strategic Digest*, Vol. 24. No. 2, (February 1994), pp. 218-221.

Seleneva, Ludmilla., "Post-Soviet Russian Foreign Policy: Between Doctrine and pragmatism",*European Security* (A Frank Cass Journal), Vol.11, No.4, 2002.

Simes, D. K., "Gorbachev: A New Foreign Policy", *Foreign Affairs*, Vol. 65. No. 3, (1987), pp. 477-500.

Simes, D. K., "The US-Soviet Relationship after the Cold War: Paper 1", *Adelphi Papers*, No. 257, (Winter 1990-91), pp. 41-63.

Sing, J., "The Strategic Dimensions", *World Focus*, Vol. 9. No. 10-12, (October- December 1988), pp. 47-50.

Spechler, Martin, C., "Gorbachev's Economic Reforms: Early Assessments", *Problems of Communism*, Vol. 38, (September-October 1989), pp. 116-120.

Stobdan, P., "Central Asian Regional Security", *Strategic Analysis*, Vol. 15. No. 5, (August 1992), pp. 465-485.

Streltsova, N., "The 'New' Soviet Economy", *European Affairs*, Vol. 5. No. 6, (December 1991), pp. 48-49.

Subrahmanyan, K., "Conceptual Approaches and General Overview of Non-Military Threats to Global Security", *Strategic Analysis*, Vol. 13, (January 1990), pp. 993-1004.

Subrahmanyan, K., "Alternative Security Doctrines", *Review of International Affairs,* Vol. 41. No. 954, (January 5, 1990), pp. 16-23.

Subramanian, R. R., "Soviet Strategic Defence Response?", *Strategic Analysis,* Vol. 9. No. 2&3, (May-June 1985), pp. 197-200.

Suganami, H., "Narratives of War Origins and Endings: A Note on the End of the Cold War", *Millennium: Journal of International Studies*, Vol. 26. No. 3, (1997), pp. 631-649.

Tadov, V. A., "Social Processes of *Perestroika*", *Russian Social Science Review,* Vol. 33. No. 3, (May-June 1992), pp. 27-49.

Temkina, A. A., "Social Base of Economic Reforms in the USSR", *Sociological Research*, Vol. 31. No. 1, (January-February 1992), pp. 18-29.

Thakur, R., "India and the Soviet Union: Conjunctions and Disjunctions of Interests", *Asian Survey*, Vol. 31. No. 9, (September 1991), pp. 826-846.

Timothy J.Colton etal., "Russia in the year 2004", *Post-Soviet Affairs*, Vol.21, No.1 (January-March), 2005, p.24.

Tsipin, K., "After the Cold War: New Tasks for Arms Controllers", *Bulletin of Atomic Scientists*, Vol. 45. No. 6, (July/August 1989), pp. 7-9.

Tsyganov, Andrei P., "Vladimir Putin's Vision of Russia as a Normal Great Power", *Post Soviet Affairs*, Vol.21, No.2 (April-June), 2005, pp.147-149.

Udalov, Vadim V., "Concept of Balance of Interests and US-Soviet Interaction", *Annals of the American Academy of Political and Social Sciences,* No. 518, (November 1991), pp. 165-176.

Umbach, F., "Control and Security of Nuclear Weapons in the Former USSR", *Aussen Politik*, Vol. 43. No. 4, (1992), pp. 362-372.

Vanaik, A., "Continuity and Change in Soviet Foreign Policy", *Economic and Political Weekly*, Vol. 23. No. 11, (March 12, 1988), pp. 547-552.

Volgyes, I., "Military Security in the Post-Communist Age: Reflections on Myths and Realities", *Studies in Comparative Communism*, Vol. 25. No. 1, (1992), pp. 89-95.

Wegner, H., "The Political Framework and the Simplifications of the INF Treaty", *NATO Review*, Vol. 36. No. 1, (February 1988), pp. 7-14.

Wettig, G., "Soviet Union and Arms Control", *Aussen Politik*, Vol. 36. No. 1, (1985), pp. 25-36.

Wettig, G. "Gorbachev's Strategy for Disarmament and Security", *Aussen Politik*, Vol. 38. No. 1, (1987), pp. 3-10.

Wettig, G., "Gorbachev and New Thinking in the Kremlin's Foreign Policy", *Aussen Politik*, Vol. 38. No. 2, (1987), pp. 144-154.

Wettig, G., "New Development of Soviet Military Doctrine", *Aussen Politik*, Vol. 39. No. 2, (1988), pp. 169-181.

Wettig, G., "New Thinking on Security and East-West Relations", *Problems of Communism*, Vol. 37. No. 2, (March/April 1988), pp.1-14.

Wettig, G., "Europe After the INF Treaty", *Aussen Politik*, Vol. 39. No. 1, (1988), pp. 24-35.

Wettig, G., "The Transformation From the Cold War to Today's Challenges", *Aussen Politik*, Vol. 48. No. 11, (1997), pp. 107-116.

Williams, P., "The New East-West Relations: The US-Soviet Relations Beyond the Cold War", *International Affairs*, Vol. 65. No. 2, (Spring 1989), pp. 270-78.

Woolskey,Lee S., "Putin's Plutocrat Problem", *Foreign Affair*, Vol.79, No.2 (March/April), 2000, pp.26-27.

Yuryev,Mikhail., "Identifying Russia's Foes" *Russia in global Affairs* Vol.3,No.1(January-March 2005), pp.114-120.

Z, "To the Stalin Mausoleum", *Daedalus*, Vol. 119. No. 1, (Winter 1991), pp. 295-344.

Zhurkin, V., Karaganov, S., and Kortunov, A., "Reasonable Sufficiency or How to Break the Vicious Circle", *New Times*, No. 12, (1987a), pp. 13-15.

Zivanov, Sava *Review of International Affairs*, Vol.LI, no.1096,(August) 2000, p.13.

Journals

American Historical Review (Washington D.C).
Aussen Politik (Hamburg, Germany).
British Journal of Political Science (Cambridge).
Bulletin of Atomic Scientist (Chicago).
Bulletin of Peace Proposal (London).
Cooperation and Conflict (London).
Current History (Philadelphia).
Foreign Affairs (New York).
Foreign Trade (Moscow).
International Affairs (London).
International Affairs (Moscow).
International Defence Review (Surrey, U.K).
International Journal of Group Tension (New York).
International Studies Quarterly (Stoneham, USA).
Japan Review of International Affairs (Tokyo).
Journal of Conflict Resolution (California).
Kommunist (Moscow).
NATO Review (Brussels).

New Perspectives (Helsinki).
New Times (Moscow).
Orbis (Greenwich, UK).
Peace Research (London).
Post-Soviet Affairs (Florida, USA).
Post-Communist Economics (London).
Problems of Communism (Washington D.C).
Problems of Economic Transition (New York).
Review of International Affairs (Belgrade).
Russian Social Science Review (New York)
Soviet Military Review (Moscow).
Strategic Digest (New Delhi).
Strategic Review (Cambridge, Massachusetts).
Slavik Review (USA).
Survival (London).
The Korean Journal of International Studies (Seoul).
World Affairs (Washington D.C).
World Focus (New Delhi).
World Policy Journal (New York).
World Politics (Princeton, N.J.).

Newspapers

Daily Telegraph, London.
Foreign Broadcasting Information Services, Washington D.C.
Hindu, Madras.
Hindustan Times New Delhi.
International Herald Tribune, New York.
Indian Express, New Delhi.
Izvestia, Moscow.
New York Times, New York.
Pravda, Moscow.
Statesman, New Delhi.
Telegraph, Calcutta.
The Times, London.
Times of India, New Delhi.
Washington Post, Washington.

Index